# no sweat

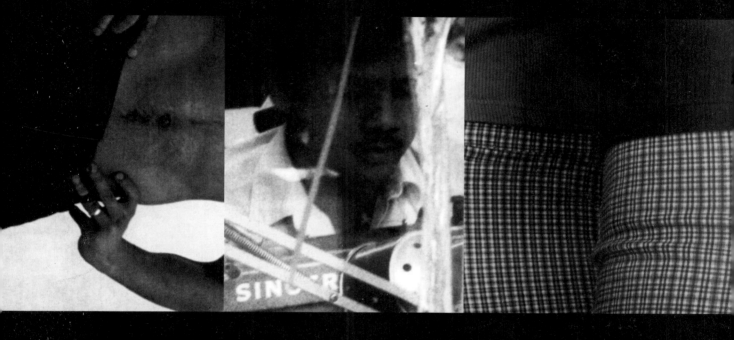

V

First published by Verso 1997
© The Contributors 1997
All rights reserved

Verso
UK: 6 Meard Street, London W1V 3HR
USA: 180 Varick Street, New York, NY 10014

Verso is the imprint of New Left Books

paper ISBN 1 85984 172 4
cloth ISBN 1 85984 866 4

British Library Cataloguing in Publication Data
A catalogue record for this book is available from the British Library

Library of Congress Cataloging-in-Publication Data
A catalog record for this book is available from the Library of Congress

design by parlour
Printed in the U.S.A. by R.R. Donnelley & Sons Co.

Proceeds from the sale of this book will be used to fund the
documentation of contemporary labor struggles.

# no sweat

fashion, free trade,
and the rights
of garment workers

edited by **andrew ross**

**VERSO**

New York  London

*The night shift begins work, El Salvador.*

# contents

*Triangle Shirtwaist Fire, NYC 1911.*

# preface and acknowledgments

This book grew out of a conference organized by the New York University American Studies Program, the garment workers' union UNITE, and *The Nation*. The conference was held in March 1996, on the eighty-fifth anniversary of the Triangle Shirtwaist fire in a building now used by NYU. The sweatshop tragedy, which took the lives of 146 young immigrants, was a decisive moment in the growth of the modern labor movement.

*No Sweat* includes the voices of workers, activists, labor lawyers, trade unionists, industry executives, journalists, and academics. One of the aims of the conference was to show how matters of style are not disconnected from labor issues, despite the fact that commentators habitually treat these two worlds as if they were mutually exclusive. Consequently, some attempt has been made here to cover the spectrum that runs from child labor in Bangladesh to runway couture in Milan, Paris, and New York. Even the latest elite retro style, as *Washington Post* critic Robin Givhan points out, has its origins in the recycling bin, not just of ideas but of real clothing, cast off by the well-heeled and then circulated throughout the Third World, ultimately re-entering the fashion world as a newly chic "look," embracing the downcast and impoverished. In a more desirable political culture, where state policy might recognize fashion as a valuable culture industry, independent fashion designers would be natural allies of labor, as Angela McRobbie argues in an essay calling for feminists to bridge the gulf that divides issues of labor from style. In his essay on comparative trade policy, McKenzie Wark argues that industrial embrace of the rhythms of pop style is a real opportunity to develop a high-wage, value-added garment sector. Paul Smith offers a case history of Tommy Hilfiger's embrace of black urban style as an example of the new industrial process known as mass customization. These are original contributions, and must be built upon if cultural analysts are to be encouraged and trained to lend their knowledge and insights to help solve labor problems.

But the bulk of this book is devoted to more direct commentary on labor conditions, and to the building of campaigns and activist coalitions in opposition to the normalization of the sweatshop. We are grateful to UNITE president Jay Mazur for the major commitment given by his staff to this project. Jo-Ann Mort gathered together a dossier from UNITE that offers up-to-date analysis, information, and testimony from officials, workers, and activists. The contributions include Alan Howard's incisive, historically informed overview of the role of organized labor within the industry; several commentaries on the labor situation in key industry locations—the

# no sweat

2

New York metropolitan area, Southern California, and Asia—from Carl Proper, Steve Nutter, and Elinor Spielberg; interviews with workers like Lina Rodriguez Meza; and an account of legal activism from Julie Su. Focusing on the case history of Central American outsourcing, Kitty Krupat has edited a National Labor Committee dossier in which she describes the history and aims of the organization, and provides a selection of their reports and campaigns. Linda Shaw reports on the Clean Clothes Campaign in Britain, and Eyal Press goes "sweatshopping."

This book would not have reached fruition without Kitty Krupat's unflagging enthusiasm, hard work, and creative ideas. Jo-Ann Mort's solid commitment to recruit and channel UNITE's hard-pressed energies kept us on track and on deadline. At Verso, Colin Robinson's zeal for the project offered a welcome haven to set sail for. At the NLC, Charlie Kernaghan and Barbara Briggs gave the book their attention at the busiest time of their lives, and Dave Dyson and Jack Sheinkman lent their voices in interviews. Thanks are also due to those who supported and participated in the conference: to Katrina vanden Heuvel at *The Nation*, Susan Cowell, Ron Blackwell, and Muzaffar Chishti at UNITE, Deborah Drier from the Guggenheim Museum, and Robyn Dutra at NYU. Alison Redick provided last-minute research assistance, Phil Mariani lent her famous editing expertise, UNITE's Keir Jorgensen, Brent Garren, Cara Metz and Carrie Kim pitched in, designers Sheena Calvert and Cynthia Madansky of parlour design miraculously pulled everything together, and Alyssa Hepburn and Gina Diaz, from NYU American Studies, lent their administrative aid throughout.

Andrew Ross, May 1997

*bottom right: International Womens Day march through the Lower East Side, New York City, in 1977.*

*Lina Rodriguez Meza.*

### Lina Rodriguez Meza

**66** **I work at 265 West 40th Street, on the sixteenth floor, making dresses. It looks like they're for the Jaclyn Smith label. I seem to have the luck of working for artists' brands.** [Here Lina is alluding to the fact that she worked previously for SEO Fashions, where clothing was made for Kathie Lee Gifford's line.] **Teresa, the supervisor, guards the tags carefully. I had to be very careful to take one. Last week we only worked for fifteen hours. And now we worked two days in a row, but it seems like we're going to be off again. There's very little work. It's difficult because you earn so little, there's almost no overtime and the small amount of money that you save you use little by little when there is no work. When it's busy, we work up to sixty to sixty-three hours. The conditions in the factory are not very good. There's no air circulation. The bathrooms are outside on our floor. In the factory where I work almost everyone is from Ecuador. Those people work hard. And since they are very far from their land, they come and are afraid of losing their jobs, so they enslave themselves. Almost no one goes to the bathroom, they feel embarrassed. The bathroom is outside. You have to leave the factory, go to the hallway. It's a bit dangerous because anyone can enter the bathrooms. Also, there is a part in the building that is unprotected. You can easily fall into that empty space.**

**I came to the U.S. because the situation in my country is really bad right now. I'm a single mother, a widow. I have three children to take care of and the salary isn't enough to sustain us. I don't want to**

## no sweat

bring my children here. The environment here is bad for them. They are with my family, with my brothers and sisters, my father and my mother. The truth is my family raised them, since I had to work and could not attend to them.

I paid $900 cash up front to cross the border. Here in New York, it's not that much, but in my country, it's a lot of money. You can work for a year trying to gather that much money.

It's difficult to cross the border. Even our own people may attack us. When a person comes here, they risk their life because sometimes they're traveling with criminals. Since you're crossing illegally, you can't choose who to cross with. On a hill there are people waiting to take the little you have, your jewelry, they even make you take off your clothes to make sure that you have nothing, not a penny. I think, rather than making laws against us, there should be a law to punish those people because they are criminals that have killed people. And they cross the border like it's a game, they come and go, they cross the border, they make fun of the law. They have found bodies in the desert.

With all my heart I would like to return. The bad part is, I see that it becomes harder every day. They are cutting off paths, choices. They are attacking us like we're the plague. They are taking everything away from us to make us leave. I don't know who writes the laws, but someone needs to speak to that person and tell them that we're not here because we want to be. If it were up to me, I would be in my country with my family. But unfortunately, as they say, bad things start close to home. We cannot do anything against our government. They have the bull by the horns. So the only choice left is to leave the country in search of work. We are small against our government. And also, you see, we want an opportunity here but they also attack us, and I don't know how we're going to end up. Immigration laws start to attack us, from the moment we enter at the border, they attack us. When you arrive here, you're denied work because everyone wants your papers. They want you to be legal. But how can you become legal if they don't give you opportunities?

In Mexico, there's a lot of talk about life here, but people don't believe it because many have returned. Some return with money, with a fortune, and many return in a bad condition, even crazy, sick. And there are people who don't return. So people will always come here. Over there people have the idea that here one can lose it all, win or lose it all, but you have to take the risk when you have no choice.

I wanted to earn enough and then rest, be with my family, my children, be a mother. At that time I didn't mind giving them up for a year to do this. But unfortunately, things are not that easy. And so the year is going by and I feel I have failed at almost everything. My daughter will turn seven this month. The boy will be six this November and my baby, my little one, turned three in July. I want to return to protect them. I know they're at an age when they need a mother, but I cannot go back. I cannot go back without at least achieving some of what I had planned. Otherwise, everything would be in vain, the sacrifice, the separation. I'd have no reason for having come.

I did the same work in Mexico. I've been in the industry for eighteen years. I started working when I was thirteen years old as a de-threader, what they call here floor work. I started at thirteen, when I was fifteen I started to work with machines. I come from a family of sewers, so we inherited our work from our mother.

My sister finished the fourth grade, I finished the fifth grade, another brother finished elementary school and one finished secondary school, and then we ended up slowly on the streets. So I finished the fifth grade and it was enough for me to study on my own. I like to read books, be informed. I'm moved by books.

Before coming here I wanted to join the auxiliary police because in my country they pay well, but they ask for a secondary school degree. So I did the secondary rapidly, I prepared for the entrance exam in three months and all I was missing to finish was the last part. But I didn't have time because the opportunity to come here presented itself, and it was now or never. I decided it was better to come here. I couldn't risk any more. Also, people spoke poorly of the police and it wasn't something I wanted to do. So here I am. **"**

# introduction

Andrew Ross

At the waning of a century that has seen the Square Deal, the New Deal, and the Fair Deal, few could be faulted for thinking that they are now paying the price of a Raw Deal. As global free trade increasingly takes center stage, the income gap between the world's rich and poor has accelerated, and is now twice as great as it was thirty years ago. In the U.S., income inequality has reverted to the levels of the 1920s, before the introduction of progressive taxation. The top one percent of families now possess 42 percent of American wealth, and the economy is governed by corporations whose ratio of CEO salaries to workers' wages is so astronomical as to mock any standard of fairness. While executive pay has swelled by 500 percent in the last fifteen years, factory pay has lagged behind inflation and actually fallen by a net 2 percent in the last five years. During the bull market year of 1995, when many large corporations recorded capital growth of 35 percent, the bottom two-fifths of U.S. workers received an all-time low 12.5 percent of the national income, and the top one-fifth received a record 50 percent. Worker termination rates escalated sharply, as did public resentment against the arrogance of layoff kings like AT&T's Robert Allen, whose 1995 compensation was $5.8 million, and IBM's Louis Gerstner, who hauled in $13.2 million.

In this context of staggering economic inequality, a revitalized labor movement has moved back onto the national stage, facing up to massive challenges at home and in the new global economy of outsourcing. The energies of progressives and activists, increasingly devoted to nongovernment coalitions between international labor, environmental, and social justice groups, are now driven as much by global inequities as by the shameful story told by statistics about the national distribution of wealth. The result is a distinct genre of moral outrage reserved for the injustices created by offshore manufacturing. Public attention has been drawn to the likes of basketball prince Michael Jordan, who earned more ($20 million) in 1992 for endorsing Nike's running shoes than Nike's entire 30,000-strong Indonesian work force did for making them. Or Disney's CEO, Michael Eisner, who earned over $200 million from salary and stock options in 1996, which, at $97,600 per hour, amounted to 325,000 times the hourly wage of the Haitian workers who made Pocahontas, Lion King, and Hunchback of Notre Dame T-shirts and pajamas, and who sewed on Mickey Mouse's ears.

041823325598

$18.00

10

It is no coincidence that these two egregious examples are drawn from the garment trade. The textile and apparel industries are a showcase of horrors for the labor abuses sanctioned by the global free trade economy, where child labor, wage slavery, and employer cruelty are legion. Conditions reminiscent of the heyday of the sweatshop at the turn of the century are being brought to light. Big name retailers and manufacturers scramble to issue statements about their honorable labor codes, and overnight are shamed by exposés of slave factories producing their lines at home and abroad. Once again shoppers in search of guilt-free clothing are scrutinizing labels, and coming up short. Price tags provide vague clues, but even "Made in the USA" labels don't tell us very much anymore, and are sometimes sewn on in Asia or Central America. For those looking for more information, the garment union UNITE's consumer guide points out that "the care tag tells you how to treat the garment but not how the worker who made it was treated."

It is a widely held fiction that most citizens of the North, however much they themselves are hurting, are not known for their discomfort at evidence that Third World workers are suffering too, and more often than not, on their behalf. On the contrary, public concern has been inflamed by revelations about labor exploitation in apparel factories in the U.S. and around the world, where workers are physically, sexually, and economically abused to save ten cents on the cost of a pricey item of clothing. This book seeks to explain how and why this has happened, and what can be done about it.

The gruesome face of the new international division of labor is all too apparent in the apparel trade, as the corporate hunt for ever cheaper labor, akin to the quest for the Holy Grail, drives wages down in entire subcontinental regions where countries compete to attract foreign investment. But the explanation for these conditions also lies in the history and structure of the garment industry, the nature of its products, and the volatility of its markets. Textile and apparel are traditionally where underdeveloped countries begin their industrialization process, since they require a minimum of capital investment—particularly in the labor-intensive sectors of sewing and assembly—and the raw materials are relatively common. Although there are many interlocking industries involved in this sector, U.S. retail giants who are in command of the vast internal market call the shots globally, while cutthroat contractors, pursuing ever tighter profit margins, crack the whip in local enterprise zones and assembly platforms. So, too,

the international mass consumer now wants the latest fashion posthaste, necessitating flexibility and turnaround at levels that disrupt all stable norms of industrial competition.

Because these industries have seen some of the worst labor excesses, they have also been associated with historic victories for labor, and hold a prominent symbolic spot on the landscape of labor iconography: from the Luddite weavers' resistance to industrialists' introduction of power looms, to the mid-nineteenth-century protest of the "factory girls" in New England mills, the early twentieth-century garment workers' strikes against conditions generated by the sweating system, the unions' role in forging pioneer labor-capital accords, and the success of the industry's labor-manufacturer bloc in winning exemption from GATT's postwar free trade rules. In the public mind, the strongest association is with labor's successes in "eradicating" the sweatshop in the first two decades of the century. Of course, it never disappeared. Severely restricted in its zone of operations, the sweatshop dropped out of view, and lived on in the underground economy. But the repugnance attached to the term "sweatshop" commands a moral power, second only to slavery itself, to rouse public opinion into a collective spasm of abhorrence. The public will to eliminate sweatshop labor often designates a significant level of development on the part of a society, in contrast to others, less democratic in their attitudes toward the rights of workers.

# no sweat

The challenge to this claim of moral superiority on the part of developed nations is one reason why the recent return of the sweatshop to the domestic workplace and its flourishing in all the offshore outposts of corporate production has provoked such revulsion in these countries. Few aspects of the corporate rollback of the postwar social contract have been greeted with the public outcry that followed revelations of sweatshops thriving at the heart of most major American cities, or that items of clothing on sale at family-brand stores like J. C. Penney, Sears, Wal-Mart, and Kmart were made by mothers and their teenage daughters toiling in inhuman conditions. These disclosures summon up the misery and filth of turn-of-the-century workplaces—tenements, lofts, attics, stables—plagued by chronic health problems (tubercu-losis, the scourge and signature sickness of the sweatshop, has also made a return of late), and home to the ruthless exploitation of greenhorn immigrants. They recall Jacob Riis's harrowing accounts of conditions in New York's Lower East Side tenements in *How the Other Half Lives*, or the social photography of Lewis Hine's labor docu-mentaries, or Henry Mayhew's profiles of the rag trade in London's East End.[1]

The dingy Victorian archetype notwithstanding, sweatshops today come in all shapes and sizes. In Central America, they are brand new, brightly lit factories policed by armed guards patrolling a barbed-wire Free Trade Zone. In Los Angeles, they are in ranch-style, suburban compounds and dwellings. The U.S. General Accounting Office (GAO) defines a sweatshop as "an employer that violates more than one federal or state labor law governing minimum wage and overtime, child labor, industrial homework, occupational safety and health, workers compensation, or industry regulation." A recent GAO report estimates that over a third of New York's 6,500 shops are sweated, as are 4,500 of L.A.'s 5,000 shops, 400 out of 500 in Miami, and many others in Portland, New Orleans, Chicago, San Antonio, and Philadelphia. In the L.A. basin, $1 an hour is not an uncommon wage in

Orange County's Little Saigon, while the New York City wage floor hovers around $2 an hour in Sunset Park's Chinatown.

Historically, "sweating" refers to the system of subcontract which, in contrast to the integrated and supervised factory system, consists of the farming out of work by competing manufacturers to competing contractors. Sweating was indigenous to garment production because of its division of labor, separating the craft processes of design, marketing, and cutting from the labor-intensive sewing and finishing, and organized around a three-tier system of

small producers—the inside shop, the contractor, and the home. To set up in the fly-by-night world of runaway shops required little more investment than was needed to rent a hole in the wall and a few sewing machines, plus ready access to a ghetto labor pool.[2] The sweatshop's primitive mode of production and the cutter's artisanal loft coexisted with semi-automated workplaces that would industrialize, with union guidance, into economies of scale under the pull of the Fordist factory ethic.[3]

Today's garment industry shows many similari-ties, with its preindustrial sweatshop sector flourishing in proximity to postindustrial, high-tech workplaces, often within the same block. The sewing machine's foot pedal is still in business, no longer competing with steampower but with the CPU. Studies by the Bureau of Labor Statistics show that, with the exception of the fast food industry's burger flippers (at $11,920), and apparel and accessory store employees (at $13,971), apparel and textile workers in the *legal* sector earn the lowest average annual wage among U.S. industries, at $19,225. Ethnic entrepreneurship is as crucial as ever, with Asian and Latino immigrants, often undocumented, denied access to the mainstream labor economy through racial labor segmentation, and thereby forced into ethnic enclaves where all labor laws are routinely neglected.[4] Where patterns of family labor are relevant, the obligations of youth to the immigrant culture of apprenticeship and to patriarchal

left: Now Hiring. A sweatshop in the
Kensington neighborhood of Philadelphia
advertises for workers, Winter 1996.

**Introduction**

15

cohesion add greatly to the degree of exploitation.[5] Women still make up the majority of
sweated labor, their sewing skills traditionally undervalued and their homework sustaining the
most underground sector of the industry. The system of subcontracting is alive and well, ever
driving wages and profit margins down.

But there are just as many differences. Seventy years of industrial regulation have left a
raft of labor laws on the books, even if they are patchily enforced. The rise and decline of union
power has left an uncertain legacy, especially among new immigrants drawn from countries
with the modern equivalent of the Russian Pale's "czarist repression," but for whom the labor
movement is no longer perceived as a messianic vehicle for socialism. The apparel industry is
now global in scope, with hundreds of countries producing for a small number of
importing nations. The balance of power among the textile and apparel industries has also
shifted toward the giant retailers, who increasingly produce their own private brand labels in
many of these countries, bypassing the manufacturer, the union shop, and the domestic
worker. The big players are no longer industrial patriarchs, accountable to workers'
communities through co-religionist ethics. For the most part, they are anonymous corporate
technocrats, solely accountable to their stockholders. More than 60 percent of the garments
sold in the U.S. are now imported, mostly from Asian countries. (Indeed, the competitive
challenge of Asian producers has been so powerful that the developing countries succeeded, in
the most recent GATT round, in winning a global agreement to phase out the tangle of trade
restrictions that have protected domestic industries for so long in the developed countries.)
The runaway shops are no longer in Trenton, New Jersey, or Scranton, Pennsylvania, or in anti-
union states in the South; they are in the maquiladoras of the Caribbean basin, a species of
labor organization that, at its worst, ranks just below the plantation on the scale of
dehumanization. Subcontracting is no longer the satanic trademark of the garment industry, it
has become an aggressive principle of all post-Fordist production, used in auto parts, building
maintenance, data processing, electronics assembly, public sector work, and every other
industry "downsizing" away from economies of scale and mass production. Disdained by
modernism's apostles of scientific management as a preindustrial relic, apparel's subcontracting system has come to be seen as a pioneer of the just-in-time flexible production that

*Garment shop, Sunset Park, Brooklyn, 1992.*
*The gate shown was always locked, creating a fire hazard.*

is geared to increasingly specialized (or niche) markets. Last but not least, the global reach of fashion (turnover not dictated by the durability of the garments) is no longer confined to elite women's wear worn in metropolitan centers of the developed countries. Long established on Main Street/ High Street, and increasingly influenced by homegrown subcultures on the side streets, popular access to style and fashion exert an influence, at times pervasive, on the social and cultural behavior of men and boys, in addition to women and girls, in ever greater numbers all around the world. This globalization of style has increasingly defined the terms on which the industry has had to respond through restructuring, adjustment, and rationalization.

The race toward globalization is often cited as the cause of labor's malaise in apparel and other manufacturing industries, but it also poses a challenge for the survival and rekindling of the labor movement in an industry that has benefited from an unusual degree of domestic protection. That story dates to the very beginning of the Industrial Revolution, when the British mercantilist system depended in part on the protection of textile and apparel trade, at that time in the technological vanguard of international production. In time, and largely in response to British trade, the U.S. began its own protectionist tradition through import substitution and developed an effective system of tariffs and embargoes in the course of the nineteenth century. Powerful enough to impose voluntary restraints upon Japan's textile export trade in the 1940s, the American industry—in cahoots with European producers with whom it has shared a "gentleman's agreement" to waive all import duties—succeeded in exempting textile and apparel trade from many of the key rules of GATT. From its 1947 inception to the Uruguay Round in 1994, GATT rules against discrimination (most favored nation treatment), tariff *below: Members of UNITE local 23-25 at a rally catch the attention of workers in a sweatshop on the upper floors of a building on 8th Ave. at 38th Street, New York City. The rally protested working conditions in Garment District factories. October 1995.*

protectionism, and quantitative restrictions on imports were all relaxed for textile and apparel, and a series of international accords culminating in the 1973 Multi Fiber Arrangement (MFA) sought to manage the trade flow from developing countries to Western markets through an elaborate system of bilateral agreements concerning import quotas and trade routes. MFA is now being slowly phased out, and in 2005 the final 49 percent of trade will be quota-free.[6]

The post-MFA free trade order is likely to intensify patterns established over the last thirty years. In each region of the world—Asian, European, and American—the respective cores are now serviced by discount-labor regions. As industries in the NICs have matured, driving domestic wages up, Japan, Hong Kong, South Korea, and Taiwan have successively established assembly operations in the least developed Asian countries—Vietnam, Bangladesh, Sri Lanka, Indonesia, and China. For the Western European industries, offshore production occurs in Northern Africa, and in Central and Eastern Europe. Because of its proximity to the largest

**no sweat**

20

*Shopping bag designed for the anti-sweatshop campaign by Barbara Kruger.*

*An advertisement which appeared in the national press, placed by UNITE in 1996.*

# no sweat

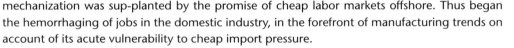

market, the situation in the American hemisphere is the most complex. In response to the first wave of Asian imports, from 1961 to 1971, lured by an overvalued dollar and the vulnerability of standardized clothing lines, the U.S. industry struggled to meet its first test of structural adjustment. Manufacturers were advised to "automate, relocate, or evaporate."[7] By the late 1980s, apparel was 40 percent automated, compared to 6 percent in the early 1960s, with textile production running much higher. Because the physical limpness of fabric precluded the spread of automation to labor-intensive sectors, the push for in-creased productivity through mechanization was sup-planted by the promise of cheap labor markets offshore. Thus began the hemorrhaging of jobs in the domestic industry, in the forefront of manufacturing trends on account of its acute vulnerability to cheap import pressure.

From 1963, manufacturers could take advantage of a special provision (Item 807) in the U.S. Tariff Schedule which allowed cut garments to be exported for assembly and reimported into the U.S. Duties were paid only on the value added to the garment through low-cost assembly. In conjunction with the creation of maquiladora free trade zones as part of the Border Industrialization Program, offshore production skyrocketed. In 1983, the Reagan administration expanded the pool of sourcing countries through the creation of the Caribbean Basin Initiative (CBI), extending special trade privileges to twenty-two countries (later increased to twenty-seven) that afforded tariff-free access for many Caribbean products. The 807 provision (now classified under the international Harmonized Tariff Schedule as 9802) remained in effect, guaranteeing that fabric was manufactured, cut, and finished in the U.S., but reducing tariffs to encourage low-cost offshore assembly.

Anticommunist politics drove the CBI as much as the need to compete with Asian imports. In association with the World Bank and the IMF's house philosophy of structural adjustment, Washington began to shift its cold war policies in the region away from support for authoritarian regimes to the active imposition of private sector development. Aggressive neoliberal penetration of state economies, backed up by low-intensity military conflict, was adopted as the most efficient way of combating Caribbean socialism. In the wake of the land

and labor reform movements of the 1970s, which gave rise to the Sandinista revolution in Nicaragua, Michael Manley's socialist government in Jamaica, the New Jewel Movement in Grenada, and rebel-peasant insurgencies in many other nations, President Reagan announced a "state of danger" in the nation's backyard and began to pour money into the region in order to secure its economic and political dependency upon U.S. needs and interests. The result was orchestrated adjustment, designed to orient each national economy toward Washington and away from regional alliances. Offshore facilities owned by U.S. firms multiplied in the export-processing zones set up by loans and grants from USAID and other government agencies. Preferred trading arrangements ensured that class alliances between foreign investors and local elites were preserved; in countries like Haiti, Guatemala, and El Salvador, the maquilas are partly owned and managed by ex-members of military juntas, while the lure of industrial employment takes peasant reformist pressure off traditional landholding elites.

So, too, the gender division of labor was consciously exploited to preserve power and maximize profit. As Cynthia Enloe points out, the hemispheric free trade market built by CBI, NAFTA, and the new Free Trade Area of the Americas—"stretching," in George Bush's words,

*Honduras shanty town.*

# no sweat

"from Port Anchorage to Terra del Fuego"—is explicitly being built on low female wages in the "unskilled" sectors of garment making, food processing, and electronics assembly. As women moved into the export enclave industries (making up 90 percent of zone labor), traditionally male manufacturing sectors like sugar, oil, and bauxite, with double the going wages of women, went into decline. Undervalued female labor also undergirds the U.S. domestic work force, especially in the immigrant economy that supports sweatshops, where it is clear that the high rate of female and immigrant employment accounts today, as ever, for the low wages in apparel. Women and children's labor is on the frontline of the new industrial investment, just as it was at the dawn of the Industrial Revolution.[8]

Whether driven by U.S. security policy or by the logic of international trade, the consequences of offshore production for regional peoples in Central America and the Caribbean amount to a disaster by several criteria: human rights, environmental, economic, and political. The CBI failed to deliver improved trade earnings, and with the exception of the export zones cranking out profit for their foreign owners to the tune of heavy subsidies from host governments, almost every other industry was hit hard. Local economies produced less and less for local consumption, economic nationalism and political sovereignty were severely eroded, and any chance of sustainable development was stillborn. Structural adjustment created a legacy of undiversified economies acutely vulnerable to every mild recession in the U.S. The combination of capital repatriation and curtailment of public spending debilitated those few resources—education, health, and monetary assets—that could stave off hardship by investing in a socially viable future.[9]

By contrast, export promotion has yielded a bonanza for U.S. firms (and for those Asian companies outsourcing in the region for proximity to the U.S. market), where wages as low as 12 cents an hour in Haitian and 31 cents in Honduran and Salvadoran maquilas can be freely maximized, and where local regulations against child labor, subminimum wages, and union repression are routinely waived by governments so hungry for foreign investment they will pay the companies' telephone and utility bills. In factories where human standards of decency are violated as a matter of routine, the U.S.'s export-promotion scheme to alleviate misery and poverty in the developing world is a sick joke. Living standards have declined as a whole in the region, as compared with the rest of Latin America, and the low-wage sweatshops of the offshore apparel industry have become notorious state-of-the-art illustrations of a transnational free trade economy going about its ruthless business: twenty-hour workdays forced on workers to fill their quotas, widespread sexual harassment, coercive birth control, brutal suppression of labor organization, and starvation wages.

These conditions are the result of programs designed to make U.S. apparel companies competitive, and if they have succeeded in filling the pockets of corporate executives and stockholders, they have done little to help American workers, forced into a downward wage spiral for jobs through competition with their maquila counterparts or with immigrant workers in the core centers. Pitting First World against Third World workers has been a highly serviceable corporate strategy. It drives wages down on both sides, and allows business to portray labor rights advocates as domestic protectionists bent on depriving maquila workers of their industrial wage ticket out of poverty. But the high-reward strategy, spurred by 400 and 500 percent retail markups, also carries some risks—poor quality control, inadequate managerial supervision, political instability. None are greater than the potentially embarrassing exposure of human rights violations in the factories of companies that cannot afford to have the names of their designers, endorsers, or merchandising labels publicly sullied.

Indeed, it is the counterstrategy of public exposure that has fired the energies of labor and human rights activists in the last few years. Media interest has been kindled by the spectacle of blue-chip names in retail and design being embarrassed by revelations about the exploited labor behind their labels. In the wake of the publicity scandals, some companies have been pressured to implement codes of conduct and to consider facilitating independent monitoring of labor conditions in their contractors' plants. Why has this strategy been necessary and why has it worked? First of all, the labor-capital accords of joint liability that used to govern the garment industry have eroded as the manufacturers lost their commanding position in the chain of production. Greater concentration and integration have afforded giant retailers the paramount power to exert downward price pressure, to circumvent manufacturers by designing and contracting their own private labels, and since retail jobs are not threatened by offshore production, to deflect union pressure. The top forty retail firms now control well over 80 percent of the market, and their chief point of vulnerability is their good name, susceptible to bad publicity and to consumer boycotts. Equally, the weak link in the global chain of design, subcontracting, and merchandising is the willingness of First World consumers to pay huge markup prices for clothing with low labor costs. Nike can move its factories from South Korea to Indonesia, China, Thailand, and Vietnam, as it has done in recent years, to exploit lower wages, but the comparative advantage means nothing if consumers are not willing to pay $120 for a shoe assembled for 70 or 80 cents. If consumer abhorrence for products made with slave labor impacts on shopping patterns, all is lost.

Accordingly, the leading edge of activism has shifted toward the high-end publicity stakes of targeting the image of large, well-known companies. This is clearly visible in the work of the National Labor Committee (NLC), the group most identified publicly with the exposure of offshore sweatshop conditions. The NLC has its origins in the National Labor Committee in Support of Democracy and Human Rights in El Salvador, founded by three union presidents in 1980 to combat the assassination of Central American union organizers. The NLC helped organized labor survive Reagan's war in the region, and began to concentrate its efforts on publicizing the ravages of the maquila system. Its 1992 report, *Paying to Lose Our Jobs* (based on an undercover operation in which NLC members posed as a small apparel company looking for an offshore opening) documented the promotional activities and the economic support (to the tune of $1 billion) offered by U.S. government agencies to induce corporations into maquila production. The report, excerpted in this volume, was released amid widespread anxiety about a new round of job losses, and its profiling on CBS's "60 Minutes," followed by two "Nightline" programs, broke the news that U.S. taxpayers were funding, often through illegal channels, the transfer overseas of their jobs. Legislation was immediately passed to outlaw USAID from funding export-processing zones and, although the funding continued, NLC's model of seeking high-level publicity for its exposés was established.

Increasingly, the NLC has turned to specific corporate targets, linking their household names and labels to detailed accounts of maquila work atrocities. The Gap, a hugely profitable nonunion company with subcontractors in Central America, was the object of a highly successful 1995 campaign aimed at national media coverage. Despite threats like the one issued by the owner of the San Marcos free trade zone, former Salvadoran army colonel Mario Guerrero, that "blood will flow," the coalition of university, religious, union, human rights, and consumer groups prevailed. The agreement reached with the Gap was unprecedented, and sent a chill throughout the industry's corporate offices. Rigorous codes of conduct would be translated and posted inside every factory, and independent monitors would be allowed to conduct regular inspections of labor and safety conditions.

In the summer of 1996, the NLC hit the publicity jackpot when, following Charlie Kernaghan's testimony at a congressional hearing, TV celebrity Kathie Lee Gifford's Wal-Mart clothing line was linked to child labor and human rights abuses, first in Honduras, and then by UNITE workers to wage violations in a New York City sweatshop. Gifford's saccharine TV personality and her precious association with children's charities were a perfect foil for revelations about child labor. Gifford was caught in a media maelstrom over which she had no control until it was stage-managed by New York's most highly paid spin publicist, Howard Rubenstein. Each step of her painful public progress was obsessively documented and dissected in the national press and TV as it segued from fierce denial and resentment toward her accusers to slapstick self-vindication (when she started endorsing, for Kraft at the age of seventeen, she "didn't think she had to check out the cows") to humanitarian sympathy with sweatshop workers and righteous anger at their bosses. The instant butt of jokes, and cartoons featuring "Sweatshops of the Rich and Famous," or "Tours of the Stars' Sweatshops," it took Gifford only three weeks to ascend to the saintly rank of labor crusader. Vowing to "shine a light on the cockroaches," she provided a photo-opportunity for Governor Pataki's signing of a Retailers Responsibility Bill to outlaw sweated products in New York State, testified in further congressional hearings, and costarred in Secretary Reich's fashion industry summit conference in Washington in July 1996. Her decision to mandate independent monitoring for her line obliged Wal-Mart, the world's biggest retailer and seller of the Kathie Lee line, to announce new codes of conduct for all its contractors.

At a time when celebrities are lining up to sponsor products, and when endorsements are the bread-and-butter of the sportswear business, Gifford's invitation to other celebrity endorsers to clean up their contracts opened a new window of vulnerability within the industry. Michael Jordan, at the top of the heap, shrugged off challenges from reporters as Nike, with 37 percent of last year's $6.86 billion sneaker market, faced a barrage of media criticism over its decision to manufacture in Suharto's Indonesia. Jordan's hardboiled nonchalance was unavailable to Kathie Lee Gifford, whose public "feminine" persona acts out a pageant of

# no sweat

emoting and caring and empathizing. Nor did much dirt stick, at least initially (see my postscript), to the cartoon celebrities of Disney, target of the NLC's other summer campaign in Haiti, where Disney's fantasy world is embellished by Mickey Mouse and Pocahontas clothing sewn for starvation wages. Disney and other companies who use Haitian factories, like Sara Lee (owner of Hanes, L'Eggs, Bali, Playtex, and Champion), make donations to nonprofit causes to launder their public image, while employing workers who often toil for fifty straight hours and can still barely feed their families at the end of the week. The NLC's letter to Michael Eisner, included in this volume, makes it clear that paying workers a living wage in Haiti by doubling or tripling their salary would have a negligible impact on the retail price of a T-shirt. From a commercial viewpoint, starvation wages are no basis for U.S. trade with its neighbors. From a human rights viewpoint, they are a criminal outcome of corporate policies.

Aside from the NLC, the two organizations centrally involved in the struggle against sweatshop conditions are the U.S. Department of Labor (DOL) and the garment union UNITE (Union of Needletrades, Industrial, and Textile Employees—the merger union of ILGWU and ACTWU). While the Clinton administration power-steered the passage of NAFTA over and against the opposition of organized labor, its first-term secretary of labor, Robert Reich, was a compensatory voice in his attempts to curtail domestic sweatshop practices, the first incumbent in fifty years to do so. After a decade of nonenforcement of most labor legislation, Reich's DOL revived the Hot Goods Provision of the Fair Labor Standards Act, and began to prosecute companies in violation of this law against the interstate transport of sweated goods. With only 800 federal inspectors to cover the industry's 22,000 cutting and sewing jobs, *in addition* to the nation's other 6 million workplaces, enforcement in the fly-by-night sector was futile in practice, and so the DOL resorted to the new action-oriented strategy of naming names.

In August 1995, a DOL raid on the El Monte compound in Southern California uncovered seventy-two undocumented Thai workers behind barbed-wire fences, locked up around-the-clock to produce garments for Montgomery Ward, Mervyn's, Miller's Outpost, and for sale at Nordstrom, Sears, Macy's, Hecht's, and Filene's. These conditions were legally recognized as peonage, and afforded the DOL the public momentum to mount what would become its NO SWEAT campaign. After El Monte, Reich announced a "white list" of companies making an honest attempt to rid their labor of sweated processes. Those excluded would be publicly shamed, and would have to submit detailed proof that they are shunning hot goods for their names to appear on this Fashion Trendsetters list. A quarterly Garment Enforcement Report commenced publication of the names of offenders prosecuted for back pay. Reich's strategy was a step in the right direction, but in the absence of any real political will to enforce regulations, it lacked teeth. Names on the DOL list barely grew from the initial thirty-six in December 1995, and a place on the list hardly guaranteed continued good conduct from any of the companies, as their workers' exposé of Guess's homework production in August 1996 made all too clear. Guess was subsequently put on indefinite probation from the list.

In response to the DOL list, the powerful National Retail Federation (NRF) established its own Retail Honor Roll for companies in compliance with labor laws, and launched a publicity war with the DOL, calling on Reich to "stop wasting millions of taxpayer dollars on counterproductive media witch hunts and devote his energies to enforcing the law."[10] It was clear which DOL strategy the retailers preferred. By July, the big retailers had been sufficiently embarrassed by the Kathie Lee Gifford–Wal-Mart scandal for many to participate in discussions about an industry-wide effort at compliance and regulation, convened at Reich's fashion summit conference at Washington's Marymount University (where a study had shown that more than 78 percent of polled consumers declared they would pay more for no-sweat clothes).[11] On hand to showcase their own codes of conduct were most favored companies like Levi Strauss (whose 1991 Global Sourcing and Operating Guidelines was a pioneer code of corporate standards), Nordstrom, Nicole Miller, Guess (the target of the homework exposé just one month later and a National Labor Relations Board complaint in November), Liz Claiborne, Patagonia, and Kmart ("we are in a learning process"), while the NRF's president, Tracey Mullin, defensively pointed a finger at immigration politics and organized crime. Union representatives and journalists told harrowing tales of child and bonded labor in factories where discipline is enforced by terror. Industry associations and the Compliance Alliance all agreed that sweatshops were bad for business. The few celebrity endorsers who attended—Gifford, Richard Simmons, Cheryl Tiegs—were greeted like social martyrs: "If you have a terrible outrage like El Monte or what Kathie Lee has gone through…"

Such industry-wide efforts at stamping out sweatshops were not unprecedented, but the distribution of power among the participants has changed over the years, none more so than the garment unions whose power to bargain was forged in the struggles to reform "industrial conduct" eighty-five years before. After the strikes of the female shirtwaist makers (the famous Uprising of the Twenty Thousand) in 1909, and the male cloak makers the following year, garment chieftains met with labor leaders to sign the Protocols of Peace, the prototype of collective bargaining agreements and the first step on the road to elimination of the sweatshop. Organized labor learned that management would make big concessions in return for uninterrupted production, while the manufacturers found a way for labor to accept their coming creed of scientific management and industrial efficiency.

Thus were sown the seeds of labor-capital's social contract, conceived as the joint control of industrial democracy, governed by the modernist creed of productive efficiency and committed to a more rational form of capitalism than that symbolized by the sweatshop. In its cold war heyday, organized labor's role in this contract was that of a powerful co-guarantor, blessed by a degree of government patronage unimaginable forty years before. The corporate breakup of that social contract, hastened by the Reagan-Bush administrations' punitive war on the basic organizing rights of labor, hit the garment unions especially hard in an industry on the front line of job attrition. ILGWU membership decreased from 457,517 in 1969 (when 70 to 80 percent of New York factories were union shops) to less than 200,000 by the time of its 1995 merger with the ACTWU. With its employment peak of 1.45 million in 1973, domestic apparel jobs had fallen to 846,000 by 1995 (which saw a year's loss of 10 percent in the first big wave of NAFTA losses). The fiber-textile-apparel complex still employs about 10 percent of the domestic work force, the nation's largest industry with a little under 2 million jobs, plus several hundred thousand other jobs in support industries. But the opportunities to increase union membership have diminished, and are more and more concentrated in the immigrant labor-intensive sector that is notoriously difficult to organize.

Industry and union endeavors to retain jobs have focused on a high-wage, high-tech, high-skill program, where Computer-Assisted Design, Point-of-Sale data, and Quick Response technologies maximize flexibility, minimize inventory, rationalize consumer preference and demand, and strengthen the capacity to deliver fashion goods. The emphasis is on craft, quality, and reliability unavailable offshore. In addition to this boost to flexibility and turnaround time, modular, team-based production systems with multitasking workers have made the domestic delivery of fashionwear more competitive than many forms of outsourcing. But escalating competition has also seen domestic sweatshops proliferate. As a result, organized labor continues to be caught between a rock and a hard place. Nonetheless, UNITE's own antisweatshop campaign, in partnership with the National Consumers League, has been an important source of consumer information. Union and nonunion workers' active role in the exposure of illegal conditions has often organized out of UNITE's Worker Centers in L.A., New York, and San Francisco. A leading participant in the Southern California coalition that runs Sweatshop Watch, the union's connections in the industry have also been crucial to maintaining public pressure on converting retailers and manufacturers' public-image concerns into effective action. Some of this pressure resulted in the introduction of Stop Sweatshop legislation in October 1996 by Senator Ted Kennedy of Massachusetts and Representative Bill Clay of Missouri, which would hold retailers and manufacturers responsible for their contractors' labor law violations. The persistence of UNITE in pursuing government inter-vention was largely responsible for the Apparel Task Force accords of April 1997 (see postscript), when a partnership of corporations, labor and human rights groups, and DOL officials proposed sweeping, if voluntary, codes of conduct for companies to adopt.

The challenge of offshore organizing is even greater, especially when the local Maquiladora Manufacturers Association, or its equivalent, can always produce a "company union" representative to mouth the regional benefits of outsourcing when U.S. reporters come calling.[12] In the developing world, activism that appeals to international human rights

*Guess Inc's domestic US sweatshops were exposed in August 1996.*
*The company moved the bulk of its production to Mexico in January 1997.*

conventions (like the International Labor Organization's Minimum Age Convention) has arguably been more successful than calls for unionization, associated with high wage levels beyond a country's stage of development.[13] At the level of trade policy, countries like the U.S. are in a position to prefer nations that raise the standard of labor protections. Animals, ivory, and prison labor, but not child labor, currently fall into that category of protection. So, too, the process of globalization does not mean that responsibility and accountability are decentralized and dispersed, especially when the chain of production and supply begins and ends with the big domestic retailers as it does in apparel. A citizen campaign, with consumer boycotts (proven effective in California grapes, South African oranges, infant formula, canned tuna fish, toys made with Chinese child labor, and sundry other items) and sustained access to publicity, can have a powerful effect in the streets, stores, and factories of the U.S., where 25 percent of the world's economic activity occurs. The movement for socially responsible investment and trade already boasts a diverse range of participating groups and organizations in different countries, and its power to mount effective international boycotts is growing. It has the capacity to serve as a powerful supplement, if not an alternative, to the feeble system of corporate regulations currently recognized by international law.

Boycotts have already taken their toll on the fashion world itself. The antifur campaigns of PETA (People for the Ethical Treatment of Animals) have had an immense impact upon the furrier and animal-skin markets. So, too, groups whose image is distorted or ignored in fashion advertising often undertake a more diffuse form of boycott. The racially exclusive face of fashion and the preternaturally thin female body types favored in modeling have been heavily condemned for almost two decades now. African Americans, conscious of their consumer power, expect to see increased representation in advertising images from companies whose products they patronize. Sometimes the response can be quite complicated.

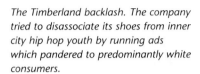

*The Timberland backlash. The company tried to disassociate its shoes from inner city hip hop youth by running ads which pandered to predominantly white consumers.*

In 1994, for example, Timberland ran some subtly racist ads as part of an attempt to dissociate its name from the inner-city hip hop youth who had adopted the trademark boots and outerwear. The ads contrasted an "out here" of white nature lovers with the "out there" of freaky black club kids, making it quite clear which group Timberland favored. As it happens, this may have been a shrewd marketing move, designed to neutralize a boycott. Hip hop youth made a public point of continuing to wear Timberland in the aim of embarrassing a company that did not want their custom. A subsequent move on the part of the same consumers to patronize the preppie clothing of Tommy Hilfiger, Nautica, and Ralph Lauren proved that the game of tag which youth subcultures play with mainstream fashionwear is increasingly part of the business cycle. The vast sportswear profits generated by endorsers like Michael Jordan, Shaquille O'Neal, and Charles Barkley have helped to create high-profile

no sweat

employment for dark-skinned African-American male models who look athletic and defiant. Such images, presented as the epitome of beauty, are a notable breakthrough in a history of public aesthetics which has either denigrated or exploited the look and physique of black males. But controversy over these issues of representation is usually disconnected from the stories about garment industry sweatshops; as Jordan or others in his position can say, "that's not my department." This is a reminder that some groups have pre-established priorities, and that labor-oriented coalitions and boycotts will have to respect and negotiate these priorities while working on a broad front.

Like Hollywood, the fashion industry is a darling vehicle for preferred causes or for fundraising on the society ladies' charity circuit: AIDS and breast cancer, for example, but not eating disorders or racial exclusion. Labor abuse within the industry is one of those topics that does not lend itself to being named as a fashionable cause, and yet in the wake of the Uprising of the Twenty Thousand in 1909, society ladies, many of them sympathetic to suffrage, were drawn to meet with the female strike leaders in Manhattan's elite Colony Club and subsequently joined their cause. Such meetings, discreet or otherwise, helped to forge a paternal welfare culture, where the dignity of labor was respected as an integral part of the nation's wardship. Today's culture of celebrity—where the images of winners are showcased as a public medium for commerce in style, entertainment, and ready-to-wear ideas—is a different landscape, explicitly laid out to obscure from view the underlying world of labor. Every so often, an event like the Kathie Lee Gifford scandal uncovers the whole line of production, bringing down public scrutiny on each of the links in the chain. Obviously, the system of celebrity endorsement will be tightened up as a result, rendering it less open to exposure, and loopholes in the elaborate system of employer's protection against liability will also be filled in. But there will be other openings, and that is why a broad, united front is all the more necessary to apply pressure at all points in the chain: from world trade policy to international human rights, workplace regulation, labor organizing, consumer politics, and fashion industry activism. The sweatshop campaigns of 1996 provided a successful model for coalitions between labor, environmental, and social justice interests: local and international, government and nongovernment, organized labor and community groups; aimed at the media, inclusive of a wide spectrum of tactics and resources, and targeting the weak links in capital's chain.

*AFL-CIO leaders support antisweatshop campaign.*
*Front row, from left: Secretary-Treasurer*
*Richard Trumka, Executive Vice President Linda*
*Chavez Thompson, President John Sweeney*
*with UNITE President Jay Mazur and Executive*
*Vice President Edgar Romney.*

# the global resistance to sweatshops

## John Cavanagh

Exploited workers in the apparel and footwear industries have seldom been silent "victims" in the face of sweatshop conditions. Workers around the world have fought these conditions, and joined with workers in other industries and allies in the religious, farm, environmental, and other activist communities to fight for dignity and justice.

Consider the Nike story. Over the past two decades, Nike closed its New Hampshire and Maine factories and increasingly subcontracted work to factories it did not own in Korea and Taiwan, where workers were paid little and denied basic rights. As unions spread in both of those countries, Nike shifted its suppliers primarily to Indonesia, China, and Thailand, countries where it could depend on governments to suppress independent union organizing efforts.

In 1991, a reporter asked Nike's general manager in Indonesia about supervisors beating workers and other labor abuses in these factories. The Nike manager replied: "It's not within our scope to investigate." He did say he was aware of "labor disturbances in the six factories that make Nike shoes," but he did not know what they were about. "I don't know that I need to know."[1]

Today, after numerous exposés and creative pressure by labor, religious, and other activists across North America and Europe, Nike acknowledges responsibility for working conditions in its subcontractors' factories overseas. Accordingly, the company has enacted its own internal code of conduct establishing labor guidelines for its suppliers. Reebok has followed suit.

But as labor rights activists remind us, there is still a long way to go. In particular, they are prodding Nike and other firms to expand their commitment by taking two more steps. First, Nike's code should require that its suppliers respect workers' rights to form unions and bargain collectively—key rights in the struggle for livable wages and benefits. Second, Nike must enforce its code through a network of independent monitors who will conduct factory spot-checks.

Meanwhile, labor rights activists at the International Labor Rights Fund in Washington, D.C., moved to pressure Nike and other firms on another front. In 1992, they filed a petition before the U.S. trade office charging that Indonesia permitted the systematic violation of worker rights and should be denied special trade privileges under a 1984 law that conditions the privileges on countries' respect for those rights. Ultimately, in 1994, the Indonesian

**no sweat**

government responded by announcing a 29 percent raise in the minimum wage. As a result, Nike and other manufacturers have been forced to raise wages. Similar, albeit weaker, labor (and environmental) language was attached to NAFTA which allows citizens to challenge corporate violations of national law before trinational commissions. By late 1996, citizen groups in the United States and Mexico had filed several challenges on worker rights and environmental violations; while all were dismissed, the cases did shine the spotlight of publicity on continuing abuses.

Twenty years ago, Institute for Policy Studies co-founder Richard Barnet (along with Ronald Muller) raised the question in *Global Reach* about which forces could pose "countervailing" power" to global corporations. Barnet focused on the strength of labor unions in the middle third of the twentieth century and the promise of more aggressive government action at local and national levels.

Today, governments are more compromised than ever in succumbing to corporate demands, and trade union movements around the world are much weaker. Yet countervailing power is emerging and it appears strongest when it derives from new coalitions of citizen movements coordinating not only across labor, environmental, consumer, and other social sectors, but also across geographical borders.

The campaign organized against the Gap was one such border-smashing initiative. (For the full story, see the contribution by Kitty Krupat in this volume.) But its success was due as well to the growing recognition among U.S. workers that their own interests now lie in helping workers elsewhere. As long as sweatshops exist in El Salvador or Indonesia, U.S. firms will use their ability to source production there to bargain down U.S. wages and working conditions to sweatshop levels here. To strengthen transnational links, in January 1996, UNITE joined with the National Consumers League and other groups to launch a Campaign Against Sweatshops at home and abroad. The alliance between these two groups was strategic. Many consumers seem willing to use their purchasing power to help workers: more than three-fourths of consumers polled in a 1995 survey of over a thousand adults by Marymount University said that they would avoid purchasing goods made in sweatshops, even if this meant paying higher prices.

Banking on consumer conscience has paid off in a number of campaigns. For instance, in May 1995, the Child Labor Coalition mobilized a consumer boycott of Bangladeshi clothing exports after investigations revealed the widespread use of child labor in the industry. The threat of a boycott convinced the Bangladesh Garment Manufacturers and Exporters Association to sign an agreement with UNICEF and the International Labor Organization (ILO) to move upwards of 25,000 children out of the garment industry and into schools. Close to $1 million from the three parties to the agreement will go toward verifying the end of child labor, education for the former child workers, and a modest stipend for their families. A novel feature of the settlement is that the Bangladesh garment firms have agreed to ILO training of independent monitors to do spot-checks in clothing factories. As with all such agreements, however, constant vigilance will be necessary to ensure compliance by the garment industry.

Some codes have prompted firms to cease subcontracting in countries with persistent records of human and worker rights abuses. The Sears and Levi Strauss codes, for example, prohibit these corporations from contracting production to firms that use prison labor or commit other specified breaches of worker rights. Chronic violations in China prompted Levi Strauss to announce that it would phase out all production contracts in that country.[2] Overall, Levi Strauss claims to have discontinued contracts with thirty-five of its roughly 700 subcontractors because of code infractions.[3] Eddie Bauer, Levi Strauss, and Liz Claiborne have all stopped subcontracting in Burma due to flagrant infringements of human rights.[4]

A major impetus behind several of the codes was a collective bargaining agreement between the Amalgamated Clothing and Textile Workers' Union (ACTWU, the union that merged with the International Ladies' Garment Workers' Union to form UNITE) and the

FOR THE GAP - THIS IS THEIR ENEMY

UNITE

SHAME ON YOU GAP

GAP

*left: Targeted by activists and consumers, GAP finally did the right thing.*

*right: Other companies which were not targeted, suffered some collateral damage.*

Clothing Manufacturers Association of the USA. Ratified on October 1, 1993, it stipulated that all employers within the Clothing Manufacturers Association would agree to a detailed set of worker rights provisions for any outsourcing contracts. European unions and development organizations working with labor rights advocates primarily in Asia likewise have begun a Clean Clothes Campaign to press retailers and garment firms on working conditions in their supplier factories.[5]

The British organization Christian Aid, working with the London-based Fairtrade Foundation and contacts in developing countries, examined these and other codes and drafted a Model Code of Practice that addresses their weaknesses.[6] In July 1995, several European and Asian organizations responded to fires and exploitive work conditions in Asian toy factories with a call on toy firms to adopt their Charter on the Safe Production of Toys.[7]

As other citizen organizations have joined the code initiative, they have employed consumer pressure to persuade more firms to adopt them. In early 1995, a coalition including the Guatemalan Labor Education Project induced Starbucks to draft a code governing conditions under which the coffee it sells is grown. In the early 1990s, citizen groups organized a "toycott" against Toys "R" Us to protest the use of child labor in China, where some 40 percent of U.S. toys now originate. The company has now endorsed a code prohibiting the use of child or slave labor by its subcontractors.

But formal ratification of a set of guidelines by itself will not deter abuses, in part because corporations attempt to limit the scope of their code or resist independent enforcement of the code. To date, several such problems have been noted. First, a lack of consensus on which worker rights and environmental standards should be protected in the codes has resulted in some egregious oversights. For instance, the codes neglect the issue of sexual harassment, an especially serious one in the textile industry since most managers are men and most workers are women. Second, the codes do not address or promote compulsory enforcement mechanisms. There is now ample evidence confirming that even when firms adopt codes of conduct to advance worker rights in their supplier factories, they seldom enforce them. A survey of codes in Guatemala by the *Wall Street Journal* revealed that corporations made next to no effort to train or encourage their own inspectors to monitor violations by subcontractors.[8] Third, wage clauses are unclear and inadequate, typically requiring only the payment of a "legal wage," which in most countries is far below the poverty level. UNITE has been lobbying for a "livable wage" based on the market value of a basket of consumer goods. Corporations claim (or feign) ignorance: the Coalition for Justice in the Maquiladoras found that many global firms do not know how much their subcontractors pay workers. Finally, many of the codes cover only their subcontractors and not the paid employees of the company. Codes should protect both.

Of these problems, the enforcement issue is perhaps the most difficult obstacle in the fight for effective codes. Corporations naturally prefer voluntary codes, but self-policing simply invites noncompliance. However, there are several avenues for advancing greater enforcement.

One strategy would be for unions to adopt the ACTWU–Clothing Manufacturers precedent and write codes into all new collective bargaining agreements. Another involves legislative pressure. Most governments offer firms incentives to invest overseas. In the United States, the Overseas Private Investment Corporation provides insurance for such ventures. A foreign tax credit allows U.S. firms to avoid paying U.S. taxes on their foreign subsidiaries' activities if the subsidiaries pay taxes in the host country. Portions of the tariff code offer incentives for firms to set up factories overseas to process U.S.-made parts and send them back to the United States.

As each of these programs comes before the U.S. Congress either for consideration or reauthorization, Congress could simply amend them to state that recipients of government resources must sign a statement agreeing to a corporate code. The code would be "voluntary" in the sense that firms could ignore it with impunity—and forfeit government benefits. Equivalent incentives exist in France, Germany, and other industrialized countries.

Even with such incentives, the question remains as to who will monitor enforcement. Concerning the labor rights provisions of codes, the United Nations ILO can offer some assistance. Funds could be set aside by each firm to pay for independent inspectors to make unannounced factory visits. As mentioned earlier, this was a feature of the 1995 memorandum of understanding governing child labor in Bangladesh's clothing factories. Likewise, in the "statement of agreement" signed by the Gap and the National Labor Committee in December 1995, the Gap agreed to work with other groups "to explore the viability of an independent industry monitoring program in El Salvador."

# no sweat

Contemporary struggles to curb corporate abuses are rooted in a number of battles in the 1970s waged by both governments and citizen groups. A strong global movement for greater corporate accountability emerged in the wake of revelations about IT&T's role in the Chilean coup of 1973. Spurred by pressure from Third World governments, the United Nations created a Commission on Transnational Corporations in 1975, which set out to negotiate a UN Code of Conduct on Transnational Corporations. The draft United Nations code prohibited bribery of public officials, required corporate disclosure of potential dangers of products and production processes, banned the export of goods from factories deemed unsafe, and a number of other measures. The Reagan administration vehemently opposed the effort, however, and negotiations collapsed.

Citizen groups such as the International Organization of Consumer Unions (IOCU) have worked hard to revive interest in the UN code or a similar set of guidelines and mechanisms on foreign direct investment. A number of groups, meeting in Delhi in February 1994 for a conference on Fairplay in Global Business, likewise committed themselves to this task. Meanwhile, other agencies within the United Nations continued to generate blueprints for regulating corporate behavior. In 1977, the ILO adopted the Tripartite Declaration of Principles Concerning Multinational Enterprises and Social Policy, a set of criteria for governments, firms, and workers covering industrial relations, employment, training, and labor conditions. Similarly, in 1976, the developed country members of the United Nations used the Organization of Economic Cooperation and Development (OECD) to pass guidelines on international investment and multinational enterprises encompassing many of these same areas.

In addition to these omnibus codes, the United Nations has developed rules governing specific issues. The most celebrated concerns the marketing of infant formula. Jointly negotiated by the World Health Organization and UNICEF, the code prohibits transnational infant formula producers from using deceptive marketing practices to sell baby food in developing countries. There have been movements to extend such marketing codes to pharmaceuticals, cigarettes, and alcohol as well.

Environmental groups spearheaded by Greenpeace launched a major campaign in the 1990s to convince governments to place restrictions on the international trade in hazardous waste products. This campaign culminated in sixty-five governments passing the Basel Convention to ban all aspects of toxic wastes by the year 1998.

Law professors Diane Orentlicher and Timothy Gelatt suggest that the Group of Seven would be a good forum for a concerted effort at adherence to a set of global principles on transnational corporations.[9] Since the overwhelming majority of the world's TNCs originate in these seven countries, this might prove a more feasible arena than the United Nations.

A number of broad-based international citizen campaigns have forced changes in corporate behavior and/or created new international mechanisms to hold corporate power in check. Many of these were launched in the 1970s, a period of growing global concern about the abuses of TNCs in the Third World. During much of the 1970s and '80s, Northern and Southern religious and consumer groups collaborated to attack Nestlé and other companies for deceptive marketing practices which induced mothers to forego breastfeeding in favor of commercially produced infant formula. Since waterborne diseases are primary killers in the developing world, powdered milk mixed with untreated water posed a significant health risk to children. Moreover, many poor families could ill-afford to spend their meager financial resources on a product that was available for free from mothers. These campaigns used the pressure of consumer boycotts which culminated in the World Health Organization/UNICEF marketing code.

An equally impressive campaign to break corporate business ties to South Africa as a protest against the racist policy of apartheid was instigated in many countries through the collective efforts of state and municipal officials, unions, religious groups, and others. Participants exploited myriad tactics and venues—selective investment, government procurement contracts, divestment—to pressure the apartheid regime to free Nelson Mandela from prison and to hold the country's first universal elections. Similar initiatives have been launched against hundreds of firms in recent years, deploying the power of individuals as consumers, workers, shareholders, and depositors. A recent issue of Co-op America's *Boycott Action News* documents campaigns against Philip Morris and fifty-seven other companies by citizen groups around the country.[10]

The Interfaith Center for Corporate Responsibility is a twenty-five-year-old association of nearly 250 denominations. Each year, ICCR members submit hundreds of shareholder resolutions to press for corporate accountability on the environment, alcohol and tobacco, equal opportunity, militarism, maquiladoras, and other issues. ICCR is part of a larger social/ethical investment movement which, through the power of large institutional shareholders, has the potential to exercise great influence in the corporate world.

Like governments, citizen groups have initiated codes of conduct in specific arenas that are prompting corporations to change their behavior. After the enormous oil spill from the Exxon Valdez, a number of leading environmental and consumer groups came together in 1992 to draft the CERES Principles, a list of ten principles of environmentally sustainable behavior that requires signatory firms to submit annual reports attesting to their compliance. Firms as diverse as Ben & Jerry's and General Motors have signed on.

The Coalition for Justice in the Maquiladoras pulled together over a hundred environmental, religious, community, labor, women's, and Latino organizations to fight the horrendous working and environmental conditions in the 2,000-plus factories that dot the 2,000-mile U.S.-Mexico border. The Coalition drew on U.S., Mexican, and United Nations criteria to craft the Maquiladora Standards of Conduct, which spells out acceptable standards for firms on the environment, health and safety, worker rights, and community impact.

These battles over the rules of trade and investment are transforming the conventional terms of political debate in the United States. For most of this century, big business and the Republican party fought for lower tariffs and fewer investment barriers; since what was good for General Motors was supposed to be good for the United States, their view was that GM should be encouraged to produce and trade anywhere in the world. Small business, labor, and many Democrats argued for nationalistic protections against imports.

Today, most Democratic and Republican presidential candidates and members of Congress preach free trade and lower investment barriers as the means to compete in a global economy. In the 1996 presidential primaries, only Pat Buchanan championed the protectionist position. His rhetoric, aimed at small business owners and workers, was anti-immigrant, racist, and intensely nationalistic. Xenophobia aside, his pronouncements were clear in naming trade agreements like NAFTA and the new World Trade Organization (WTO) as responsible for speeding up corporate globalization without any protections for workers, who have seen their wages and benefits eroded by mobile firms. Buchanan scored more political points among the "anxious class" of insecure workers by joining Ralph Nader in blasting a January 1996 WTO decision which challenges U.S. regulations requiring stringent environmental standards on gasoline imported into the United States.

Yet the debate is now much wider than Clinton and Dole's free trade dogma versus Buchanan's protectionism, thanks to the hundreds of efforts to press firms to abide by codes, and the move to attach labor and environmental conditions to trade agreements. Although it is a position that will rarely be featured on the nightly news, the emergence of a "third way" offers a path between the extremes of free trade and nationalistic protectionism.

This third way includes three prominent and often overlapping currents. Closest to the Buchanan end of the spectrum are the radical environmentalists and localization advocates who say "no" to large corporations and globalization through campaigns to kick Kentucky Fried Chicken out of India, liberate small-town America from Wal-Mart, and prevent pharmaceutical firms from patenting products derived from trees and other life forms. Another stream includes Ralph Nader and much of the anti-NAFTA and anti-WTO coalitions whose intent is to "slow down" globalization by defeating trade agreements that accelerate trade and investment by lowering barriers.

Finally, there is a wide array of citizen movements that are seeking to reshape globalization by rendering it more "socially and environmentally responsible." These include the mobilizations to add enforceable labor and environmental standards to trade agreements, the pressure on Starbucks and other firms for tough corporate codes, and the growing alternative trading movement that bypasses large corporate channels to deliver products made under more humane and sustainable conditions from cooperatives directly to consumers.

The overall message of these efforts to reshape globalization is that if you combine strong twenty-first-century global rights for corporations with weak twentieth-century national rights for labor and the environment, the result is a return to something more like the brutal capitalism of the nineteenth century. Hence, activists struggle both to curb the global rights of firms and to extend labor and environmental rights and standards to a global level.

Despite some tensions, these various strains of a third way came together dramatically in North America in the grass-roots, cross-sectoral, and cross-border alliances that opposed NAFTA. Since the NAFTA fight, these forces have linked together with other citizen movements in Europe and parts of the Third World in venues like the International Forum on Globalization. Headquartered in San Francisco and including participants from nineteen countries, the Forum organized a teach-in on globalization in New York's Riverside Church in November 1995 that drew 1,800 people. Similar strands came together that same weekend in Japan when more than 120 Asian citizen groups met to protest plans for a NAFTA-style free trade area in Asia.

These forces are united by an internationalist, anticorporate stance that counters Buchanan's nationalistic populism. Canadian anti-NAFTA activist Tony Clarke is leading an International Forum on Globalization effort in several countries to bring together activists around the theme of "challenging corporate rule," by which he means challenging not only corporate abuse of workers and the environment, but also their deepening purchase on political agendas worldwide.

The success of these citizen campaigns will depend in large part on moving beyond labor, environmental, and religious alliances to harness and organize consumer power. The United States still accounts for a quarter of the measured economic activity on the planet. Hence U.S. consumers hold the power to demand significant changes in the way goods are produced. As yet, however, there is little experience in the kind of consumer-labor-environmental-community coalitions that will be required for success. The future of efforts to transform trade and investment in a global economy will depend on innovations in organizing that break down traditional barriers among constituencies and across borders.

### The Child Behind the Label

August 1995, San Pedro Sula, Honduras—At 6:30 a.m., workers arrive at the gate of Orion Apparel, a Korean-owned factory in San Pedro Sula that produces Gitano shirts and sportswear for other American manufacturers. Each worker is searched as she goes through the door. Standing in line with them are Charles Kernaghan and Barbara Briggs of the National Labor Committee Education Fund in Support of Worker and Human Rights in Central America. Dressed as American business executives, they walk through the door unquestioned. With them is a camera crew, filming the line as it passes into the factory. Once inside, Kernaghan and Briggs begin asking questions: How old are the workers? What do they earn? How are they treated? One fifteen-year-old tells them she works till 8:30 most nights. She is the sole support of eight people in her family. She earns 38 cents an hour. *"Es suficiente*—Is it enough?"* Briggs asks. The girl shakes her head and whispers, *"No."* This same girl tells Briggs that supervisors yell at the girls and hit them. Another says workers are forced to take birth-control pills in the presence of plant supervisors.

Later, the outraged owner of Orion is caught on video, shouting at Kernaghan. "This is a private company. What right do you have to come in here?" Kernaghan, who is executive director of the National Labor Committee (NLC), answers disingenuously, "The door was open." In the war against sweatshops, the simple truth is NLC's greatest weapon. That night, Kernaghan, Briggs, and their camera crew are escorted to a factory garbage dump by Lesly Rodriquez, a fourteen-year-old Orion worker. The camera surveys piles of garbage, zooming in on hundreds of aluminum packets that once contained birth-control pills.

Kernaghan estimates that 500,000 people in the free trade zones of Central America and the Caribbean work in conditions like these, producing goods for U.S. markets. Most of them are women and young girls. The defense of their rights has become the mission of the NLC. "What that implies," Kernaghan says, "is bringing the system out into the light of day. So many companies have fled the United States—set up this enormous low-wage export platform—and nobody knows a thing about it. An hour and a half from our border. Who's investigating it? We took a part of the global economy and put a human face on it."

In the final analysis, NLC operates on populist faith. "Our job is to make the system translucent. There's something profoundly political about doing that," Kernaghan says. "In

*Outside ZIP Continental Free Trade Zone, Choloma, Honduras.*
*Trucks wait late at night to transport workers from the factories.*

a true democracy—if you have enough faith in people—you'd let them see how the system works, and they would decide what to do about it. Americans are not so cynical. They don't want to buy clothes made by kids who are being paid slave wages." Shoppers *are* becoming squeamish about buying clothes made in conditions like these, and NLC can take some credit for helping to rouse the public conscience.

Since beginning its investigation in 1990, NLC has made so many trips to the free trade zones that NLC associate Barbara Briggs has trouble accounting for every one. Her best recollection is eighteen. In the course of those trips, Briggs and Kernaghan have collected data on conditions in at least a hundred different garment factories. They get leads about these shops from religious and human rights groups operating in the region. Through this same network, they meet workers who tell them about conditions in the factories. Once they establish a relationship with the workers, Kernaghan and Briggs teach them how to collect the evidence—labels that tell NLC which American companies to go after.

The issue of manufacturer responsibility in the apparel industry is not a new one. For eighty years or more, it has been a driving force of union organizing and contract enforcement in the garment centers of major American cities.[1] Globalization has complicated the issue, at a time when the apparel industry is increasingly dominated by a few giant retailers, all of whom consign production to independent, offshore contractors.[2] They do not own these companies or hire the workers. Motivated by the desire for cheap labor, they have been happy to rely on local wage standards and local labor law enforcement—though factory owners are often unscrupulous, law enforcement is weak, and minimum wages (where applied) are incommensurate with the standard of living. Like the Gap, some retailers have issued company codes of conduct to their offshore contractors and may send company representatives on occasional inspection tours. Until recently, they have felt secure enough to leave it there. In 1995, however, the Gap was made to confront the extent of human rights violations in a Salvadoran sweatshop where Gap merchandise was produced, and every other retailer felt the shock waves.

In January 1995, NLC met a group of teenagers employed at Mandarin International, a factory in the San Marcos free enterprise zone of El Salvador. They were sewing garments for the Gap, Liz Claiborne, J. C. Penney, Eddie Bauer, and J. Crew. At 56 cents an hour,[3] they

# no sweat

Honduras, 1995: Charles Kernaghan
(back row, center) and Barbara Briggs
with fourteen-year-old Orion worker,
Lesly Rodriquez, and her mother.

worked eighteen hours a day, when orders from the U.S were heavy. They had to get a ticket to go to the bathroom and were punished if they stayed too long. Under these conditions, the Mandarin workers were trying to organize a union. Management was retaliating swiftly. Already many of the union activists had been fired. NLC recognized an opportunity to dramatize the plight of these teenage workers by targeting the Gap, whose fortunes depended so heavily on American teenage consumers.

Briggs, Kernaghan, and NLC research associate David Cook discussed ideas for a campaign against the Gap with Reverend David Dyson, the pastor of Lafayette Avenue Church in Brooklyn. A trade unionist of long standing, Dyson had been an aide to Cesar Chavez of the United Farm Workers. Later, at the Amalgamated Clothing and Textile Workers' Union, he had developed support campaigns for major organizing drives, including those at Farrah Pants and J. P. Stevens. One of NLC's closest advisers, Dyson helped to bring a cadre of religious activists into the Gap campaign.

In February, NLC issued an alert to its network of supporters, asking them to write letters of protest to the Salvadoran labor ministry. One NLC bulletin followed another, as mass lockouts, firings, and physical violence continued.[4] By June, 200 were fired, and NLC decided to bring workers to the U.S. for a speaking tour. Their first stop was the founding convention of UNITE (Union of Needletrades, Industrial, and Textile Employees).[5] For the next sixty days, teenagers Judith Viera and Claudia Molina traveled from city to city, talking to local advocacy organizations, business and professional groups, students and journalists. UNITE members in Dallas, San Francisco, and New York turned out to support them at rallies in front of Gap offices and stores. American youth, in particular, responded with enthusiasm and, according to former

# no sweat

**May 18, 1995**

**To: NLC Contacts**
**From: Charles Kernaghan**
**Re: Urgent Action Alert/**
**Request for Immediate Solidarity**

**Women maquiladora workers under attack in El Salvador at a plant producing for J.C. Penney, the Gap, Eddie Bauer, and Dayton-Hudson.**

At Mandarin International, a Taiwanese-owned plant in El Salvador where goods are being assembled for export to the U.S. under contract with major U.S. companies, 850 mostly women maquiladora workers are under attack.

In late January 1995, the women at Mandarin organized a union — the first union ever established in a free trade zone in El Salvador. At the time, the Salvadoran government and the Maquiladora Association pointed to Mandarin as living proof that workers rights and unions are respected in El Salvador. Reality proved otherwise.

Mandarin International immediately lashed out at the new union, at first locking out the workers and then illegally firing over 150 union members. The company hired two dozen ex-military plainclothed, armed "security guards." The women workers were told their union will have to disappear one way or another, or "blood will flow."

NLC staffer Ralph Rivera, uniformly across lines of gender, race, and ethnicity. Students at the United Nations high school in New York had received a grant from the Gap to bring high school students from across the country to a program at the UN General Assembly. After learning about the Mandarin situation, they returned the money and invited Charles Kernaghan to speak at the event. In Minneapolis, the Central America Resource Center sent out an appeal to some 7,000 students and got 2,000 to sign up for the campaign.

Hundreds of news accounts put the Gap under increasing pressure as the campaign went on. The *New York Times* alone published five op-ed columns by Bob Herbert. UNITE members continued to demonstrate at stores in Boston, Philadelphia, Chicago, St. Louis, Baltimore, and Freeport, Maine. Responding to the pressure, Gap senior vice-president for sourcing, Stan Raggio, met with Kernaghan and the Mandarin workers at corporate headquarters in San Francisco. Raggio pointed out that the company had a code of conduct, which it monitored for compliance periodically. The code of conduct had not been translated into Spanish, and the workers had never seen or heard of it, Kernaghan countered. Raggio went on to say that investigators had been following up on allegations of abuse but had found nothing to substantiate them. Nevertheless, he said the company was disturbed by the allegations and was thinking about withdrawing its orders from Mandarin, which it ultimately did.

This was not the outcome NLC wanted at all. "We didn't want the Gap to walk away from these workers, leaving them without jobs," Kernaghan explains. "If that happened, workers would learn a terrible lesson—you lose your job if you dare to speak up in defense of your rights." Caught in the dilemma of economic globalization, NLC's campaign might have been misconstrued as an effort to bring

jobs back to the United States at the expense of jobs to poor workers in El Salvador. So, continuing to press for reinstatement of the fired workers, the campaign redirected its energies toward driving the Gap and other retailers back into Mandarin. What NLC now demanded was the promise that Gap would install an independent, third-party monitoring system. "We put as much as we did into the Gap because we felt an independent monitoring system there would be a blueprint for independent monitoring not only in the garment industry but for other offshore industries as well," Kernaghan says.

The campaign continued unabated through December. "What we were discovering," Kernaghan recalls, "is that we had, not one Gap campaign, but many. We had left them behind in almost every city we'd visited." Several times during the campaign, fifteen or more of these local groups would coordinate their activities by conference call. In October, twenty-seven Salvadoran human rights activists sent a letter to Raggio, disputing outright the benign reports of the Gap's company monitors. That month, NLC drafted a strategic plan of action: continued calls and letter-writing; outreach to students and progressive business investment funds; participation from international advocacy groups; consumer actions during the holiday shopping season. In New York, on December 4, UNITE and NLC cosponsored a lunch-time rally at the Gap's Herald Square store. Protesters held signs saying, "The Real Gap Kids Work 12-

# no sweat

**October 13, 1995**

**Fired Mandarin Union Workers Demand a Meeting with the Gap to Set the Record Straight**

Translation from Spanish

**San Salvador**

**Mr. Stanley P. Raggio**
**Senior Vice-President**
**The Gap**

**Dear Mr. Raggio:**

**We, the undersigned members of the Union of Workers of Mandarin International (SETMI), are among the 332 unionists who were illegally fired by the management of Mandarin International.**

**We, along with many of our fired compañeras, could tell you of the abuses that we suffered at the Mandarin plant, including: forced work shifts until 4:00 a.m.; frequently being robbed of our overtime pay; being put out in the blazing sun all day as a form of punishment ... of how Colonel Luis Alonso Amaya and his "bullies" beat us when we organized our union, and of the death threats.**

**If you want to hear the truth, we will meet with you, but only in the presence of the National Labor Committee.**

**Sincerely,**

**The Union of Workers of Mandarin international, SETMI-CTD**

Hour Days." They also passed out copies of a statement issued earlier by the Gap, saying it would consider returning to Mandarin under certain circumstances.

Acting as intermediaries, David Dyson and his colleague Reverend Paul Smith met with Gap executives at Smith's church in Brooklyn Heights to discuss a meeting between the Gap and NLC. Angered by NLC's aggressive tactics, Raggio and his associates refused to meet with Kernaghan. Dyson refused to meet without him and walked out. The Gap executives left for the airport. As Dyson recounts it, standing in line for the San Francisco flight, Raggio suddenly decided they were headed in the wrong direction. They returned to Brooklyn to plan the meeting, which took place on December 15, 1995. In one long, hard negotiating session, Raggio, Smith, Dyson, and Kernaghan worked out the first independent monitoring agreement in the history of the apparel industry.

Under the agreement and an accompanying Statement of Purpose, the Gap agreed to restore production to the Mandarin plant, provide religious and human rights groups with access to all its Central American facilities, and work with them toward the development of monitoring procedures.[6] The resolution also called upon Mandarin to reinstate fired union activists.[7] A second agreement was signed in El Salvador by Mandarin management, independent monitors, and worker representatives. As a result, the monitoring system is up and running, under the care of Salvadoran organizations, including the human rights departments of Jesuit University and the Catholic Archdiocese and Centra (Centro por Estudio de Trabajo, a labor rights and research organization).

Four months after the Gap agreement was reached, NLC hit Wal-Mart by taking aim at TV talk-show host Kathie Lee Gifford. A line of clothes under Gifford's name was bringing her $9 million a

year in royalties. Some of those clothes were being produced for Wal-Mart at Global Fashion, a Honduran sweatshop where workers earned about $900 a year. NLC first encountered the Kathie Lee Plus label during a visit to Honduras on Gap business. Briggs and Kernaghan arranged to meet thirty workers from Global Fashion behind a lunch stand, across a four-lane highway some distance from the shop. When they got there, however, the workers recognized three young men they believed were company spies and wouldn't talk. On the sly, they gave Kernaghan and Briggs some labels and left. Later, twenty workers came to the headquarters of CODEH (Co-mmittee for the Defense of Human Rights in Honduras). In the presence of CODEH officials, they told NLC about working conditions at Global Fashion.

All through the Gap campaign, NLC kept in touch with workers at Global Fashion. With evidence in hand, they decided upon a public-relations strategy, focusing on Wal-Mart's celebrity endorser, Kathie Lee Gifford. They wrote to her directly on March 15, 1996, and again on March 28. The letters were passed along to Wal-Mart, whose senior vice-president, John Lupo, told NLC the company had pulled out of Global Fashion when it learned of child labor in the factory. "After exploiting these kids for a year or more, Wal-Mart thought it could put the problem to rest by dumping them out on the street," Kernaghan says. Determined to prevent other companies from sweeping labor violations under the rug, NLC decided to hold Wal-Mart

# no sweat

**Gap Returns to El Salvador Agrees to Independent Monitoring – Setting New Standard for the Entire Industry**

*Watershed Victory for Worker Rights*

*Agreement Reached with Gap*

On Friday, December 15, the Reverend Paul Smith convened a meeting between Gap senior vice-president Stan Raggio; sourcing guidelines director Dottie Hatcher; Gap consultant James Lukaszewski; Reverend David Dyson; and Charles Kernaghan.

**Excerpts from agreement:**

1. In Honduras and Guatemala, and across Central America, human rights officials will be allowed immediate access to plants producing Gap clothing to monitor compliance with Gap's code of conduct.

2. With this interim monitoring process in place, the Gap will work with the Interfaith Center for Corporate Responsibility (ICCR) and other interested groups to design and imple-ment a long-term system of independent monitoring of its contractors' plants.

3. By taking this step, The Gap becomes the first retailer to agree to independent monitoring.

accountable. Citing past violations, Kernaghan named Global Fashion and Kathie Lee Gifford in testimony at an April 29, 1996, hearing of the Congressional Democratic Policy Committee, chaired by California congress-man George Miller. He had a worker waiting in the wings to back him up.

Fifteen-year-old Wendy Diaz had been working at Global Fashion since she was thirteen. Brought to the U.S. for a speaking tour by NLC, she addressed the congressional committee and spoke at a press conference afterward:

> At Global Fashion, there are about 100 minors like me – thirteen, fourteen years old – some even twelve. On the Kathie Lee pants, we were forced to work almost every day from 8:00 pm to 9:00 pm... Sometimes they kept us all night long, working.... Working all these hours, I made at most 240 lempiras which is 31 U.S. cents. No one can survive on these wages... The supervisors insult us and yell at us to work faster. Sometimes they throw the garment in your face, or grab and shove at you. The plant is hot like an oven. The bathroom is locked and you need permission and can use it twice a day. Even the pregnant women they abuse. Sometimes the managers touch the girls, our legs or buttocks. Many of us would like to go to night school but we can't because they always force us to work overtime. We have no health care, sick days, or vacation. After we met with Charlie and Barbara the company threatened us with firing. They [said] they would fire all of us if we tried to organize. I am an orphan. I live in a one-room home with eleven people. I have to work to help three small brothers.

For millions of Americans who watch "Live with Regis & Kathie Lee" every morning at nine, Kathie Lee Gifford is virtually an icon of family values. Charged as an accomplice in the exploitation

*Frank Gifford meets the press after big handout at SEO.*

of children, America's mom was hard-hit. She nearly cried as she told her audience she was innocent: she wasn't the factory owner or the retailer; how could she know about conditions at Global Fashion? Then she threatened to sue Kernaghan. Losing it in front of four and half million people all but guaranteed the torrent of publicity that followed.[8] All through it, Kernaghan kept asking the key question: Didn't Kathie Lee have a responsibility to see that her name was well used?

Meanwhile, UNITE had discovered Seo Fashions, a sweatshop in the garment district of Manhattan, where Kathie Lee clothes were made and where the workers had been cheated out of overtime pay. Outflanked by NLC and UNITE, Kathie Lee and husband Frank Gifford took the high road, handing out money to the workers in New York, urging Wal-Mart to accept independent monitoring in Honduras, and pledging at a press conference with Labor Secretary Robert Reich to lead a star-studded campaign against child labor and sweatshop conditions the world over. After Governor George Pataki of New York announced passage of antisweatshop legislation on June 25, 1996, Kathie Lee modestly accepted the congratulations of her TV sidekick, Regis Philbin.

The Giffords had hired Howard Rubenstein, a high-priced public relations consultant, to help them orchestrate this conversion. While some reporters praised the Giffords, others speculated on their sincerity. Likewise, though Kernaghan was hailed as a crusader in most news accounts, his research methods and aggressive tactics were assailed by industry executives.[9] It hardly mattered. By the P. T. Barnum standard of name recognition, the publicity was a bonanza all around. On the level of survival skills, these adversaries were well matched. The Giffords had fame, money, and an adoring public on their side; NLC had the moral authority of teenaged Wendy Diaz. Under the circumstances, Kernaghan didn't care too much about being villainized. "We fight to win," he says. At the same time, he gives credit where it's due.

"Kathie Lee met with Wendy Diaz, and I think she had the same reaction all decent people have. She apologized to Wendy and gave her word she would do what she could,"

**"You can say I'm ugly. You can say I'm not talented. But when you say I don't care about children and that I will exploit them for some sort of monetary gain, for once, Mister, you'd better answer your phone because my attorney is calling you today. How dare you?"** — Kathie Lee Gifford  May 1, 1996

Kernaghan said. Following the meeting, Gifford issued a joint communiqué with NLC and other participants, including UNITE president Jay Mazur and Reverend David Dyson. Essentially a statement of principles, the communiqué called for worldwide codes of conduct and an alliance of manufacturers and retailers, committed to the creation of a universal third-party monitoring system. Specifically, Kathie Lee Gifford would urge Wal-Mart to reverse a decision to remove its production from Global Fashion, providing Wal-Mart worked with the local management to correct violations and establish independent monitoring procedures.[10] Though Wal-Mart did not immediately agree to return to Global Fashion, it did agree to return to Honduras and to set up independent monitoring in its contracting shops. Whether or not Wal-Mart and Global Fashion continue to do business, the Kathie Lee affair is momentous for its impact on the larger issue of "responsibility." The world's largest retailer, Wal-Mart has brought others along in its wake. Liz Claiborne has begun talking to NLC about independent monitoring. Though Reebok did not meet directly with NLC, the company told Jesse Jackson it would consider plans for independent monitoring. After Kathie Lee's personal ordeal, celebrities are on the alert and will almost certainly start asking questions before selling their names.

Kathie Lee and the Gap are fixtures in American popular culture. NLC picked them above other big names in the apparel industry, hoping to cash in on their public appeal. Their calculations were correct. The impact of these two campaigns has been global. In a front-page story on June 6, 1996, *Women's Wear Daily* acknowledged that NLC is "shaking up the issue of labor abuses in the apparel industry like nothing since the Triangle Shirtwaist fire." When Robert Reich convened an apparel industry summit meeting on July 16, some 200 industry executives, union leaders, journalists, and celebrity endorsers showed up. NLC remained in the background of that meeting, but its influence was discernible, if only in the prominence of Kathie Lee Gifford. More gratifying to NLC, however, was the prominence of independent monitoring, a subject that dominated discussion throughout the day.

Media attention has given NLC an opportunity to push its campaign against another American icon, Walt Disney. Soon after the Kathie Lee exposé, *Newsday* carried a front-page photo of Haitian garment workers amid piles of Disney T-shirts. What Kathie Lee did for the issue of child labor, Disney should do for starvation wages. Disney markets Mickey Mouse shirts and Pocahontas pajamas in the U.S., made by workers earning the legal minimum wage of 28 cents an hour in Haiti. Some earn even less. In Haiti, as elsewhere, NLC rejects local wage standards based on legal minimums or market rates. What it demands instead is a *living* wage. In July 1996, a *Los Angeles Times* reporter followed Briggs and Kernaghan on a trip to Port-au-Prince and documented the desperate situation of workers in one of the poorest countries in the world, where unemployment runs to 70 percent. Totaling the cost of carfare to and from work, a breakfast of fruit juice and cornmeal, and rice and beans for lunch, reporter Barry Bearak calculated that a garment worker spent nearly her entire daily earnings of $2.40 before returning home.[11] Case histories like this fill a thirteen-page open letter to Disney CEO Michael Eisner. In the letter, NLC calls for a 30 cent an hour wage increase, an amount determined by workers themselves. With that additional 30 cents, they told NLC, workers would still be poor but they would not be miserable. (The Eisner letter and accompanying documents are reprinted in this volume.)

*Kathie Lee Gifford: Positive or negative?*

**NLC's Legacy: A Challenge to Foreign Policy**

In the speed of a two-minute sound bite, NLC achieved name recognition. If publicity gave the Committee a great push forward, it also suppressed nearly two decades of activist history. The daring investigative style of NLC owes much to its predecessor organization, the National Labor Committee in Support of Democracy and Human Rights in El Salvador. The Committee goes back to 1980, when a handful of New York unionists began meeting after-hours at the headquarters of the Amalgamated Clothing and Textile Workers' Union. Dave Dyson, then on ACTWU's staff, was a founder of the New York committee.[12] The group was concerned about U.S. involvement in the civil war, just beginning in El Salvador. They were equally concerned about AFL-CIO support for U.S. foreign policy in Central America. On both counts, it seemed, El Salvador could turn into another Vietnam. According to Dyson, the Vietnam factor cannot be overemphasized: "Almost all of us involved with the local committee and eventually the national committee had been in some way affected and traumatized by the war in Vietnam."

Though a number of unions and thousands of individual union members joined the antiwar movement, they were marginalized inside the institutional labor movement. All through the war, even when public opinion was divided on the issue, the AFL-CIO under George Meany's leadership had maintained steadfast support for administration policies in Vietnam. According to retired ACTWU president Jack Sheinkman—who was one of the dissenters—union leaders who opposed the war were under heavy pressure to toe the line. Now, Lane Kirkland seemed to be leading the Federation down the same path in Central America. "We got squashed on the Vietnam debate inside the labor movement," Dyson says. "We didn't want it to happen again."

The committee, whose members came from several unions in New York, were skeptical of solidarity groups whose politics seemed to them sectarian. Nevertheless, they were impressed by a documentary film, *El Salvador: Another Vietnam?*, produced by the Committee in Solidarity with the People of El Salvador (CISPES), and used it as the centerpiece of educational forums held at union halls around town. By the end of its first year, the committee had a presence in New York and captured the interest of Sheinkman, then secretary-treasurer of ACTWU. He began talking to Dyson about the possibility of going national. Taking the initiative, Sheinkman floated the idea to a few other national labor leaders. Two union presidents at the time, Doug Fraser of the United Automobile Workers and William Winpisinger of the International Association of Machinists, agreed to co-chair a national committee with Sheinkman. Six other union presidents signed on by November 1981, when the National Labor Committee in Support of Democracy and Human Rights in El Salvador was launched with a full-page ad in the *New York Times*. The Committee ultimately grew to include the presidents of twenty-three unions.

The NLC was a part-time operation with a staff of one. (Dyson did the work, along with his full-time job.) A top-level, internal leadership project at first, the Committee sought to challenge AFL-CIO policy on El Salvador by influencing members of the Federation's Executive Council. As a personal matter, Dave Dyson interpreted the challenge more broadly. He was interested in addressing the role of organized labor in American life. "What is the role of the AFL-CIO in confronting an issue like Vietnam or Central America?" he now asks. "Should it be lock-step patriotic support of U.S. foreign policy, regardless of its effect on workers? Or should the AFL-CIO be an advocate for workers, regardless of American foreign policy?"

Until its first trip to El Salvador in 1983, the Committee functioned like other opinion groups, issuing press releases and taking out ads. After that visit in 1983, however, the NLC was launched on a course of human rights activism that foreshadowed NLC's work today. Through NACLA, the North American Congress on Latin America, the Committee had established contacts with the Salvadoran labor movement and learned a great deal about repressive measures taken by El Salvador's military regime against opposition union leaders. Many were in prison or had disappeared. Others had been tortured or murdered by El Salvador's gestapo, the infamous death squads. At NACLA's urging, NLC sent a delegation to El Salvador in 1983 to investigate these atrocities.

In the course of their investigation, the NLC discovered the presence of U.S. apparel firms in El Salvador. "We ran into Bali Bra, Kimberly Clark, and Levi Strauss," Dyson recalls. Salvadoran trade unionists, who had been unable to organize these companies, told them the United States Agency for International Development (USAID) was helping U.S. apparel manufacturers get established in El Salvador. They heard it again from U.S. embassy officials, who talked candidly to members of the NLC, assuming they were an official delegation of the American Institute for Free Labor Development (AIFLD). An affiliate of the AFL-CIO

# no sweat

International Affairs Department, AIFLD was created after the 1959 Cuban revolution to train and support anticommunist unions in Latin America. Though by 1980 AIFLD's board was composed entirely of union officials, its founding board had included executives of United Fruit, Pan American Airlines, and the W. R. Grace Company. Controversial from the start, AIFLD was implicated in a series of anticommunist intelligence operations in the Dominican Republic, Guyana, and Brazil. In 1964, AIFLD-trained workers participated in the coup that ousted Brazilian president João Goulart. Speculation about the extent of AIFLD's ties to the CIA was widespread by 1983, when NLC made its first mission to El Salvador.[13]

The experience was a revelation, Sheinkman recalls. While many NLC members had suspected it, here was compelling evidence that workers and unions in the U.S. and El Salvador were victims of a self-serving relationship between cold war politics and neoliberal economics. Though references to the effects of free trade appeared in almost every NLC publication thereafter, the economic issues remained secondary as the war intensified and more labor leaders were marked for death. "It seemed wrong to talk about something that could be interpreted as our own self-interest, while Salvadorans were getting slaughtered," Dyson explains. A report issued by the 1983 delegation went out to about 1,200 trade unionists, a range of activist organizations, and government officials. In addition to the original New York committee, other local NLC chapters were springing up around the country. NLC continued to make dangerous missions to Central America. In July 1988, the author represented District 65 of the United Automobile Workers on a fact-finding tour that included New York state assemblyman Frank Barbaro and *Newsday* reporter Ken Crowe. One day, a group of Salvadoran union leaders took us on a tour of militarized work sites in San Salvador. Traveling along a main thoroughfare, our van was stopped by Treasury Police, and the Salvadorans were ordered out. Slapped up against a wall at gunpoint, they were searched as we watched from the windows of the van. Terrified we might bring harm to our comrades, no one said a word. After about ten minutes, the Salvadorans were allowed back into the van. An elegant-looking military man thrust his machine gun through a window, straight into my face, it seemed. "We want you to know that we know who you are and what you are doing here," he said in flawless English. Then, withdrawing his gun, he wished us a nice day and waved the van on. When we arrived at our destination, we saw a crowd gathered on the corner and went to investigate. There was a

*Members of farmworkers' collective, "disappeared" by Salvadoran death squads during the civil war.*

large pool of blood on the ground. An ambulance had just carried off a seven-year-old girl, shot in the midst of the crowd by a young soldier no more than seventeen. He was trembling visibly as he gave a report to his superior officer. What union leaders learned from experiences like these had already contributed to mounting concern about Central America inside the AFL-CIO.

Though NLC had confined its campaign to El Salvador, it was the civil war in Nicaragua that finally brought Central America to the floor of an AFL-CIO convention in 1985. First to speak out was Kenneth Blaylock, president of the American Federation of Government Employees. A member of NLC, he had made a trip to El Salvador and Nicaragua and described what he saw:

> I sat in a church [in El Salvador] late one night and listened to mothers… tell about the atrocities being perpetrated against them and their families… This technique of military operation, it would literally bring tears to your eyes… We see… square miles and miles of homes and farms destroyed, it makes you wonder what our government is about.… When I look at Iran, I look at Vietnam, I look at Nicaragua… El Salvador, Guatemala, I would like for one time for my government to be on the side of the people, not on the side of rich dictators living behind high walls…

After that, a succession of delegates rose to condemn Reagan administration support for the antirevolutionary contra forces in Nicaragua. None of them were radicals. Like Jack Sheinkman, most had probably grown up committed anticommunists. They were reacting from a working-class instinct. If Reagan and the rich corporations were for the contras, labor had better be against them! This floor debate on Central America was the first open challenge to AFL-CIO foreign policy anyone could remember. It ended with a compromise resolution that condemned the left-wing Sandinistas of Nicaragua but called for a negotiated settlement of the war there and in El Salvador.[14]

The contacts NLC had made on its first trip developed into a network of personal relationships with Salvadoran unionists, human rights activists, and opposition political leaders, including democratic socialists Guillermo Ungo and Reuben Zamora.[15] Such relationships made it possible for NLC to gather information and develop a rescue operation modeled on the style of Amnesty International. NLC enlisted the support of trade unionists and Social Democratic party leaders in Italy, France, England, Germany, and Scandinavia. Sensitive to international opinion, the governments of El Salvador and the United States could not easily ignore letters and calls from these NLC supporters. With the help of sympathetic legislators—Congressman Joe Moakley and Senator Edward Kennedy, among others—NLC was able to negotiate the release of imprisoned trade unionists and arrange for political asylum with the embassies of *left: El Salvador, 1989: Sister and children of union leader Ricardo Lazo, moments after Lazo and his wife were taken from their home.*

Holland, Mexico, and Canada. In the course of NLC's campaign, thirty to forty prisoners were released by the Salvadoran Treasury Police to representatives of the International Red Cross. But, once released, they were sitting ducks for the death squads, and NLC had to get them out of the country in a matter of hours. It reached the point, Dyson says, where NLC's network could react instantly to an SOS from El Salvador.

Activists were galvanized by events in Central America, but something was missing, Dyson says—"People on the street." CISPES had organized a few protest demonstrations, but its open support for revolutionary forces in Central America drew a limited response from working people and trade unionists. Shifting the emphasis to U.S. foreign policy, a coalition of religious leaders and trade unionists called for a mass demonstration in Washington, on April 25, 1987. An ordained Presbyterian minister and a trade unionist, Dyson was a natural choice to coordinate the rally. The demonstration drew a crowd of 100,000 to the nation's capital. Dyson is still amazed by the numbers as he recalls the freezing rain that day. He estimates that 35 percent of the turnout was union.

There was a great deal of tension in the background to this success story, however, and some ugly incidents. In the months leading up to the demonstration, Dyson reports, the offices of the coalition had been vandalized and his co-coordinator was under surveillance, he assumes by the FBI. By the day of the rally, he was worn out. Till the final hour, he had continued to mediate ideological differences between participating organizations, ranging from militant solidarity groups to relatively conservative unions. For some time, the AFL-CIO had been putting pressure on NLC committee members to resign. No one did, but the demonstration was a source of anxiety to some Committee members, who feared an open confrontation with the Federation. Ultimately, the Committee hung together in support of the demonstration, despite a memorandum issued by the AFL-CIO denouncing the event. On the day of the demonstration, the AFL-CIO building was closed and surrounded by security guards.

A year before the march on Washington, free-lance photographer Charles Kernaghan joined a peace march in El Salvador. While there, he spent three days occupying the cathedral in San Salvador, lying in the catacombs of the church with 500 campesinos, one bathroom, and very little food. "Being in the cathedral was tough for me—not speaking Spanish," he

69

recalls. "I can do a lot of hard things, but then I wished I was in the woods, lying under a tree." He was assigned by march organizers as a bodyguard to Humberto Centeno, the president of ASTTEL, an association of telephone and telecommunications workers fighting for union recognition and the right to bargain. In one year alone, six leaders of the campaign had been murdered and one had disappeared. Centeno's life had been threatened and his sons were in Mariona Prison. Kernaghan met them there, got drawn into their lives and into the ASTTEL campaign. The experience radicalized him, and when he returned to New York, exhausted and overwrought, he sat down to write about it. "I haven't stopped since," he says.

Without knowing anything about the National Labor Committee—with no copy machine, no mailing facilities, and only his private phone—Kernaghan set out to organize a labor rights campaign from his apartment on Manhattan's Lower East Side. To help him finance the campaign, his parents split their Social Security checks with him. He worked alone for two years until he met Dan Kane, president of Teamster Local 111. Kane's was a local of communications workers, so he had a particular interest in the ASTTEL campaign. He offered Kernaghan office space and facilities at Local 111, and Kernaghan moved in.

As a result of the move, Kernaghan began to establish labor contacts. After meeting Dyson in 1988, he joined the New York chapter of NLC, which adopted the ASTTEL campaign.

Within a year, Kernaghan assumed leadership of the New York chapter, which now included Barbara Briggs, who had returned to the U.S. after several years of study in Central America. Needing additional staff, Dyson asked them both to join the national committee.

### Workers' Rights: A Fundamental Human Right

In 1990, the peace accords in El Salvador were signed, ending a twelve-year civil war. Though many trade unionists and human rights workers were lost, many others are alive today as a result of NLC's rescue missions.[16] Around the time of the peace accords, Dave Dyson made a decision to return full-time to the ministry. The NLC could have folded then and there, but Kernaghan lobbied to redirect the Committee's efforts toward workers' rights. Few human rights organizations at the time had given full attention to this issue, and Kernaghan thought NLC could help bring workers' rights to the fore, as a fundamental human right. Some people thought Chile or Brazil, controlled by powerful military dictatorships, were better targets for such a campaign than the tiny nations of Central America. But Kernaghan argued strongly to stay put: "Over the years, NLC had built up deep contacts on the ground in Central America. They were precious, based on real trust and real faith. We were hooked up to labor groups, religious groups, women's organizations, students. We had local chapters all across the United States. It seemed nuts to throw it all away." With the Caribbean Basin Initiative in place since 1983, American companies were rushing to Central America and the Caribbean in search of cheap labor. With trade liberalization replacing cold-war conflict as the axis of U.S.–Central America relations, Sheinkman also wanted to continue the Committee's work. As the human rights agenda of NLC developed, he agreed that an independent Committee was desirable and hired Kernaghan as a full-time director, using foundation money and private contributions to cover his salary.

Under the Foreign Assistance Act of 1961, USAID was mandated to help raise living standards for poor people in developing countries. But on its first trip to El Salvador in 1983, NLC had already learned that USAID was directly helping U.S. corporations profit from depressed standards in a poor country. In 1990, NLC turned its attention to the role of USAID in facilitating capital flight to the free trade zones. A two-year period of research and undercover activities had revealed a lavish USAID promotional program to lure U.S. companies to free trade zones, including the development of industrial parks in more than 200 export-processing zones, tax incentives for relocation, technical assistance, and worker training programs. To finance these projects, the Reagan and Bush administrations had funneled over a billion U.S. tax dollars to USAID.

NLC began compiling lists of U.S. apparel companies that had moved to the free trade zones and compared them to WARN statistics on plant closings and job loss in the U.S. (The Worker Adjustment Retraining Notification Act, WARN, requires sixty days' notice of closings.) A partial list from 1988 to 1992 showed eighty-one companies (owned by such corporations as Calvin Klein, Levi Strauss, Gitano, Sara Lee, and Kellwood) operating in the free trade zones at a cost of more than 15,000 U.S. jobs. To all intents and purposes, U.S. workers were paying to lose their own jobs.

To field-test its data, NLC invented a New York–based company called New Age Textiles. As business entrepreneurs looking for a good deal in the free trade zones, Kernaghan and Briggs went to the Bobbin Contexpo apparel trade show in Miami. Among the exhibitors they encountered were promotional organizations funded by USAID. Some of these promoters later sponsored New Age Textiles on a tour of the business circuit in Central America. While Briggs and Kernaghan hobnobbed with the promoters in El Salvador, Honduras, and Guatemala, they were secretly meeting with human rights activists to get information about working conditions in the maquiladoras. Their exploits are documented in *Paying to Lose Our Jobs*, a research report issued by NLC in 1992. (Excerpts are reprinted in this volume.)

Before the report was released, Kernaghan accompanied a "60 Minutes" producer and camera crew to El Salvador. Posing as an executive of New Age Textiles, the producer talked directly to USAID officials. New Age Textiles was encouraged to lay off its New York workers and relocate to El Salvador. New Age would be very happy with the quality of work in El Salvador, and—since union activists are fired and placed on a blacklist—they could be sure of a union-free environment. "We know names of people you probably will not want to hire," agency official John Sullivan told them.

Back in the U.S., "60 Minutes" sent sweater manufacturer Bernard Lax to the State Department to ask how USAID could help him move his Los Angeles company to Honduras. Lax was sent to a Honduran business promoter, who told him about tax provison 936. Under

936, Lax could get a loan so cheaply the startup cost would be negligible. "It's as if someone's giving you the money to start business," he said.

Aired Sunday, September 27, 1992, the "60 Minutes" exposé triggered a media chain reaction. The following Tuesday and Wednesday, Ted Koppel featured the story on "Nightline." Within the week, presidential candidate Bill Clinton and his running mate Al Gore had taken up the issue. On the Phil Donahue show, with laid off workers from Decaturville Sportswear Factory in Tennessee, Gore blasted George Bush for the tax scam that helped Decaturville relocate to El Salvador. In a matter of days, USAID got the message. On October 2, a House-Senate conference committee banned the use of tax dollars to provide incentives for offshore business relocation and for projects resulting in human rights violations.

The "60 Minutes" experience taught NLC an important lesson about the angles. "If you wanted to move human rights issues in the U.S., you could do two things," Kernaghan says. "You could talk about union busting and put the whole country to sleep. Or you could talk about the use of taxpayers' money to send jobs overseas and impact on a presidential election. You can have the greatest issue in the world, but if you don't know how to move it, that issue doesn't exist."

### Defining a Human Rights Agenda

After "60 Minutes," the Committee found a distinctive, if idiosyncratic, style that served it well in the case against the Gap and Wal-Mart. With an annual operating budget of $250,000 and a staff of three, NLC has developed compensatory work habits, based on unlimited hours and total commitment. They have learned how to conduct a campaign on several levels simultaneously and have acquired a taste for realpolitik. Every campaign is underwritten by research, but NLC sticks to basics at the public level. An experienced speaker by now, Charlie Kernaghan still takes a shopping bag up to the podium with him. As he reels out statistics on wages and working conditions in Haiti, he pulls out a Pocahontas T-shirt and says, "A Disney worker in Haiti gets 7 cents for making this shirt. It sells in the U.S. for $11.97. It isn't right." For a combination of reasons, NLC has become synonymous with its director. The Committee has no bureaucratic tier of leadership. With his powerful personality, Kernaghan is a media natural—a passionate man whose image can be shaped to fit the American ideal of rugged individualism. To the extent NLC has been personified, however, the complexities and multidimensional character of its work have been obscured.

The National Labor Committee makes no self-conscious or theoretical claim to global significance. Yet it is a player on the stage of globalization, where human rights rise to the level of universality as they transcend national borders. To prosecute its campaign, NLC has adopted a transnational strategy: exposing a system of economic globalization that gives rise to local abuses; teaching workers in the free trade zones to defend themselves; bringing them face-to-face with U.S. workers and consumers; demanding remedies that link transnational corporations to regional groups. In a lengthy interview on August 14, 1996, Kernaghan talked about NLC's philosophy, some of its most successful tactics, and its plans for the future.

"We've issued three reports since *Paying to Lose Our Jobs*. We do thorough research. But then we translate it into a human story. We use anecdotal examples and language that's accessible to people."[17] Though the accuracy of NLC's research has been questioned,[18] Kernaghan takes pride in the fact that he is not a professional—not a trained organizer, economist, or academic. Hard as they try, he claims, U.S. companies have been unable to refute NLC's findings and are stumped by the simplicity of their techniques. "They can't figure out how we get information out of an obscure company in Haiti. 'How in the hell do they get the labels? How do they get a worker to talk with them in a country where being seen with a foreigner will get you fired?' How? It's because of the longstanding personal relationships NLC has developed over the years with the religious community, human rights and women's groups, with unions and universities. At this point, we have a reputation. People trust us. When workers come to the U.S. to speak for NLC, we tell them they'll be fired when they go back. But we also tell them NLC will always protect them. We've raised money to send a number of them to school." The money sometimes comes from unlikely sources. A government official, who Kernaghan declined to identify, is paying for Wendy Diaz's schooling back in Honduras.

Young workers have been NLC's best campaigners. "We wanted the most authentic, direct, virtually naive workers we could find. We had faith that these young kids would simply tell the truth, and that would be more damaging than anything an academic could say." In reality, it's more complicated than it sounds. Kernaghan and Briggs have developed an intensive educational technique to help workers like Wendy Diaz and Judith Viera become eloquent witnesses once they come to the United States.

"They stay in our apartment. We're together constantly, talking and learning from one another. In my opinion, it's filthy and rude to bring a young worker up from Central America and just say, 'Here's a speech. Go ahead.' She'd say, 'We're oppressed.' What does that mean? No one ever asked her to define it. Why? How? Name it. We do that. We really press them to be specific. 'They yell at us.' 'What do they say?' 'They just yell at us.' 'How?' 'They call us chicken heads, we're born of whores.' 'They hit us.' 'Well how do they hit you?' 'They hit us on the head.' 'How?' 'With their knuckles.' We make them write it down and practice their delivery till it's polished. They're so elevated by the fact that someone has given them their own voice and the chance to speak for all their co-workers, they dig inside themselves, and they're unstoppable."

With little more than a good strategy and wide-ranging support, the National Labor Committee has shamed the apparel industry into taking stock of its labor practices. It has been able to accomplish this precisely because it travels light. Structurally lean, NLC is flexible and independent. It has moved around, made decisions quickly, reacted to situations as they develop, taken risks a more encumbered organization could not. It is supported by relatively small funding agencies, including the Unitarian Universalist Veatch Program at Shelter Rock, ARCA, and the New World Foundation. Unions continue to provide a third of NLC's budget and remain an important ally. "On the Gap and Kathie Lee campaigns, we coordinated very closely with UNITE and it was very effective," Kernaghan says. Nevertheless, NLC regards autonomy as essential and defines its distinct role accordingly.

"Independence is essential for our work in the free trade zones. People trust you when they know your only agenda is helping them defend their rights. The right to organize is fundamental, of course, but I don't think it's our job to do it. Our job is education. Most maquiladora workers don't know a thing about how profitable U.S. companies are; they never heard of codes of conduct. So the companies have got their hands around defenseless people. Knowledge is power. Once people have it, they may be able to organize. We do education on two fronts. In effect, we always have two campaigns going on simultaneously—one in the U.S. to educate consumers, and one in Central America to inform the human rights and religious communities about U.S. companies. The companies say they have codes of conduct and

monitoring systems. But these local groups don't know what that means. Yet, they're the ones who will have to develop independent monitoring procedures.

"We've acted as cultural interpreters. After the Gap agreement was reached, we went to El Salvador and met with the people from Jesuit University and Centra. We've been in continuous dialogue with them about what independent monitoring requires in the context of a U.S. system. Ultimately, they told *us* what to do and designed the independent monitoring system themselves. They'll figure out how to enforce human rights, codes of conduct, labor law in their own country."

Does NLC have the capacity to expand upon its current achievements? Can it move on to other regions and other industries without compromising the gains it has already made in Central America and the Caribbean? Kernaghan has no hesitation acknowledging that NLC needs to double its funding and its staff in order to move forward. Following the "Kathie Lee" campaign, NLC hired a part-time communications associate and organizer. Her job is to reactivate, expand, and coordinate the international network of students and advocacy groups that developed during the Gap campaign. If it can be put to work, NLC will have a strong base of operations. NLC has also reconfigured its board, adding international human rights leaders and academics who are instrumental in the Committee's work.

*left: Fifteen-year-old Wendy Diaz (center)
with Global Fashion co-workers.*

The religious community has been one of NLC's most important allies. "They give us credibility and put enormous moral pressure on the companies," Kernaghan says. NLC is working closely with People of Faith, an activist religious coalition, put together by David Dyson and a number of other prominent theologians. With an emphasis on poverty and racism, the coalition aims to be an alternative to the Christian Right. "Our work with them is the most exciting new thing we're doing," Kernaghan says. And that's as far as he wants to go for now. "Our options are open. Our mission is to promote human rights. If companies get too used to us in Central America, we may decide to go to Indonesia. I haven't the slightest idea. Everything is done at the moment it feels right."

**Postscript:** In October 1996, the NLC extended its campaign eastward to Burma, whose military dictatorship has been charged by the UN Commission on Human Rights with abuses ranging from forced labor to rape. According to an NLC report on October 10, workers in the Yangon apparel factory worked sixty hours a week, at 6 cents an hour, to produce Mickey Mouse T-shirts for the Disney company. Charlie Kernaghan bought one of these shirts at Macy's for $17.00, the equivalent of four and half weeks' wages for a single Burmese worker. Wittingly or not, Disney shared the profits with the Burmese government, a 45 percent owner of Yangon. After public pressure from the NLC and others, Disney pulled out of Burma (see Postscript).

*Charlie Kernaghan: "Sweat Detective".*

edited excerpts from a report
issued in 1992 by
the National Labor Committee

# paying to lose our jobs

## Charles Kernaghan

### U.S. Tax Dollars at Work

A striking ad appeared recently in a prominent U.S. trade journal. It shows a woman working at an industrial sewing machine. The bold-print caption reads:

**Rosa Martinez produces apparel for U.S. markets on her sewing machine in El Salvador. You can hire her for 33 cents an hour. Rosa is more than just colorful. She and her co-workers are known for their industriousness, reliability and quick learning. They make El Salvador one of the best buys.**[1]

U.S. tax dollars paid for this ad. In fact, the little-known organization that placed the advertisement, the Salvadoran Foundation for Economic and Social Development (FUSADES), has received $102,397,000 in U.S. government funding since 1984. U.S. assistance accounts for 94 percent of FUSADES' total budget.[2]

With U.S. tax dollars, FUSADES operates investment-promotion offices in New York and Miami, and is about to open a third office in California. In a 1991 funding agreement, the U.S. Agency for International Development (USAID) directed FUSADES' U.S. operation to pursue a "proactive, direct and systematic sales effort involving direct contact with targeted U.S. firms to…convince them to explore opportunities in El Salvador." According to the USAID agreement, "The initial focus will be on companies likely to engage in assembly [maquila] operations, either through direct investments (including joint ventures) or contract production. The industry focus will largely be apparel, but could also include electronic/electrical assembly and other labor intensive assembly activities." To complete the strategy, USAID informed FUSADES that "within the U.S., the regions with the greatest concentration of relevant firms are likely to be in the Northeast and Southeast."[3]

Once a targeted U.S. company is convinced to relocate production to El Salvador, it can—in the words of USAID—"take advantage of one of El Salvador's best resources: plentiful, low-cost labor, with a strong work ethic."[4] The promotional materials FUSADES distributes to U.S. businesses highlight the same benefits: "Salvadoran workers are known for their high productivity and quick learning abilities. The country has a large pool of skilled, semi-skilled and unskilled labor, totalling some 1.6 million workers. Unskilled labor can be easily trained at reasonable costs."[5]

# no sweat

The U.S. Department of Commerce—which jointly runs, with USAID, the Latin America/ Caribbean Business Development Center—is also actively promoting El Salvador as a low-wage offshore production site. A Commerce Department "Investment Climate Report" recommends that, "Business with significant labor requirements should consider the positive factors of the Salvadoran labor market," the most attractive of which are the starvation wages.[6] However, what good is a 40 cent hourly wage if there is no place to put people to work? This problem was met head on by USAID when "a major effort was undertaken to develop, finance and promote free trade zones" in El Salvador.[7] In 1988, the U.S. government contributed more than $32 million to startup costs for the eventual construction of 129 factory buildings, which will house U.S. and other foreign maquiladora assembly operations targeting the U.S. market.[8] In addition to the $32 million allocation, $5 million of U.S. Food for Peace Aid to El Salvador was used to build a 72,000-square-foot free zone factory which is now occupied by a U.S. manufacturer.[9]

But what good are low wages and new factories if the Salvadoran work force is largely unskilled? USAID also met this challenge head on by creating the Foundation of Entrepreneurs for Educational Development (FEPADE) "to meet the immediate training needs of firms in El Salvador..."[10] To date, the U.S. government has allocated $27 million for its worker training programs in El Salvador.[11] These funds can be drawn upon to provide a 50 percent subsidy to cover the worker training cost of U.S. firms relocating to El Salvador.[12]

Furthermore, as the Commerce Department points out, "Recognizing the shortage of venture capital for investment in non-traditional export enterprises, USAID and [FUSADES] have collaborated to create specialized lines of credit to promote export projects." USAID established a $15 million credit line, available for "favorable-term loans" to "export-oriented light industrial or drawback operations in El Salvador."[13] Assistance was also provided to the Salvadoran foreign trade ministry "in revising laws and regulations which affect development of non-traditional exports and investments."[14] The Salvadoran government responded by developing the following "Foreign Investment Incentives" package: a 100 percent exemption on corporate income tax, all import and export duties, and all dividend and equity taxes.[15]

And finally, drawing the investment-incentive package full circle, El Salvador's exports to the U.S. market enjoy unlimited access, with specially reduced or no tariffs. At this point, USAID could boast that "El Salvador is thus an exceptionally attractive location for U.S. apparel manufacturers with offshore production sites."[16]

In effect, the U.S. government has spent hundreds of millions of tax dollars since 1980 to promote company flight. FUSADES is just one of at least eleven U.S. government–funded Central American and Caribbean investment- and export-promotion organizations with operations in the United States. Since 1983, USAID has obligated more than $289 million to these groups.

### "Trade, Not Aid": A New Government Strategy

U.S. funding for these investment-promotion programs was the result of a dramatic change in foreign assistance policy initiated by the Reagan administration. The new policy stipulated that foreign aid would increasingly be shifted from government support to private sector assistance, "to foster the growth of productive, self-sustaining income and job producing private enterprise in developing countries."[17] This became identified as the "Trade, Not Aid" policy.

In 1982, as Vice President George Bush lobbied for passage of the Caribbean Basin Initiative, he explained the new foreign aid rationale:

> We want to maintain a favorable climate for foreign investment in the Caribbean region—not merely to protect the existing U.S. investment there, but to encourage new investment opportunities in stable, democratic, free market–oriented countries close to our shores. CBI will not only provide direct incentives for this investment, but encourage follow-on investment.[18]

After passage of CBI, U.S. assistance to the Caribbean Basin increased nearly 40 percent in the first two years. "Much of it," Bush said in 1985, "is going to help build trade associations, chambers of commerce, business training facilities, financial institutions and toward removing structural barriers to productive trade and investment."[19]

By 1991, USAID could state that "to stimulate and foster positive, free-market policy changes in Latin America and the Caribbean has become A.I.D.'s strategy for the LAC [Latin America and Caribbean] region." This was now "a government wide strategy." Just how inclusive the policy was intended to be, and that nothing would interfere with it, is made evident by USAID:

> There are no restrictions on the types of funds or modes of assistance applicable to the pursuit of the private enterprise objectives. ESF [Economic Support Funds], DA [Development Assistance], and PL480 [Food for Peace] loans or grants are all appropriate ways to support private enterprise development. Forms of assistance such as studies, short or long term technical advisors, commodities, training or resource transfers can be used either as components of project or non-project assistance in exchange for appropriate policy changes or for support of country performance in areas of significance to private enterprise development. Local currency generated from non-project assistance can also be programmed effectively in support of private enterprise development.[21]

An investigation by the National Labor Committee revealed that since 1980, the U.S. government has obligated $1,306,111,000 to ninety-three investment- and trade-promotion projects in the Caribbean Basin region. Many of these projects have been and continue to be used to foster company flight from the United States.

### Companies Close U.S. Plants

As the Reagan and Bush administrations were spending hundreds of millions of U.S. tax dollars promoting low-wage offshore production in Central America and the Caribbean, 497,000 textile and apparel workers  and 194,800 electronics workers lost their jobs in the United States.[22]

An average of 41,416 textile and apparel jobs have been lost each year in the United States since 1979, a rate of 3,451 jobs per month. Apparel employment in the U.S. has declined 18.9 percent since 1980. Between 1978 and 1991, real wages for U.S. apparel workers fell 17 percent. Seventy-six percent of all U.S. apparel workers are women; 36 percent are minorities.[23] The typical apparel worker in the U.S. earns $6.85 per hour and works a 37.4-hour week, at the end of which she earns $256. This comes to an annual wage of $13,321. Studies by the U.S. Department of Labor's Bureau of Labor Statistics show that apparel workers who have been displaced from their jobs return to the job market earning, on average, only 85 percent of their former pay.

In 1980, 70 percent of all apparel purchased in the United States was produced domestically. Today, imports account for half of the U.S. apparel market. A National Labor Committee study found thirty U.S. apparel manufacturers operating plants in El Salvador, Honduras, and Guatemala, as well as sixty-eight other U.S. clothing manufacturers and retailers outsourcing to the "Three Jaguars." The National Labor Committee was able to determine that these same companies were involved in fifty-eight plant closings and eleven mass layoffs in the U.S. since 1990, which left 12,234 U.S. apparel workers jobless.

### The New Age Textiles Story

The National Labor Committee staff formed a company to see firsthand why business moves offshore. Our shadow operation, New Age Textiles (NAT), was an environmentally conscious firm manufacturing reusable, 100 percent natural cotton canvas bags, which we proposed could eventually replace the waste-producing plastic and paper throwaway bags used in supermarkets across the country. Despite this ambitious business plan, NAT remained a very small company, and our total production over the course of nearly a year amounted to only a hundred bags. But, NAT did have a mailing address, business cards, stationary, a phone, and a fax.

NAT's first foray as a company was to Miami in April 1991, where we attended the annual Bobbin Contexpo Apparel Show of the Americas along with nearly 6,000 other participants. Its organizers said the event "targets executives seeking new business opportunities through sourcing, joint ventures, 807/9802 or other programs." As expected, many of the USAID-funded Caribbean and Central American investment-promotion organizations attended as exhibitors.

NAT decided first to approach the Jamaica Promotions Corporation, or Jampro, which had a prominent exhibit of several adjoining display booths. We knew that Jampro was receiving USAID support under the Export Development and Investment Promotion Project, which allocated $7,500,000 for Jampro between 1990 and 1994. And in the 1980s, Jampro had received over $15,000,000 from the Reagan administration. However, even we were surprised when, within a matter of minutes, we were approached by a Mr. Stuart Anderson who immediately began pitching NAT on the advantages of moving offshore to Jamaica. Anderson is a USAID employee assigned to Jampro.

Of course, Anderson told us, the biggest selling point Jamaica can offer is that "your labor cost is real light," by which he meant 60 cents an hour. Also, there are no taxes on Jamaica's export-processing zones, and there never will be. Nor would we have to be overly concerned about unions. "We're not union," Mr. Anderson told us. Jamaica is like the U.S. Where "they had weak management in the U.S.," he explained, they "had labor troubles coming out of their ears." Cost-wise, we were told, "you're gonna be ahead of the game" if NAT's production moved offshore.

As we were leaving, Anderson gave us a package of Jamaica's promotional materials, which explained that "USAID works in partnership with Jampro" to make Jamaica "an attractive alternative to more expensive 'on shore' production facilities in the United States." "Overseas expansion is a big decision," Jampro acknowledges. "But with Jampro's help and encouragement, it doesn't have to be a difficult one." Further, Jampro could help us secure financing and technical assistance should we decide to relocate, and could put us in touch with another USAID-funded project, the Human Employment and Resources Training Trust (HEART), which offers subsidized worker training programs. HEART could afford to be generous. It was part of the Basic Skills Training Project which was allocated over $52 million in U.S. foreign assistance since 1983.

### What El Salvador Offered

NAT next approached the Salvadoran exhibit, which was hosted by FUSADES. El Salvador was in the midst of developing a booming export-processing zone infrastructure. Factory space was available, and export firms were tax-exempt. Labor was cheap and plentiful. There were no quota limits on access to the U.S. market. Also, NAT could tap the subsidized worker training programs offered through the Foundation of Entrepreneurs for Education Development (FEPADE). FUSADES could assist us with direct investments, joint ventures, or sourcing out, and help us secure financing.

When we questioned FUSADES concerning its connections to the U.S. government, we were told the organization enjoyed a close working relationship. FUSADES was "receiving funding from the U.S. Agency for International Development." Asked how much this amounted to, they responded "substantial" (more precisely, $102,397,000). What proportion of their budget came from USAID? "Very, very substantial" (that is, 94 percent). They asked us to visit El Salvador, and we told them we probably would.

The U.S. Commerce Department urges businesses considering relocation to "make technology decisions reflecting the availability of an eager supply of inexpensive labor." What "technology decisions" is the Commerce Department referring to? The technical editor of the U.S. textile and apparel journal *Bobbin* offered a clue when she wrote, "Apparel production is highly labor intensive, yet can be carried out without extensive capital investment in automated equipment if the labor prices are low enough." In other words, why invest in upgrading the infrastructure of U.S. factories when, as FUSADES points out, "El Salvador's productive, low cost labor force" is "ideal for establishing facilities or expansion of labor intensive investments"?

USAID's strategy calls for El Salvador's maquiladora apparel industry to become the country's leading export sector by 1994, at which time textile and apparel exports should total $664 million. USAID has reason to be satisfied. In 1991, foreign investment in maquiladora industries in El Salvador tripled over the previous years.

This maquiladora export strategy rests on a fully loaded wage—benefits included—of 62 cents an hour in El Salvador. USAID and FUSADES have neglected to mention that real wages in El Salvador were cut by more than half between 1985 and 1991. Today's 62 cent prevailing wage covers only 15 percent of the overall minimum basket of food and other basic necessities required for the survival of the Salvadoran family.

### The Blacklist in the Honduran Free Trade Zones

New Age Textiles' visit to Honduras was hosted by FIDE, a USAID-funded investment promotion group. The first stop on our itinerary was the ZIP Choloma Export Processing Zone, which had been constructed with U.S. government financing as well as receiving technical assistance from FIDE. There were eight U.S. apparel firms with assembly operations in the zone. FIDE first took us to see the manager of BestForm Foundations, Inc., a private women's undergarment manufacturer headquartered in New York, which has annual sales of over $100

**no sweat**

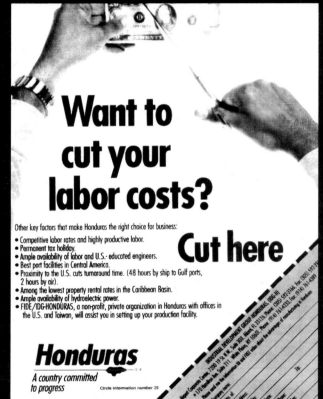

*These ads, luring American manufacturers to the Carribean,*
*were paid for by US taxpayers through the Export Development*
*and Investment Promotion Project of USAID.*

million. Asked if there were union troubles at ZIP Choloma, the BestForm manager explained that this was not an issue since zone management maintains a computerized blacklist to screen and protect companies from potential agitators. The blacklist is constantly updated with new names of those fired for attempting to organize. The BestForm manager described one such incident: a young girl was caught "passing a note here a couple of weeks ago. We just called the administration out there, 'Somebody slipped through,' and we got her out of there."

Everywhere FIDE took us we heard about the blacklists. At the INHDELVA Export Processing Zone, we met with the zone manager, who explained that the blacklist includes all the names of people dismissed for whatever reason from any zone in the country. NAT would be able to present a list of job applicants to the zone management and "we check it out and will see problems with union members or anything like that. We tell you, okay, you have to get rid of this one or you have to get rid of that one."

At the San Miguel Industrial Park, which is being financed by the U.S. Overseas Private Investment Corporation (OPIC), the zone manager also assured us that NAT would not have to worry about unions. Every new hire was screened through the computerized blacklist.

In a phone conversation with Scott Taylor, a USAID official in Honduras, NAT learned that the agency was financing FIDE as well as the development of the industrial parks. NAT asked Taylor if the managers could deliver on their promise to keep the zones union-free. Taylor responded, "Oh, yes." Labor unions "haven't penetrated the zones, nor will they, is what they will tell you. And I think they can deliver on that. I think they run in Honduras topnotch operations, and precisely to keep them out."

Taylor mentioned that the U.S. Shoe Corporation had just signed a deal to open a large plant in Honduras. In 1991, the U.S. Shoe Corporation closed three U.S. plants and laid off 1,147 workers.

### Cheap Loans for Offshore Operations

A National Labor Committee researcher accompanied a U.S. manufacturer to a series of meetings with USAID and Commerce Department staff in Washington, D.C. We said we were exploring the idea of going offshore and were especially interested in what, if any, financing sources were available. At the Latin America/Caribbean Business Development Center—a joint

**no sweat**

## Quality, Industriousness and Reliability Is What El Salvador Offers You!

Rosa Martinez produces apparel for U.S. markets on her sewing machine in El Salvador. <u>You</u> can hire her for **57-cents an hour\***.

Rosa is more than just colorful. She and her co-workers are known for their industriousness, reliability and quick learning. They make El Salvador one of the best buys.

In addition, El Salvador has excellent road and sea transportation (including Central America's most modern airport) . . . **and** there are **no** quotas.

Find out more about **sourcing** in El Salvador. Contact **FUSADES**, the private, non-profit and non-partisan organization promoting social and economic development in El Salvador. Miami telephone: **305/529-2233** **Fax: 305/529-9449**

\*Does not include fringe benefits/exact amount may vary slightly depending on daily exchange rate

## Quality, Industriousness and Reliability Is What El Salvador Offers You!

Rosa Martinez produces apparel for U.S. markets on her sewing machine in El Salvador. <u>You</u> can hire her for **33-cents an hour\***.

Rosa is more than just colorful. She and her co-workers are known for their industriousness, reliability and quick learning. They make El Salvador one of the best buys.

In addition, El Salvador has excellent road and sea transportation (including Central America's most modern airport) . . . **and** there are **no** quotas.

Find out more about **sourcing** in El Salvador. Contact **FUSADES**, the private, non-profit and non-partisan organization promoting social and economic development in El Salvador. Miami telephone: **305/529-2233** **Fax: 305/529-9449**

\*Does not include fringe benefits/exact amount may vary slightly depending on daily exchange rate

1990

1991

USAID–Commerce Department project—we were encouraged to consult with the Puerto Rican Caribbean Development office about a possible "936 loan." Before leaving the Commerce Department, we were informed that the $800,000 loan figure we had been mentioning was most likely too small to qualify for 936 monies.

Section 936 of the Internal Revenue Code exempts U.S. companies from all federal corporate tax on income derived from their subsidiaries in Puerto Rico. The untaxed 936 profit pool in Puerto Rico is now estimated to contain $19 billion, and to be growing by $2.7 billion each year. U.S. subsidiaries are also exempt from Puerto Rican income tax under the island's Tax Incentive Act. Further, interest earned on 936 deposits in Puerto Rico's financial institutions is also untaxed. Given these multiple incentives, the U.S. corporations accept a lower rate of return on their 936 deposits, which then permits the banks to lend 936 funds at reduced interest rates; 936 funds are lent to offshore investors in the Caribbean Basin region at one to two points below market rate, which represents a 20 to 25 percent savings in project financing costs.[24] As of May 1992, $911,215,000 in 936 loans to Caribbean Basin projects either had been disbursed or were pending. The Johnson and Johnson Company alone receives $112 million each year in federal tax credits or exemptions. On the other hand, the entire training component of the Trade Adjustment Assistance (TAA) program, which is meant to address the retraining needs of U.S. workers who lose their jobs through government trade concessions, is capped at $80 million a year for the entire country.

After listening to our story about opening a manufacturing facility in Honduras, the representative of the Puerto Rican Caribbean Development Office in Washington, D.C., responded quite positively. For one thing, they were interested in giving out more "small" loans, such as our financing request of $800,000 represented. The staff at the Caribbean Development Office were willing to work with us on our loan request and business plan.

### Costs and Overhead That Are "Very Difficult to Explain"

On July 25, 1988, a remarkable meeting was held at USAID headquarters in Washington, D.C., the purpose of which was to discuss a damaging internal evaluation of FUSADES' activities. A USAID consultant who attended the meeting kept what he described as "verbatim notes" on the discussion, remarkable in itself. Among the major points raised were the following:

## no sweat

"Evaluation doesn't build a case for continuing FUSADES, particularly given the pressure on the Hill for BHN expenditures. How do we defend a $70 million expenditure on this?"

"I fail to see that $70 million has had any great impact."

"FUSADES has no expectation that AID funding will continue."

"FUSADES has had tremendous costs and overhead which are going to be very difficult to explain."

The concern about "pressure on the Hill" is probably a reference to a congressional debate over government spending on Basic Human Necessities (BHN) programs in the U.S. The $70 million figure refers to the fact that as of September 30, 1987, USAID had already allocated more than that amount to FUSADES, and knew how difficult it would be to explain this expenditure to Congress and the public.

A second USAID-commissioned audit of FUSADES drew the following conclusions, despite the fact that the agency was $70 million and three years into its FUSADES project: "None of the A.I.D.-funded activities administered by [FUSADES] had been independently evaluated to determine its impact on achieving planned objectives or its cost-effectiveness." Moreover, "Neither USAID/El Salvador nor [FUSADES] had established adequate criteria or a system for measuring project accomplishments." "As a result," it was impossible for the auditing team to begin to "accurately assess the cost-benefits or impact of project activities." The auditor did find, however, that "USAID advanced more funds to the foundation than authorized by AID regulations." In one case concerning an unnamed company, the audit found that FUSADES had used USAID project funding "to alleviate the company's cash flow problems." And despite the lack of even a single independent review of FUSADES' effectiveness, the auditor found that: "Some program activities had been amended to increase their funding and to extend their project assistance completion dates without benefit of independent evaluations."

The next move the Bush administration took with FUSADES has major and disturbing implications. In 1991, USAID essentially gave FUSADES a bank so that the organization could "become an independent financial institution with its own loan portfolio." Under this arrangement, USAID noted, "FUSADES could reasonably project interest earnings on the A.I.D.-funded credit programs of approximately $5 million per annum in 1994 and beyond." The Investment Fund credit line USAID originally established under FUSADES' management in the 1980s was capitalized at $15 million. USAID allocated an additional $600,000 to cover FUSADES' administrative costs. The money was to be used "for the purpose of stimulating the establishment of new and expanded" assembly plants. But FUSADES also controlled two additional USAID-financed credit lines worth $20.8 million.

By 1988, there were approximately $170 million in USAID-funded credit lines established in El Salvador, making it difficult to pin down precisely how much money USAID has provided for the new FUSADES bank.

Under the Bush administration, USAID capitalized an offshore endowment controlled by FUSADES, providing self-sustaining project support outside the reach of congressional control. If this arrangement stands, it becomes a precedent for removing U.S. foreign assistance programs from congressional oversight and public awareness. Indeed, a consultant working for USAID to review FUSADES' projects was puzzled as to why, after countless interviews with the organization's staff, USAID was barely mentioned. This struck the consultant as odd given that USAID funds at least 94 percent of FUSADES' budget. When he asked USAID officials in El Salvador about this, they stated it was "simply preferable to maintain a low profile in certain elements of A.I.D. activities." How else could one run an unauthorized offshore operation?

In Honduras in 1990, the USAID mission's deputy director, Donald Enos, was caught skimming nearly $100,000 in payoffs for awarding USAID contracts. According to newspaper accounts, the chairman of the USAID-funded Haitian Promotion Center for Investment and Exports (PROMINEX) misused $2 million of the Center's funding between 1986 and 1989. USAID responded by dumping the chairman and changing the name of its project to the Promotion of Business and Exports (PROBE). Funding was then increased. Between 1986 and 1992, USAID allocated $8,334,000 to its Haitian investment program. USAID awarded a $9,000 per diem to a U.S. business consultant to oversee the planning, management, and promotion of export-processing zones in Honduras. In Guatemala, the USAID mission paid the Virginia-based consulting firm Free Zone Authority, Inc. (now The Services Group) $34,937 for a contract lasting all of one day. In what was perhaps an illegal use of U.S. tax dollars, USAID in Costa Rica lent $1 million to "a Japanese-owned company to upgrade two hotels to five and four-star ratings respectively." According to a USAID consultant who reviewed the project, "both hotels have gambling casinos." USAID/Costa Rica lent another $100,000 to finance the purchase of sewing machines made in Japan.

### Planning to Mislead Congress

In 1990, USAID commissioned a review of its private sector trade- and investment-support projects, most of which were operating in Central America and the Caribbean. Chosen to conduct the survey and evaluation was the Washington, D.C. consulting firm, Development Economics Group.

Janet Ballantyne, associate assistant director of USAID's Bureau of Program and Policy Coordination, wrote a preface to the final draft of the Group's findings. Ballantyne explains that it was the "large volume of A.I.D. resources committed to trade and investment projects... and the expected increase of funding for export promotion and investment promotion... that prompted this review." The report presents several startling recommendations for USAID consideration in order to ensure "the expected increase."

For instance, one way to achieve sufficient funding while still maintaining flexibility in actual program implementation is to design a "Christmas tree" project that purports to provide "a wide range of services to any and all target groups." This approach "implies a shotgun multiservice strategy" that would have "the appearance of serving broader equity objectives as well as narrower growth objectives." This way, "Project designers do not have to make any early hard choices concerning the target group—choices that may be politically unacceptable."

Once the funding is obtained, however, "a Christmas-tree project needs to be transformed into a targeted promoter project as quickly as possible." According to the Group:

> At issue in any development project is the trade-off between equity and growth goals. Growth goals generally involve working with larger producers that are capable of generating significant investment and exports. Equity goals focus on providing assistance to smaller producers in an attempt to promote social reform and income distribution.

Of course, "these two goals are not always compatible." And it is the USAID-funded projects, which focus "more on bottom-line impact results" (e.g., increased jobs, investments, and exports) and "weight the project portfolio toward 'winners' and growth objectives," that are "more successful."

But, the Group believes, "the problem of sustaining promotional services in… developing countries can be resolved if approached realistically." Listed among the possible solutions: USAID could capitalize "endowment funds," which would permanently sustain offshore investment and trade-promotion programs. Another source of financing could include local host government funding, which in reality would be almost exclusively drawn from other nonproject U.S. foreign assistance such as general Economic Support Funds or PL480 food aid. USAID is, in fact, presently using both endowment funds and host government counterpart contributions to finance some of its more than 120 trade and investment programs worldwide.

Quoting from an earlier USAID-commissioned study, the Development Economics Group notes that the "quick responses" necessary for program flexibility may "not allow for A.I.D. project approval through the normal channel." Though the Development Economics Group's report never mentions the U.S. Congress, it is abundantly clear that one of the central targets of the study was how best to mislead the elected representatives who control appropriations.

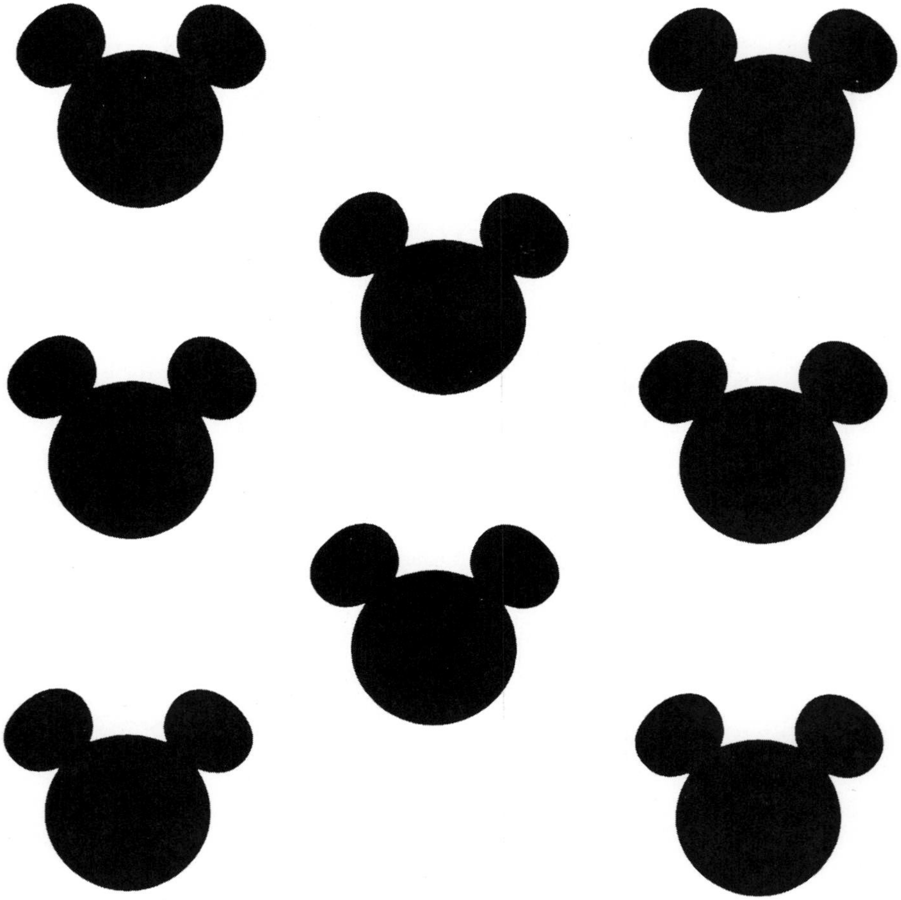

*Disney repeatedly states that, despite vigorous and numerous attempts to investigate conditions, it can find no violations at its apparel contractor plants in Haiti. The enclosed letter, to which we have received no formal reply, tells a different story.*

**An Open Letter to Walt Disney**

May 29, 1996

Michael Eisner
CEO Walt Disney Company
500 South Buena Vista Street
Burbank, CA 91521

Dear Mr. Eisner:

The National Labor Committee (NLC) fully supports Walt Disney's decision to source production in Haiti. The Haitian people desperately need investment and jobs, but they need jobs with dignity, under conditions which respect their basic human rights, and which pay wages that allow them and their families to survive.

The NLC would like to open a serious dialogue with Walt Disney representatives regarding working conditions and wages in Haitian factories where Disney children's clothing is currently being produced. The issues raised in this letter and the proposals which follow are the result of ongoing discussions with the workers in Haiti, as well as with concerned consumers and human rights activists across the United States and Canada…

Neither the NLC nor the Haitian workers we are in contact with want this attempt at dialogue, or the documentation of conditions under which Disney garments are produced, to result in Disney's pulling out of Haiti. Leaving Haiti would be a terrible mistake. Rather, in all good faith, the National Labor Committee and the coalition of religious, labor, student, human rights, and grass-roots organizations we work with, want to join the Walt Disney Company in an attempt to improve conditions in these Haitian factories.

*A shanty town where sweatshop workers live in Haiti.*

Currently, the Walt Disney Company has licensing agreements with two U.S. apparel manufacturers, L.V. Myles and H.H. Cutler, which in turn contract production to four assembly factories in Haiti: L.V. Myles, N.S. Mart, Classic, and Gilanex. Children's clothing carrying the images of the Hunchback of Notre Dame, Pocahontas, Mickey Mouse, and the Lion King is sewn in these factories and then exported to the U.S. for sale in Wal-Mart, J.C. Penney, Kmart, and other retailers.

### Living on the Edge of Misery

On a recent trip to Haiti in late April, I had the opportunity to visit the home of a Disney worker who lived in the Delmars neighborhood of Port-au-Prince. She worked at N.S. Mart (Plant Number 32) in the Sonapi Industrial Park where she sewed Pocahontas and Mickey Mouse shirts. Her home was typical of those of other Disney employees.

She was a single mother with four young children. They lived in a one-room windowless shack, 8 by 11 feet wide, lit by one bare light bulb and with a tin roof that leaked. The room contained: one table, three straight-backed chairs, and two small beds. This is all the room would fit. I counted four drinking glasses and three plastic plates. There was no fan, no TV, no radio, no toys, no refrigerator, no stove, no running water. She had to buy water by the bucket and carry it home. The toilet was a hole in the ground, shared with ten other families.

The children were 3 1/2, 8, 11, and 14 years old. They were very small for their age. The mother told us that when she left for work that morning, she was only able to leave them 6 gourdes [the Haitian currency], or 30 cents U.S. The four children had to feed themselves for the day on *30 cents—7 1/2 cents per child.* Her children had been sent home from school two and a half weeks before because she had been unable to pay their tuition. Tuition for the three older children totaled $2.63 a week, but this was more than the mother earned in a full day sewing Disney shirts.

One child had malaria, another a painful dysentery, but their mother was unable to afford the medicines, so they had to go without and simply bear it.

A Jesuit priest with whom we spoke in Haiti, who had had a similar stomach infection, told us it cost over $30 to purchase the necessary antibiotics. But this woman's salary making

Pocahontas shirts was only $10.77 a week! Antibiotics for her daughter would have cost nearly three weeks' wages, which was impossible to afford.

Before leaving, I asked the family what they would eat that night. *"Nothing,"* they responded. There was no food. For this family, there were many days when they could not afford to eat. Instead of eating, they would just go to bed. The mother slept in one small bed, the daughters in the other, while the two boys slept on the ground under the table. No one in this home had ever seen a Disney movie.

### Working at N.S. Mart Sewing Shirts for Disney

The mother had years of experience as a sewer. The production quota set at N.S. Mart is excessively high. On her assembly line, working furiously under constant pressure, she handled 375 Pocahontas shirts an hour—shirts which sell at Wal-Mart for $10.97 each. Yet her average weekly wage was only $10.77! She earned the minimum wage of 28 cents an hour.

No one can survive on 28 cent an hour wages—even in Haiti, which is not a cheap place to live. Seventy percent of what Haiti consumes is imported, including basic staples like rice, beans, and cornmeal. Food can actually be as expensive in Haiti as in the U.S. Workers producing Disney garments in Haiti are thin and tired looking. They and their families are always at the edge of hunger, sinking ever deeper into debt and misery. Far from being the exception, this woman's life and her story are typical.

The following day, we met with a large group of N.S. Mart workers… They told us that the majority of workers at N.S. Mart earn just 28 cents an hour, which is $2.22 for a full eight-hour day. And, they reported, at times they are shortchanged on their hours and pay.

The workers also told us the plant is hot, dusty, and poorly lit. Some complained about having trouble with their eyesight and respiratory problems. According to the workers, the production quotas and piece rates the company sets are impossible to reach. Supervisors put enormous, constant pressure on the workers to go faster. Supervisors yell, scream, threaten, and curse at the workers. Among the management, Saint Hillaire is particularly abusive. If you are young and pretty and a supervisor wants you as his mistress, you either give in to him or you are fired. Sexual harassment is common.

# no sweat

The toilets are filthy. Rats are everywhere. The holding tank for drinking water is covered only with a light piece of metal, which the rats have no trouble getting under. In the last week of April, the N.S. Mart workers told us, rats that had been poisoned were floating in the water tank.

If you dared to speak up, to complain to N.S. Mart management about these conditions or about the pay scale, you would be fired, period. Every worker we spoke with told us that if the company even suspected that they were interested in organizing to claim their rights, they would be thrown out of the factory immediately.

The most fundamental human and workers' rights of the N.S. Mart employees are being violated on a daily basis.

### Payday for Disney Workers at the L.V. Myles Factory

Friday, April 26, was payday for the workers sewing Disney garments at the L.V. Myles plant (Number 30) in the Sonapi Industrial Park. A meeting with the L.V. Myles workers had been set up by our colleague and contact person in Haiti…

L.V. Myles management describes their factory as *"a model,"* as *"the best you will find."* Also, Disney has had a long sourcing relationship with L.V. Myles, dating back some twenty years. Albeit a little reluctantly, one L.V. Myles officer explained to a U.S. journalist that L.V. Myles definitely pays its workers above the legal minimum wage in Haiti. When pressed, he said that L.V. Myles pays between 38 and 42 cents U.S. an hour, which would amount to weekly wages ranging from $16.72 to $18.28.

At 4:00 p.m., the workers began to leave the park. Soon there were forty or fifty L.V. Myles workers crowded around us…We had a chance to review dozens of pay stubs. We could find no workers who earned more than 30 cents U.S. an hour. We were also told that some workers in the plant, perhaps a dozen, did not even earn the minimum wage. One possible explanation for these discrepancies could be that L.V. Myles factory representatives include managers' salaries in their calculations, which would drive up the average wage paid in the plant.

The weekly earnings recorded on the pay stubs we reviewed ranged from $9.97 to $15.23, the latter including seven hours of overtime pay. L.V. Myles workers are paid biweekly. The pay stub of one woman provides an example. For two weeks of work, this woman, a sewing machine operator, earned 384.75 gourdes, or $23.67. This equates to $11.84 a week, or 28 cents an hour.

At the L.V. Myles factory, as at N.S. Mart, the daily piece-rate quota is set impossibly high. For example, in eight hours, the workers must attach 1,600 collars on Disney T-shirts or close to 1,600 shoulders, which means completing 200 pieces every hour. The work pace is relentless. If you get up to wash your face, the owner yells at you... *"They treat you like garbage,"* the workers said, *"they don't look at you as a human being, but as a piece of shit."* They continued, *"The owners won't even talk to us, and if they don't like your face, or you're sick, they fire you."* The supervisors pace the assembly lines clapping their hands and shrieking at the workers to go faster. At the end of the day, the workers are exhausted.

### Crying Out in Disbelief

Prior to leaving for Haiti, I went to a Wal-Mart store on Long Island and purchased several Disney garments which had been made in Haiti. I showed these to the crowd of workers, who immediately recognized the clothing they had made...I asked the L.V. Myles workers if they had any idea what these shirts—the ones they had made—sell for in the U.S. I held up a size four Pocahontas T-shirt. I showed them the Wal-Mart price tag indicating $10.97. But it was only when I translated the $10.97 into the local currency—178.26 gourdes—that, all at once, in unison, the workers screamed with shock, disbelief, anger, and a mixture of pain and sadness, as their eyes remained fixed on the Pocahontas shirt...In a single day, they worked on hundreds of Disney shirts. Yet the sales price of just one shirt in the U.S. amounted to nearly five days of their wages! (G178.26/36 minimum daily wage = 4.95 days.) In fact, one production line of twenty workers assembles 1,000 Disney shirts in an eight-hour period. In effect, each worker assembles fifty Disney shirts in a day which, at $10.97 each, would sell for a total of $548.50 in the U.S. For her eight hours of work sewing these shirts, the L.V. Myles employee earns just $2.22!...

### Surviving on 28 Cents an Hour

Is it possible to survive in Haiti earning 28 cents an hour?

The maquila factories start operating at 7:30 a.m., and demand that the workers be there at least ten to fifteen minutes early. Most factory workers get up at 5 a.m., when it is still pitch dark. They literally squeeze themselves into overcrowded tap-taps, small pickup trucks converted into buses, which crawl through the morning traffic jam to reach downtown. To get to and from work costs about 37 cents a day.

A cheap breakfast of spaghetti and coffee from food stands out in front of the factory will cost 62 cents. A modest lunch of rice, peas, and cornmeal soaking in oil, with a cup of juice, will cost the same, another 62 cents.

In total, the transportation and a small breakfast and lunch combined cost $1.61. But the factory workers only earn $2.22 for the entire day. So 73 percent of what they earn each day goes to just surviving. At the end of an eight-hour day, they have only 61 cents left over.

Since the workers have no money left over from their last paycheck, the only food they can get must be purchased on credit from the food vendors. The workers literally come to work each day to eat, but they eat only on credit. If they did not come to work, they literally would not eat.

Most workers try to, or would like to, leave $2.50 or $3.00 behind with their families when they leave for work in the morning, so that their families can eat. But that is more than a day's wages. Most families are left with only 31 cents to 62 cents a day to survive on.

The average rent for the typical one-room hut the workers and their families live in costs around $7.10 a week. This means that someone sewing Disney shirts must work for more than three days a week just to pay the rent.

If you have a child in school, that costs another $1.42 for tuition each week. And since the parents—given their own lack of education—cannot help their children with their lessons, they have to pay for a tutor, which costs an additional 71 cents a week.

A small can of powdered milk, which if stretched could last a week for an infant, costs $3.08, or more than the mother earns in an entire day of work. If a worker or her child are sick, a visit to the doctor costs between $3.08 and $4.62. Chloroquine pills for malaria cost 62 cents. For children suffering from diarrhea, a small bottle of medicine costs $1.54. Medicine for dysentery, which is very common, costs $4.68—over two days' wages—while a decongestant costs $2.77, and cough syrup costs $1.54.

If you or your children need glasses, you might as well forget it. Eyeglasses cost $40, or three weeks' wages!

In Haiti, in the neighborhoods the workers live in, there is no running water so you must buy your water by the bucket. To wash clothes, for example, two buckets of water and two bars of soap cost 37 cents, or more than you make in an hour.

No serious observer could reach any conclusion other than that the wages being paid to Haitian workers sewing Disney garments are sub-subsistence wages. No one should use the term lightly, but these are definitely starvation wages.

### The Classic Apparel Factory—Again Workers Treated as Dirt

At the Classic Apparel factory, which is under contract with H.H. Cutler (the label reads "The H.H. Cutler Fun Factory"), hundreds of workers sew "Mickey's for Kids Stuff" and other children's clothing for Disney.

Are conditions at Classic any different, any better, than at N.S. Mart or L.V. Myles factories?…

When we inquired about conditions at the Classic factory, worker after worker responded that *"conditions are miserable."* They continued: *"They treat us badly, like we are dirt, like we were dumb, with no respect. You can't even speak to the bosses. If you try, they fire you. The supervisors are always screaming at us to work faster. The pressure to make the quota is great. If you even try to get up to use the bathroom they scream at you."*

The plant is very hot, we were told. It is poorly lit and dusty. The workers say the lint-filled dust gives them headaches. Rats are everywhere. The drinking water is right next to the toilet, which is filthy. Women are getting infections from the water, so the company dumps in more chlorine. Nor does the company pay sick days properly…

The production manager at Classic Apparel is John Paul Medina, who has been identified by the workers as a former member of the Fraph death squad, which killed thousands of civilians during the coup. He has told the workers that if they ask for a raise, *"the Americans will come and take the jobs to the Dominican Republic."* However, in June 1995, when President Aristide increased the minimum wage, Medina did not hesitate to increase the daily piece-rate quota by 66 percent. Instead of sewing 720 collars on Disney garments in eight hours, now the workers must complete 1,200 pieces in order to earn the minimum wage, or a little above.

Similar to the other factories, sexual harassment is common. Also, when U.S. representatives—presumably from H.H. Cutler—tour the plant to check on production quality, they never bother to speak with the workers.

When we asked them how they were able to live on their wages, we heard the same sad story. More often than not, they and their families went to bed hungry, having no money left for food that night. They never eat meat; they cannot afford it.

When asked, they told us that their children were *"tired and weak"* and often had *"to go to school without food for lunch."* At the time of our visit, many of their children were sick, either with malaria or stomach infections.

Like the rest of the workers we had spoken with, no one had ever heard of "Corporate Codes of Conduct" nor had Haitian Ministry of Social Affairs officials ever spoken with them. They were alone to face the working conditions in which they were trapped.

### Haitian Workers Make a Proposal to Disney

The workers at N.S. Mart, L.V. Myles, and Classic Apparel asked the NLC to carry a message back to company representatives at Walt Disney. The Haitian workers sewing Disney clothing have several modest proposals they would like to discuss. They are as follows:

1. Primary among them is that Disney representatives come to Haiti to meet with the workers, to learn their story and see how they live. These workers want to continue sewing Disney clothing; in fact, they would like more orders. They are good at what they do and they work hard. They only want to be treated with respect.

2. They would like to work with Disney to clean up the factories, to guarantee respect for human and worker rights, including their legal right to organize. These workers want the factories to be even more productive and efficient, but they also want their rights as workers restored.

3. A very modest increase in wages from the current 28 cents an hour to 58 cents would allow the Disney workers and their families to survive. They would remain poor, very poor, but they would no longer be trapped in misery.

4. To guarantee respect for basic rights, local human rights organizations should have access to Disney's contractors' plants to monitor conditions. Such an independent monitoring agreement has already been signed with the Gap.

### Not That Sort of a Trip

The NLC is aware that, following our trip to Haiti, Disney representatives did in fact visit the N.S. Mart, L.V. Myles, Classic, and Gilanex factories during the week of May 6. Before that, H.H. Cutler Company officials were also in Haiti.

However, this is not the type of meeting the workers are requesting. The workers want a meeting with Disney representatives, but in the presence of the NLC and independent local human rights organizations, away from the factory and local management, and in a secure place. The workers want to speak the truth, openly, frankly, and without the threat of being fired or retaliated against for doing so. Disney should provide their word that no harm will come to the workers for attending such a meeting and speaking truthfully.

### Could the U.S. Companies Afford It?

The workers' demands seem very reasonable, perhaps even overly modest, to the NLC. The wage increase the workers are calling for would allow them to earn 58 cents an hour, which is only $4.62 a day, $25.38 a week, and $1,320 a year.

Would such a wage increase make Haiti less competitive? Available research is clear in documenting that this would not be the case. Through interviews with assembly-line workers in Haiti, the NLC is documenting production schedules and labor costs.

# no sweat

### At the L.V. Myles Factory

For example, at the L.V. Myles plant in the Sonapi Industrial Park, twenty workers on a production line sew 1,000 pairs of purple Pocahontas pajamas in a single day. The pajamas are then exported to the U.S., where they sell at Wal-Mart for $11.97. L.V. Myles claims it is paying its workers 38 cents to 42 cents an hour (which, as we have already seen, is inflated since the vast majority of sewers in the plant are actually earning between 28 cents and 30 cents). Even if we grant that the L.V. Myles Company is paying 42 cents an hour, this would mean that the twenty workers, each earning $3.32 a day (8 hours x $.42 = $3.32), collectively are earning only $66.40 for the day (20 x $3.32 = $66.40), while at the same time producing $11,970 worth of Pocahontas pajamas ($11.97 x 1,000 = $11,970). In other words, the wages the Haitian workers earn amount to just .55 percent—about one-half of one percent—of the retail price the pajamas sell for at Wal-Mart! In effect, the workers earn just 7 cents for each $11.97 pair of Pocahontas pajamas they sew.

Now, if wages were raised to 58 cents an hour —as the workers are requesting—what would be the effect?

At 58 cents an hour, or $4.64 for an eight-hour day, the Haitian sewers would earn 9 cents, instead of 7 cents for every $11.97 pair of Disney pajamas they made. The Haitian sewers would still be earning less than eight-tenths of one percent of the sales price of the garments. If the workers earned 9 cents per pajama, this would still leave Walt Disney, L.V. Myles, and Wal-Mart with over 99 percent—$11.88—of the $11.97 sales price.

### At the Classic Apparel Factory

At Classic Apparel, forty workers in one production group sew 2,400 Disney Lion King children's outfits in an eight-hour day. Given the recent raise at Classic Apparel from 28 cents to 35 cents an hour, this means that forty workers earning 35 cents an hour would collectively earn $110.77 a day (8 x $.35 = 40 x $2.77 = $110.77), while producing $28,776 worth of Lion King outfits selling in the U.S. for $11.99 each (2,400 x $11.99 = $28,776)…

Right now, workers at Classic Apparel are earning only 5 cents for every $11.99 Disney garment they sew, their earnings amounting to only four-tenths of one percent of the sales of the Lion King garment.

What would happen if the Haitian workers' modest demand for 58 cents an hour was met? Instead of 5 cents for each garment they sewed, they would earn 8 cents, or six-tenths of one percent of the $11.99 retail price, leaving the U.S. companies with well over 99 percent of their share.

Not only is the 58 cent an hour wage—or higher—a desperately needed improvement for the people of Haiti, and one easily afforded by the U.S. companies, it is also good for the U.S. people. No one earning 28 cents an hour, who cannot even afford to feed his or her family, will ever purchase anything made in the U.S. You cannot trade with someone making 28 cents an hour…

The Haitian maquila workers are very isolated. The Haitian government's Ministry of Social Affairs, which is responsible for factory inspections and implementation of labor regulations, is not functioning. It has no budget, no money, no presence. Even the factory owners will confirm this.

On the other hand, sadly, the Haitian workers are not receiving any assistance or support from the U.S. Embassy. In a February 1996 cable to the State Department in Washington, D.C., the U.S. Embassy in Port-au-Prince reports that in the maquila plants producing under contract for U.S. companies, the average pay is 46 cents an hour and not the 28 cents an hour (or even less) that the NLC documented. The Embassy's cable notes that a *"greater analysis of the Group's [NLC] charges will follow."*

But how did the Embassy reach its conclusions? The Embassy simply sent out a questionnaire to the maquila factory owners and waited for them to mail back their responses! This, of course, is ridiculous in a country like Haiti, where the tiny elite which controls these factories has an unparalleled record for corruption, tax evasion, cheating on bills owed to the state electrical, phone, and port agencies, and massive violations of the internationally recognized rights of their employees…

Currently the "global economy" which links the U.S. and Haiti is pitting U.S. workers against Haitian workers in a bitter race to the bottom over who will accept the lowest wages and the most miserable working conditions. Under these conditions, one of the only remaining avenues to break this destructive cycle, raise social standards, and level the playing field is to

110  involve the U.S. consumer. Consumer pressure can move the whole system forward, as it did with the Gap, which became the first company to agree to open its contractors' plants to independent human rights monitors…

Disney could continue to well serve its commitment to family values by going to Haiti to meet with the workers and raising their wages to 58 cents an hour.

For its part, the National Labor Committee will go anywhere at any time to meet with Disney representatives to discuss the proposals put forth by the Haitian workers.

When we left Haiti, the people told us, "we are counting on you." It is a responsibility the National Labor Committee takes very seriously. We are committed to raising their needs with the U.S. people. Thank you.

Sincerely,

Charles Kernaghan
Director

cc:
Mr. Peter F. Nolan, Vice President, Assistant General Counsel, Walt Disney Company
Peter Levin
Chuck Champlin, Director of Communications, Disney Consumer Products

**Model Letter for the Walt Disney Company**

Date

Michael Eisner, CEO
Walt Disney Company
500 South Buena Vista Street
Burbank, CA 91521

Dear Mr. Eisner:

We support Walt Disney's decision to produce in Haiti. The Haitian people need jobs. However, we hope that the high level of unemployment and poverty is not used to exploit the workers.

Walt Disney Company has licensing agreements with two U.S. companies—L.V. Myles and H.H. Cutler—who in turn contract with several companies in Haiti to produce Mickey Mouse and Pocahontas pajamas. Three of these companies—Quality Garments, National Sewing Contractors, and N.S. Mart Manufacturing—are openly violating Haiti's wage laws, paying their employees as little as 12 cents per hour.

We ask the Walt Disney Company to sign the attached pledge to respect Haiti's wage and benefit laws.

We also ask that you translate Walt Disney Company's corporate code of conduct into Creole, to post it in your contractors' plants, and distribute it to the workers. We ask you to agree that independent human rights observers will have access to your contractors' plants to monitor compliance with your stated human rights concerns. Also, we know that Haitian women are being paid 7 cents for each pair of $11.97 Disney pajamas they make. This seems unjust—even criminal—to us. Is there any reason Walt Disney cannot work with your contractors to double, triple, or even quadruple the wages these women are being paid in Haiti? If you were to quadruple the wage, the women would still be earning 28 cents for every pair of $11.97 Disney pajamas they produced. Disney and the other companies involved would still keep $11.69—or 98 percent of the sales price. Couldn't the Walt Disney Company afford this? Wouldn't the $11.69 provide plenty of room for an adequate profit?

Lastly, can you explain to us how the U.S. people can trade with Haitian people earning 30 cents an hour? Of course, it is impossible. What do the U.S. people gain when U.S. companies pay such starvation wages in Haiti? Without fair social standards in international trade—linked to sustainable wages and human rights protections—the North American people cannot prosper, as we will be forced to compete for jobs in a race to the bottom over who will accept the lowest wages and the most miserable working conditions.

As we are sure Walt Disney Company stands by its human rights principles and has nothing to hide, we look forward to your company's promptly signing the attached Pledge. We await your response. Thank you.

Sincerely,

Attachment: Pledge

**Walt Disney Company: Please Sign the Pledge**

We Pledge

We, Walt Disney Company, pledge to immediately comply with all Haitian labor lawscovering all employees producing goods for our company, especially:

- To pay at least the legal minimum wage of 30 cents an hour, including proper overtime rates;
- To pay all legal benefits, such as health, pension, sick days, and 7th day bonus pay;
- To end sexual harassment;
- To respect the workers' right to organize and the right to a collective contract;
- To improve working conditions and to cease arbitrary and unfair production speedups;
- To translate our code of conduct into Creole, post it in our contractors' plants, and distribute it to all employees; and
- To allow independent human rights observers to monitor our contractors' compliance with our corporate code of conduct.

# the myth of nimble fingers

Elinor Spielberg

There's a saying among girls in the slums of Bangladesh: If you're lucky, you'll be a prostitute—if you're unlucky, you'll be a garment worker.

Pinky was both lucky and unlucky. She was sold into a brothel when she was eleven. At thirteen, she was living at a shelter for victimized women and girls in the capital city of Dhaka and working at Expo World-Wide Garments. Undernourished since birth, then fed according to the nutritional standards of a pimp, the bird-boned girl stood on her feet for up to fourteen hours a day, six to seven days a week, for the equivalent of $12.50 a month.

The foreman came on to her all the time. No doubt he could sniff out her background. But that wouldn't have made a difference. No, not for a pretty one like that in a garment factory. Just threaten to fire them and they're yours. A girl in the labor force means she's unprotected: either her family has abandoned her, or the family men are too poor and desperate themselves to make trouble.

There are at least 10,000 children, many far younger than Pinky, working in the Bangladeshi garment industry, according to a survey done by an International Labor Organization inspection team. Pinky was, indeed, lucky to be under the protection of the Bangladesh National Women Lawyers Association (BNWLA), where I met her in 1994. This gave her the courage not only to talk about the foreman's sexual advances, but actually reject them. Should it be necessary to set him straight, Salma Ali, director of the organization, would storm into the factory with her lawyer's briefcase and a temper as hot as the color of her sari. She had leveled her guns several times before, when Pinky's salary was overdue. Village girls and women are easy to cheat. They have no concept of what an hour is; a workday is from sunrise to sunset. And the hand is quicker than the eye when the paymaster deals out their salary in cash—no check, no records of anything. His skim is business as usual.

Pinky dreamed of "marrying a good man and raising a good, secure family," which I took to mean financially immune to a daughter's slipping into the hands of a brothel dealer. Her friend Shafia, another garment girl, dreamed not of marriage but of "being independent." Perhaps the rickety girl was simply being realistic. A penniless girl turned out by her family could only win a decent groom with her beauty. As if following my thoughts, she pointed at her feet. "Look," she said, "from standing all day at the factory."

*Young boy making silk saris in Varansi, Uttar Pradesh, India, May 1996.*

Whatever early malnutrition had started doing to her chances of marriage, the garment trade had finished off. The mind cannot register, in the first few seconds, that these appendages are attached to a creature that walks upright on the ground. They have flattened and spread out to such a degree they seem more suited to one that propels itself in water. Like fins. Like flounders, but curved in toward each other: bottom fish that got trapped, and grew, inside a kidney-shaped pan. The mind tries to grab hold of something more noble, something scientific, perhaps, to explain why a child, a child who is now admiring her new plastic bangles and smoothing the hem of her best dress, has been cursed with feet like that on which to toil. Compensation: now that's a scientific word. The bones of her feet were too weak to support the weight of the body, so they accommodated the floor. A voice breaks in. Shafia is saying something.

"...to be single, but with a good job, not a garment factory." Salma Ali's keys are jangling as loud as a landlady's in a Bengali film. She's waiting for me in the hallway. She is taking me to meet three children who have just arrived.

There's something wrong right away when Salma Ali opens the door. Not the room itself, which is no more spartan and monsoon-stained than any room in South Asia. What's wrong is that it's so quiet. Three children have been shut into a room together and have not become a hundred monkeys. They are sitting still in a way that suggests they haven't budged or talked for hours. Certainly not the girl sitting on the edge of the bed, wrapped up like a cocoon in this heat, whose face I can see only by peeling back the woolen blanket. She looks about twelve or thirteen. Her eyes are glazed over. "She is mourning her family and her village. She will never see them again because she brought shame upon them," Salma Ali said, rolling her eyes—"bringing shame" meant some man forced his way inside her. "Even when parents of girls like these are willing to take them back, the village won't. They will chase her out, throw rocks."

She, too, will eventually find work in a garment factory.

I hold out a piece of bubblegum to the boy. He looks slowly at my face, at my hand. He is extremely confused. Perhaps the seven-year-old thinks I am buying him from Salma Ali. I stroke open his clenched hand, put the gum on his palm, and stand back. Very slow, his jaw drops open, and his tongue slips out when he finally realizes that he has been given something. My own understanding took a little longer. I was going on the premise that the boy, like any kid, would anticipate a gift for himself when a grown-up is giving out treats in the room. But it's obvious now: *He did not even have the sense of self to think that.* This child, too, will wind up in the labor force.

The thin, leggy girl sitting on the floor in the corner is certainly filled with anticipation, holding out both wrists for the perfume I brought along. She certainly knows about perfume, this lively one. After I dab her wrists, she turns her neck to expose one ear. Then the other. But what is it about her motions? They are stiff, jerky. And why is she still sticking out her wrists? The reason hits home. God, the assumptions we make! That even a five-year-old knows how to put on perfume like mommy. Or that a girl sold as cheaply as this could afford to buy perfume for herself. All along, she'd been observing me anoint the girl in the stupor and is just imitating her movements.

She smiles when I put her wrists to her nose, and looks up at me for approval. When I stroke her hair, she presses her head against my legs and holds my hand. I think of Shafia, motherless, then rejected by her stepmother. Stabbed in the biceps by her father and left in the river. Some fishermen found her. From the hands of her father to fishermen to the police, to BNWLA to the hands of a factory foreman. From this little dormitory room, her future does not look much better than her past. The place starts feeling like a cross between a home for battered children and a nightmare employment agency: Girlpower, Inc. Yes, this is the labor pool from which garment manufacturers recruit.

# no sweat

One prays that these girls will find their way into the Bangladesh Independent Garment Workers Union, whose founding convention I had attended a week earlier. A thousand seamstresses had stood on line for hours despite two bomb explosions, compliments of industry thugs, earlier in the day, and filed into an enormous tent to ratify their constitution and elect their officers. The temperature inside was hardly kinder than the Bengali sun. The women of BIGU are among approximately one million garment workers laboring in Bangladeshi sweatshops, or under grueling conditions in the "formal sector": big factories represented by government-controlled unions that are hardly democratic and do not have workers' interests at heart. These BIGU women, largely illiterate, whose self-assertion is frowned upon by their own community let alone their employers, who have withstood brutal beatings, arson, sexual attacks, and sadistic intimidation, had finally launched their own, independent union.

To those of us in countries where we return from rallies in one piece, unionists in countries like Bangladesh are heroic. On November 22, 1995, the BIGU office was attacked by over twenty well-dressed men armed with pipe bombs, guns, and Molotov cocktails. The goons announced they were there "to stop the union's work." They poured gasoline on staff lawyer Fawzia Karim Feroze and throughout her office. Fortunately, the match landed in another room. They beat people up to the degree that several had to be hospitalized. Windows were smashed, files destroyed, shots fired into the air, a bullet promised to anyone who dared speak.

It is not only these activists, who must face attacks like this from time to time, who seem to be made of stronger stuff. So, too, do the regular workers—members of BIGU, active or not, the unorganized and the child laborers—for whom simply waking up in the morning and facing the workday is an act of courage. At UNITE's founding convention in June 1995, first-time delegates as well as longtime activists reached into their pockets and raised $5,000 to help build a school for liberated carpet children in a faraway Pakistani village. They had just heard about the Iqbal Masih Project, launched by elementary school children in Massachusetts, to carry out the dream of a twelve-year-old former carpet boy and activist, murdered that year.

Union members and other consumers have also been supporting the Rugmark Campaign, run by the Child Labor Coalition in Washington, D.C., initiated by the South Asian Coalition on Child Servitude in New Delhi. While SACCS director Kailash Satyarthi continues to free children sold into India's carpet-weaving industry, Rugmark activists in the U.S. continue to boycott carpets made by such children. The alternative offered to consumers is to buy carpets from factories approved by the fledgling Rugmark inspection team. Oriental rugs with the new, child-free label are already on the market. The Rugmark Campaign also lobbies for the Harkin Bill, which would ban goods made by children from entering the U.S. market, and has many enemies in Congress.

Such elaborate, hand-knotted carpets, with or without the child-free label, are too expensive for the average person to buy. But that has not stopped even low-wage earners from supporting a campaign that seeks to eradicate child labor. Nor is there a handmade rug industry in the U.S. in which workers could lose out to overseas competition. The reasons why this fight is the human thing to do are not very complicated, after all.

One reason can be found in Iqbal Masih's death. The small twelve-year-old boy, bent over the loom since age four, won his freedom through the Bonded Labour Liberation Front of Lahore, Pakistan. He had since learned how to read and write, freed hundreds of other children, spoken at government hearings in Europe and America, won the Reebok Youth Action Award, and received a standing offer for a scholarship from Brandeis University. He planned to become a lawyer much like Ehsan Ullah Khan, the man who heads BLLF and freed him. On Easter Sunday in 1995, during a visit with his mother in their village of Muridke, thirteen bullets from a sawed-off shotgun were fired into Iqbal's stomach, chest, and head, while riding his bicycle. "I used to be afraid of the master," Iqbal was fond of saying at rallies. "Now the master is afraid of me."

Other reasons can be found seared on the bodies of glass-factory boys, branded for life from working without gloves, goggles, shoes, or even long trousers. Or in the lungs and eyes of the tannery children. In the stunted growth and hunched-up posture of the loom children. In the erect, graceful posture of toddlers—balancing baskets of rocks on their heads in the quarries. In a saying among girls in Bangladesh. In the shape of Shafia's feet, or in the work-roughened, enlarged, laborer's hands that dangle incongruously from the arms of the carpet children—hands crisscrossed with ugly, permanent scars, often as gnarled as an old arthritic's.

It is a myth that small children are employed because of their "nimble fingers." Anyone who remembers idolizing their first-grade teacher because she knew how to use scissors can

*Iqbal Masih, Pakistani Child Activist.*

figure that out. In fact, children are used only in the production of low-end rugs, meaning less than 250 knots, usually single, per square inch: "The more expensive carpets are made by adults because of the strength it takes to press down a high number of double knots," said a Pakistani rug dealer who asked to remain anonymous. He has seen hundreds of children in the cheaper rug loom houses.

These children cut themselves with shears all the time, and are rubbed raw by taut woolen yarn. When they bleed, matchstick powder is poured into the open wounds and lit, often by the master himself.

Contrary to the legitimizing myth that they are prized for their deft hands, children are hired because they are the most exploitable work force in the world. Adults can organize, oxen can kick, and donkeys balk. If children resist in the mildest way, they are physically punished. I know of one situation in which a boy was beaten for the offense of crying for his mother. Iqbal used to talk about the beatings, about being chained to his loom and, on several occasions, being hung upside down by the feet for the entire day.

Nor are the fingers of Asian children any more agile than the fingers of other children. The often heard statement, "but things are different over there," as if certain workers have a special capacity for suffering, is just another rationalization for child labor, promoted by businessmen. Yet another is that child labor is a result of poverty, and until nations develop economically, it is just an unfortunate fact of life. People like Kailash Satyarthi of SACCS in India, and Ehsan Ullah Khan of Pakistan's BLLF, see it differently, arguing that child labor is a cause, not an effect, of poverty. For every child working, who earns a third or less than the market wage, one or more adults are unemployed.

As horrific as it is for children to be robbed of their childhood and health, what happens to their minds is worse. Satyarthi once liberated a twenty-year-old man bonded since early childhood who "did not know what money was, or even the name of the country he lives in." If this is the generation to participate in a nation's economic advancement, what are the real chances of leaving child labor behind?

Satyarthi and Khan have seen countless numbers of enslaved adults and children like this young man. I will never forget the day I saw the face of a slave for the first time. There was not even sorrow in his eyes. They seem dead, their limbs animated by an unearthly force.

Both Satyarthi and Khan have been midwife to the miracle of such faces becoming human again. Bonded children and adults have won their freedom solely through labor groups like theirs. Without their organizing campaigns, the nations of South Asia would not advance, either economically or in the field of human rights. Not until those governments enforce the laws against the ingrained practices of *peshgi*, or generational debt, and the dowry. Asian labor coalitions cannot afford to wait. How many decades will that take? Especially in countries like Pakistan, where even Prime Minister Benazir Bhutto employs children on her estate? Although "Benazir does say hello," according to one little boy interviewed on video by BLLF, "she does not know my name or ask if I go to school."

*Peshgi* is the curse of entire families in South Asia. Most bonded children throughout the world are handed over to their employers as a means to pay off longstanding family debts, by parents who are desperately poor, illiterate, and often indentured themselves. "Often the parents do not even know which ancestor owed money, to whom it was originally owed, or that person's relation to the current master," Satyarthi says. He adds that the masters sell them off to other masters, which contributes to the confusion. The new or extended loan that parents get in exchange for their child multiplies rapidly by trumped-up fees, such as the cost of mistakes made by unpracticed hands. On top of that are usurious interest rates. So the loan is virtually impossible to pay off and passes to the next generation. The master takes his payment in hours. This is why the twenty-year-old man, bonded since childhood, did not know what money was.

Marrying off a daughter is a major reason for a family to borrow money. Not only must the bride's parents pay for the wedding, they must pay a dowry, in the form of cash or goods, to the groom's family. A daughter signifies money leaving the family, a son means money coming in. For poor families, the dowry is a stranglehold. This is why thousands of girls are turned out, like Shafia, and wind up in garment factories.

Compared with the life of children enslaved by *peshgi*, the garment girls in Bangladesh don't seem to have it so bad. Many of them over the legal working age of fourteen are being organized by BIGU, and younger ones are released into schools established for them by the union. At least they get wages and are not isolated from society. And because they make products for North American and European export, the powers of publicity and boycott are on their side. Those who are not producing goods for export are invisible. They, and often their whole families, making bricks or matches or Asian garments or tilling the fields, are kept hidden from public view. How can slaves who are the children of slaves, and surrounded by slaves, even conceptualize freedom? Labor coalitions like BLLF and SACCS are showing them the way out of hell.

When you enter the wrought iron gates of Mukti Ashram outside of New Delhi—the small, Gandhian oasis Satyarthi created for children rescued from bonded labor—you notice tame little rabbits darting around the well-laid gardens. They are, actually, rather necessary staff members. When children first arrive, they are afraid to be touched by adults. Hence the bunny-surrogates, which they love to hold. Bonded children are terrified after they are freed from slavery. I watched a videotape of one factory raid, when Satyarthi found dozens of children hidden high up in the trees by their master. These masters threaten to shoot them and their families if they run away. One boy Satyarthi rescued pretended not to know his own father when the man went to release him. No matter how often Satyarthi tells these children they are being taken to freedom, they don't believe it. A man putting himself to all that trouble could only be a new master.

At Mukti Ashram, the children get medical and nutritional attention. All castes must eat, wash, and live together. They are taught self-sufficient labor skills. In pleasant wooden sheds surrounding the main garden and the gazebolike Hindu shrine, children were in workshops learning carpentry, cobbling, electrical wiring, and other trades. This is to help them from slipping right back into bondage or into factories after returning to their villages. They also get an education. Both native and international labor coalitions know that it is not enough to simply free children from labor. They may wind up on the street in even worse situations, selling drugs or their bodies. Education is the single most important way to break the cycle.

Iqbal Masih's murder, which BLLF believes was carried out by order of the carpet manufacturers, has never been solved. International statements by Bhutto's government on the subject proved to be a joke. The "culprit," they announced, had been taken into custody: he had found Iqbal sodomizing a donkey and had shot him out of moral outrage. Then the story changed. The man himself was sodomizing the donkey, was discovered by Iqbal, and shot him. "Pakistanis had a good laugh when those stories came on the news," said a friend of mine in Lahore. "Even we didn't believe them."

So new accusations abounded. Iqbal was not a stunted carpet child, but a dwarf dressed up as one, paraded around by Khan to enrich himself with foreign contributions to his cause. Then, jealous of Iqbal's international fame, and wanting to get his hands on the $15,000 Reebok award, Khan murdered his Frankenstein and took off for Sweden. I cannot imagine the exiled man's desolation when learning he was accused of Iqbal's murder.

The only consolation in Iqbal Masih's death is that it galvanized the movement against child labor. Since his murder, Pakistani rug imports to North America and Europe have dropped by more than $10 million. There are now preliminary meetings and a growing interest in the Rugmark label in that country. Still, the forces against these children are overwhelming. So is their number: at least 200 million worldwide—most of whom will not be reached in our lifetime. But the people fighting for these children carry on. People like Sister Rosaline Costa, a Bangladeshi human rights activist working with BIGU, who must travel with bodyguards. Pictures of the former nun were plastered all over Dhaka with the word "whore" printed boldly beneath. Or her colleague Father Timm, also part of the labor movement. A tall, energetic, handsome man in his seventies with sandaled feet as tough as any native's, who speaks fluent Bengali and "stopped peddling Christianity years ago," he was denied overseas travel for desperately needed eye surgery. "The government is happy to let me out, but not back in," he said, clapping his helmet on his head and starting up his motorbike. It took years of pressure from international labor groups to guarantee a round-trip for Father Timm.

There are people like Craig Kielburger of Canada who, at age twelve, read a newspaper article about Iqbal Masih's death in 1995, began researching child labor, and founded Free the

*Craig Kielburger, Canadian Child Activist.*

Children. A year later, he was able to travel through South Asia on a fact-finding mission. Canadian prime minister Jean Chretien happened to be there at the same time, promoting free trade. Kielburger met with Chretien for fifteen minutes and got child exploitation put on the official agenda of the trade discussions.

He spoke so movingly before the Ontario Federation of Labor, that delegates, among them UNITE workers, raised $150,000 for his organization, which he operates out of the den in his parents' house. It has since grown and become international. Kielburger convinced Toronto's officials to ban fireworks made by children, appeared on CBS' "60 Minutes," and went to Washington to tell Congress about the horrors of bonded child workers. The Canadian government has pledged $700,000 for the International Labor Organization's campaign against child labor and is funding a study on independent monitoring of factories which would bolster the Rugmark Campaign. In a speech at the Canadian labor convention, he quoted then foreign minister Andre Ouellet's remark that "Canadians can't be Boy Scouts" about the world's human rights abuses. "Well, I'm a Boy Scout," Kielburger said, "and this just means we the children will have to work all the harder to end exploitation of Third World children."

Like all of those in the movement against child labor, Kielburger will not wait for government leaders to see the light. "Because childhood does not wait," says Satyarthi.

# rat-catching: an interview with Bud Konheim

## Sally Singer

Nicole Miller, Inc., a manufacturer of women's apparel with a $100 million turnover and an annual growth of 20 percent, is one company that emerged with special credit from the Kathie Lee Gifford scandal. Founded in 1982 by Nicole Miller, a carrot-topped designer with a special talent for cocktail dresses, and Bud Konheim, a feisty businessman from a garment-making dynasty, it is the company put forward by UNITE as the model for how to run a clean, no-sweat operation. What has set Nicole Miller, Inc. apart from its neighbors on Seventh Avenue is that its line of women's wear—brightly colored, fashionable sportswear and slinky evening dresses—is produced entirely in New York and not in some distant corner of the globe. It is also an all-union operation, from the CEO, Konheim, to the pressers. Its own employees (as distinct from the contract labor in the factories) receive an exemplary package: free education, transport vouchers, free cooked lunches, and generous maternity leave.

Konheim's business philosophy, in which employees are treated as members of an extended family and productivity is linked to worker contentment, has old-fashioned noblesse oblige origins. Raised in a twenty-three-room house run by a mother who breakfasted only in bed, Konheim observed his parents' respectful treatment of domestic staff and company employees and learned the social and commercial benefits that flowed from this. He also gratefully acknowledges the debt he owes to the English designer Jeff Banks, from whom he borrowed many of his management strategies.

The success of Nicole Miller, Inc., however, is not solely the result of this homespun, family-firm approach. The name has been licensed—for leather goods, accessories, and such novelty items as the Nicole Miller Barbie—and these goods are primarily produced in Hong Kong and China. Currently, the licensees account for 40 percent of the annual turnover. The company, then, is not exempt from the commercial pressures and aspirations that affect others in the industry.

Nevertheless, Konheim became a pivotal figure in the U.S. Department of Labor's campaign to publicize and eliminate abusive labor practices. At the "fashion summits" organized by Labor Secretary Robert Reich in the wake of the Kathie Lee revelations, Konheim argued forcefully that industry self-regulation is essential to eradicating sweatshops in the U.S. Occupying the ground between the mass producers (the "major perps," as he calls them) and the antisweatshop activists, he has criticized both for failing to realistically address what he

124 considers to be the essentially soluble problem of unethical production in the U.S. In his view, the perps are involved in a destructive, blinkered price war, while the activists are preoccupied with mounting a misdirected and overambitious global campaign. What Konheim argues for is nothing less than ethical capitalism, whereby the gratification of consumer needs, the fair treatment of the work force, and the satisfaction of stockholders go hand in hand.

At once hardheaded and idealistic, his vision merits close inspection. In the fall of 1986, I interviewed Konheim at his offices on Seventh Avenue. He is outspoken and unpious, prone to offering—and yet suspicious of—anecdotal evidence to back up his opinions. What I discovered was a man wedded to business and to his social conscience, who is attempting to ally these uneasy partners.

*Bud Konheim.* *Nicole Miller.*

**sally singer**

*I know that you worked with Nicole Miller on another garment line in the 1970s for which production was based abroad. When you founded Nicole Miller, Inc. in 1982, why did you choose to return to the U.S.?*

**bud konheim**

To begin with, Nicole and I were the first people to seriously manufacture in the Orient in the early 1970s. In the beginning, of course, there was a price incentive to go to the Far East, and the expertise and quality were good. However, as time went on, prices went up. There was nothing unusual about that—it happened here too. But prices continued to go up, freight went up, and suddenly we were looking at costs that were not dramatically different from what we could do in the United States.

**ss** *That was why, in 1982, you returned to New York?*

**bk** No, that was not the clincher. We moved back because of a bunch of dramatic changes. Here's what happened. Everybody was going to the Orient and projecting long deliveries—three months, six months—because that is what you have to do when you're that far away from your factories. And everybody was overprojecting their quantities, because you cannot just go back and get more. The result was that the marketplace became saturated with product, and the extra product that landed had to go somewhere. It was dumped on jobbers who quickly sold it into discount stores— Loehmann's, T. J. Maxx, you name it. And that started a round-robin of phony business. The department stores were not blind, and they demanded a rebate so that they could mark down the merchandise to keep the customers happy. So we gave the rebate. What happened next was unprecedented in the industry: everybody anticipated that the stores would ask for a rebate, and to hedge against this, the manufacturers started raising their prices, which put the merchandise further out of reach of price-conscious consumers.

We decided that the way to sell merchandise is either by design or by winning the pricing competition—a competition we did not want to be in since we are not interested in selling

# no sweat

for zero. So design was the answer. Now, innovatively designed merchandise cannot be made where you have to guess on quantities. It has to be made close at hand, and the supply has to be one unit under the demand. You have to make one less than what everybody wants. We decided that the only thing to do was to manufacture in New York City, right across the street from the office. It worked. Since we did not have to bring in product from the Orient, we did not have to give rebates or hedge against markdowns. We sold on the basis of design only, with the guarantee that nothing would be marked down or sold in discount stores. We were only going to sell in a credible way to one level of retail customer. What happened over time was that stores realized that our brand was not saturated and they felt comfortable buying it in without feeling pressured to put it on sale within twenty minutes. This led to a great bottom line for us. So that was our story, and it became very, very efficient to work across the street.

**ss** *Does the consumer benefit from any of this?*

**bk** Of course. Our retail prices actually end up lower than those of manufacturing in the Orient now. Prices there have continued to rise because of labor demands. To beat this, manufacturers are now scurrying around to countries you cannot spell, but that is absolutely death to quality. Quality control is proportionate to how close the manufacturing is to the main office, to where the designer actually works. That is quality control. When the telephone rings here, the production person is at the factory in one minute.

**ss** *So American workers do not make goods of better quality. It is just their proximity to the designer.*

**bk** I am new in the business. I have only been in this for forty-one years. In my lifetime I have manufactured products from Irkutsk to Israel, and I can tell you that the workers of Scranton, Pennsylvania, or of Latin America are only as good as the forelady trains them to be. There is nothing genetic about an Italian sewer that makes that sewer any better than his descendant in New York. This is the greatest myth in the world.

Nicole Miller
new york city

**ss** *How do you organize your work force?*

**bk** We have seventy-five employees, but our labor is all contract labor, and all union. We believe that labor price is not important. The downside of the business is not the cost of labor, or even the initial cost of the fabric: the downside is missing delivery dates or making bad merchandise that people want to take back. We work routinely in about ten factories, and have about 450 people working there. Every factory is in New York, within two blocks of each other.

**ss** *But Nicole Miller products—the bags and umbrellas, for example—are made in other countries. How can you ensure that there is no unethical production when you are producing in China and Hong Kong? How do you know it is not being subcontracted?*

**bk** You cannot. Across the street I can guarantee our product is not made in a sweatshop. Now let us take Yung Sin province, which none of us have heard of. If you are manufacturing in Yung Sin and have got a worker in chains at four o'clock in the morning and are putting amphetamines under his nose to wake him up, can you expect a beautiful design to be made by that worker? It is not going to happen. Good products are made by good people with good materials. Our guarantee is that we have the best factory in whatever country in which our licensees operate because we want the best product.

**ss** *But is the quality of a garment a satisfactory indicator of the labor conditions in which it was made? Why not send an inspector to Yung Sin?*

**bk** It is not productive to send an inspector on a human rights mission through Yung Sin province, south of Wang Nan, east of Win Chu, to see whether there are any abuses going on on the day he arrives. By the time he gets to Wang Nan, someone will know that some honky from America is headed for Yung Sin, east of Win Chu. The moment the guy gets off the train in Yung Sin, the whole town is abuzz. "Where is this guy going? I've never seen a guy like this, he's headed for the factory." So he walks into the factory, and everything is wonderful. He goes back with a report, "Everything is wonderful at that factory." As soon as he's gone, the girls go back in chains.

# no sweat

**ss** *Could you define what a sweatshop is, or what you consider a sweatshop to be, both in the States and abroad, if you think there is a distinction?*

**bk** I know what a sweatshop is in the U.S. A sweatshop goes into business when you ask your main contractor to make a thousand dresses by Friday. Although he is too busy, he takes the work and subcontracts it to a factory that has nothing to do. Why is this factory not busy? Because it is a sweatshop. It is not a sweatshop because it has low labor costs or abuses immigrant workers, but because it makes bad things. By the time the goods come back, the seams are wrong, the fit is not quite right—either that, or I never get the garments because the operation has been closed down for unpaid taxes or violations of fire regulations. I lose out.

**ss** *And what does a sweatshop abroad look like?*

**bk** I have been to factories all over the Pacific Rim—Korea, Japan, Hong Kong, Szechwan, Singapore. I have seen workers in all kinds of situations but have never seen what I would call hazardous or abusive conditions. But the issue is complicated. Take child labor. Child labor is child labor: it is disgusting. I went to Morocco and saw seven-year-olds working in the kilim factories. In Morocco, that is not against the law, that is fine for them. I found it disturbing and could not buy a kilim. However, nobody in Morocco is picketing the streets about their daughters working in a rug factory. It is not slavery and the families have donated the girls to do this kind of work. Little boys working in leather-dyeing are running around in tanning acid; it cannot be good for them, but this is what they do. So am I going to rewrite the social conduct of Morocco? It is very difficult.

**ss** *You believe then that the antisweatshop campaign should focus on the States, where at least there seems to be some measure of agreement about what a sweatshop is?*

**bk** Absolutely. The U.S. has the laws. We have the Standard Minimum Wage Act, which is a piece of federal legislation. Fair labor is an issue of national morality.

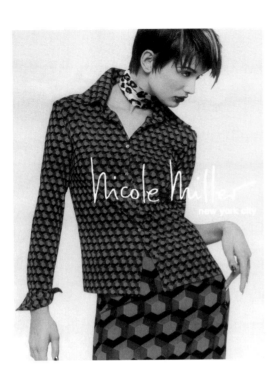

**ss** *What is Secretary of Labor Reich's role in upholding this morality?*

**bk** Reich is involved in enforcing the Fair Labor Standards Act of 1938, and in accordance with that act he is labeling "hot goods" and busting high-profile manufacturers like Kathie Lee Gifford, Kathy Ireland, Guess Jeans, and the Gap, who were producing in illegal shops. Of course, every one of those manufacturers has professed ignorance that their stuff was being made in sweatshop conditions. It is probably true—they probably never gave it a thought. After the busts, though, people are thinking. Now everybody sends out denials: "This cannot be. This is not corporate policy." Everyone wants to be perceived as clean in the States. Reich is responsible: he alerted everyone to the issue.

**ss** *What do you think of the National Labor Committee? I know that in the past you have been critical of Charlie Kernaghan.*

**bk** The problem with Kernaghan is that he is an anecdotalist and a rabble-rouser. He picks up the amphetamine story, that some drugged kid was forced to work until two or three in the morning. But you cannot characterize an entire industry with one anecdote. I know people that make in Honduras and Guatemala and they observe all the laws of those countries. Phil Knight makes Nikes in such squeaky clean factories that they would put their American equivalents to shame. It is easy to say, as Kernaghan does, "Phil Knight is paying $25 million a year to Michael Jordan and 20 cents an hour to his workers. He could pay Jordan $20 million a year and spend the remaining $5 million to double everybody's salary in those plants." But Kernaghan isn't running Nike, he's running the NLC. The charges he makes may get him an audience, but he has not changed Nike's business at all. He has not done anything.

**ss** *Do you really think Reich would have paid attention to Kathie Lee and the Gap, and the conditions under which their garments are produced, if the NLC had not conducted this type of campaign?*

**bk** As I said, Kernaghan is a rabble-rouser—and rabble-rousers get attention. Kernaghan did get Reich's attention, but Reich is the one who has actually brought people to the table.

# no sweat

130

**ss** *You were an outspoken participant at the Department of Labor fashion summits which followed in the wake of the Kathie Lee scandal. At the Marymount conference in July 1996, you proposed a controversial system to tackle sweatshop abuse.*

**bk** Mass producers are under enormous pressure to go out and get the cheapest price, no matter what. You give it to a contractor, you close your eyes. You don't care where he gets it subcontracted, or whatever. Now, are you going to get inspectors to every factory? No. So you use the rat principle. Y undercuts X by using cheap, sweatshop labor. So X rats on Y to the retailer and says, give me the contract. Reich said, "That's not a bad idea." If we invoke the rat idea, he would not need inspectors. If we do not have enough inspectors, let everybody point out competitors who are ratty, who are illegal.

**ss** *So you're asking the industry to regulate itself.*

**bk** Exactly. Use the industry to point out abuses. If Y says, "Well, I don't care. Who are you? You're just saying that because you've lost the order," then X will go to the government and say, "Look, I'm losing business. What's happening?"

**ss** *It is more complicated than that. For your rat principle to work, at least one contractor who produces at the mass level for, say, Wal-Mart or Kmart would have to believe in ethical production. And isn't the bottom line the only priority when manufacturing for this market?*

**bk** The only way the economic pressure would work is if the retailer issued a statement saying, "We will only accept merchandise from quality makers and quality factories."

**ss** *Do you think that it is possible to be a major player at that level without sweatshop labor? When your numbers are that large and you are trying to keep prices so low, can you afford to entertain ethical concerns?*

**bk** Probably not. If Y is in competition with X, and X is producing in prison camps and has a willing buyer, Y is out of business.

nicole miller
new york city

**ss** *What do you think will come out of the Department of Labor summits?*

**bk** First, everybody's interested in self-preservation and that means preserving the status quo. Kmart and Wal-Mart are in a death struggle with each other for market share—and for them, market share does not mean making something more beautiful than the other guy. But what's happened as a result of these meetings is a level of consciousness and pious talking. If I had walked into a Wal-Mart office a year ago and said, "You are doing business with guys that make stuff under abusive conditions," they would have thrown me out. Now this is an issue they pay attention to.

**ss** *Do you think Reich and the NLC's efforts have had a lasting effect?*

**bk** No. It has got to be a nonstop effort.

**ss** *One way to keep manufacturers, retailers, and consumers aware of the issue of sweatshop production is to label garments as fairly produced. Representative George Miller (Calif.) has proposed such a label, but I understand that you would take the idea a step further.*

**bk** If you can figure out how to tell consumers which goods are made in great conditions and which aren't, you will have an incredible economic lever. But you must be able to ensure that not only are the goods made in great conditions but that they are made to the manufacturer's specifications. For example, if a manufacturer says a garment can survive fifty washings, then the label guarantees it will stand up to fifty washings. As the Japanese learned when they added a gold seal to their exports, if you tag a quality issue onto the workers' rights requirement, you have a very powerful label.

**ss** *Who would regulate it? There are too few federal inspectors as it is.*

**bk** First of all, you sell the label to interested manufacturers. Then there could be an agency made up of fashion-school graduates around the country who would visit participating factories and test the products on a random basis. The labels

would pay for these inspectors. Of course, it would have to be independent.

**ss** *But if you're imagining ex–fashion students as inspectors, isn't quality your primary concern here? Aren't you really concerned with the number of stitches to the inch?*

**bk** I believe that at the end of the day, the customer who is standing at the counter choosing between two piles of jeans is asking, "What is the difference?" And if one represents better value, better design, better something, then it will be bought. If you just say, "This represents good working conditions," maybe it will, maybe it won't. A recent survey indicates that only about 50 percent of consumers care about fair practices.

**ss** *How do you think more people could be made to care?*

**bk** Raise them differently. Change all the television programs. How do you change an entire culture? Why do people now care about the environment? They had to have it drilled into their heads that we were going to be choked to death if we continued to put crap into the air. When they first put catalytic converters on cars, do you know what the big industry was? Taking the cars from the factory and removing the catalytic converter because a lot of macho guys said that they hindered the car's performance. With that going on, what hope is there for the culture?

**ss** *But you think that one way to educate consumers is to piggyback concern for ethical labor onto the desire for high-quality merchandise?*

**bk** You can always appeal to self-interest. It's a great motivator for everyone. Take manufacturers. The apparel business is not made up of rocket scientists. We believe in survival of the fittest—which here means cheap, cheap, cheap—but few actually make it. A lot of people who are producing in sweatshops right now will soon be out of business because they are competing on such low levels as to have no margin—after all, in a price competition, the winner's goods cost zero. Most manufacturers who survive in a saturated market make good designs.

Nicole Miller

**ss** *For your customers, who are relatively affluent and style-conscious, good design and quality matter, and so it is in your self-interest to ensure against shoddiness. However, people who are shopping for a Pocahontas T-shirt or something similar are not looking for precision cutting and tailoring. They're buying a souvenir. What, then, do you imagine the self-interest of manufacturers of these garments to be?*

**bk** The Pocahontas T-shirt is a good example. Let us say that it is the lowest level of product you can make—no imagination, no style, just a plain white jersey cotton knit with one of three Pocahontases striking a pose. Say you are in the business of making millions of these three shirts. Do you know what your self-interest tells you to do? Make the whole thing by robot. It is so cheap to produce, so repetitive, that you can find a machine to do it better than any worker.

**ss** *So why did Disney choose to produce in Haiti?*

**bk** Haiti had the lowest labor base in the world, even lower than Burundi. Haiti appeals to the self-interest of the guys who do not want to invest in machinery and do the robot thing because they do not believe they have a long-term business. They want the lowest labor paid by the day. But even these manufacturers are leaving Haiti now. Haiti cannot keep work down there. The workers are not dependable, they get sick, whatever. The statistics show that Haiti, with its lowest labor price, is not actually gaining in work.

**ss** *Are these statistics a reliable indicator? Isn't Haiti a place you'd go only if you had to crash out production very cheaply? Isn't it the ultimate expression of the sweatshop?*

**bk** It could be. But to return to our earlier discussion of the priorities of the No Sweat campaign: If you are willing to say, "I would like to correct 90 percent of the problem," Haiti falls in the bottom 2 percent. If you want to attack the problem, you should start with the U.S., then Canada (easy), then Mexico (not so easy). You start with something you can get your hands around, for God's sake. In Haiti and places where military dictatorships are in power and nobody has any rights, everybody could be sitting eating dinner and the police could

come in and haul two people away. These are not countries for us to start worrying about whether sweatshops are in operation.

**ss** *Because it is harder to define what a sweatshop is in such situations?*

**bk** It is harder to define what human rights are. What is a human right in China? There are none.

**ss** *But to return to the idea of quality/fair labor labeling: How could you be sure that the bags you produce in China would qualify for such a label? How could labels be applied to merchandise made abroad?*

**bk** I think it would be difficult. Let's see if—and it is a big *if*—we can first make labeling work in the States. The real success of such an effort will only be realized when the labeled goods sell better than those that are not. Then what you will see is everyone acting in their self-interest, which is the way I like it.

**ss** *How you behave as a manufacturer, and how you believe your peers should act, rests on a belief that capitalism can be forced to behave ethically, and that corporate imperatives can coexist with ethical imperatives—this seems to me to lie at the heart of both your labeling and ratting proposals. Yet we both know that capitalism is not an ethical system, and that the bottom line is always the bottom line. How do you reconcile your position on these facts?*

**bk** The bottom line could be ethical. Capitalism does not have to mean "somebody wins, somebody loses." I do not believe in that. I believe that if capital wins, everybody wins. At Nicole Miller, it is my job to ensure that everybody wins. In business, capital without labor is meaningless. I say good equipment, good material, and good labor make a good product, which makes good sales, which make good business. It is not a difficult formula.

# the economics of the sweatshop

## Michael Piore

The revival of the sweatshop in the American garment industry is surely one of the great ironies of our time. The popular press at the end of the twentieth century is filled with the same kinds of stories about sweated labor that scandalized Progressive era reformers: immigrant women, and sometimes their children, paid by the piece at subminimum wages, packed like sardines in cramped quarters under the ruthless supervision of predatory floor managers. The inventory of hazardous working conditions—aisles and exits clogged with materials, no ventilation or heat, frigid in the winter, stifling in the summer—matches the worst found in the gilded age of sweatshop production.

Contemporary exposés suggest that the problem has been generated by competition from imports produced by low-wage labor in China and Mexico. But the irony is even greater than it appears. While the sweatshop is certainly a feature of the economic landscape in developing countries, these shops generally cater to their own domestic markets and face similar competitive pressures from manufacturers exporting to U.S.-based retailers like Wal-Mart and Kmart. Moreover, most of the export-oriented garment factories do not *look* like the ones uncovered in Los Angeles or New York City, in fact, seem like models of modernity by comparison: orderly, spacious, well lighted, well ventilated, and equipped with ample machinery.

What accounts for the sweatshop's return after virtually disappearing for so many decades? The explanation lies in a more rigorous definition of the sweatshop and a better understanding of the historical forces that led to its decline in the first place. These days, the term *sweatshop* is applied very loosely to almost any set of conditions considered inhumane or unfair. Using this broad criteria, the export-oriented factories of the developing world could be labeled sweatshops. After all, their quasi-Fordist veneer often masks conditions that are extremely exploitive of labor. These conditions are not limited to wage levels which, deemed extortionate by Western standards, are not necessarily so from the perspective of the people who earn them abroad. They may involve a work force rounded up in distance provinces and confined to factory compounds under close supervision in prisonlike settings. They include grueling workloads, frenetically paced production schedules, and protracted shifts, all of which deplete the physical health of workers and push them out of the industry. Repugnant as these operations are, however, they do not constitute bona fide sweatshops, at least as conventionally understood.

# no sweat

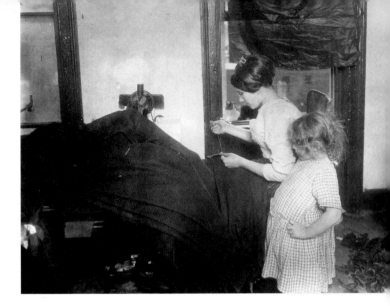

The genuine sweatshop is symptomatic of a particular economic logic, the manifestation of a specific organization of work. To understand what is driving the garment industry today, we must trace that logic and clarify its functional arrangement. This arrangement involves the violation of a host of legal provisions that developed out of campaigns to eliminate the use of sweated labor in the late nineteenth and early twentieth century, campaigns that finally came to fruition in the labor legislation of the New Deal. These include prohibitions on child labor, the regulation of homework, piecework, and overtime, as well as a series of health, safety, fire, and building codes (normally the purview of local authorities). The sweatshop is typically in violation of not one but virtually all of these regulations simultaneously.

Why this is so lies in the distinction drawn by economists between fixed and variable costs. In the typical production process, some costs are fixed (at least in the short run) irrespective of how much is produced, and the employer is obliged to pay these costs no matter what. Other costs vary with the level of output. When fixed costs are large, the employer is motivated to scrutinize an operation's productivity in terms of hourly output. As productivity rises, the fixed costs of an operation are spread over more and more units of output, and the cost of each unit declines. The reverse holds when fixed costs are low relative to variable costs: the employer has less incentive to worry about productivity.

The sweatshop is characterized by very low fixed costs. The worker is paid by the piece; other hourly costs—rent, electricity, heat—can be transformed into variable ones by passing them along to the worker through the homework system. Typically with homework, the worker either leases or buys tools and equipment, and it is common for the worker to pay for at least part of her materials. When work is done in the employer's shop, the major fixed disbursement

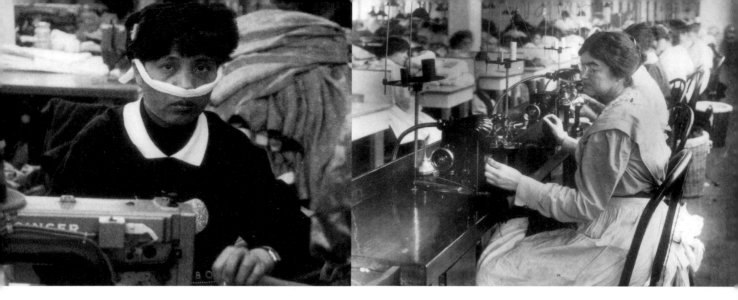

is rent. To minimize that cost, the employer will seek out cheap—that is, substandard—factory housing like cellars and attics, and cram as many workers into the space as possible. The attempt to reduce the rent paid per worker is the chief cause of congestion in sweatshops, affecting the way in which material inventories, supplies, equipment, and work-in-progress block aisles and exits. It is also the source of the unhealthy and dangerous conditions (poor wiring and ventilation, unsanitary or nonexistent bathrooms, fire hazards) for which the sweatshop is notorious.

One might reasonably expect that such conditions have an adverse effect on worker productivity. They do. But since workers are paid by the piece, most of this effect is borne by them. If productivity drops, the employer can simply add fresh workers. As long as any reduction in turnout does not outweigh the savings obtained by overcrowding, the employer is unlikely to care. The sweatshop employer's relative freedom from concern for the rate of hourly productivity also encourages the use of child labor.

In industries with a heavy capital investment or where workers earn hourly wages, an employer has a stake in productivity. (In fact, if capital investment is large enough, an employer will be concerned with productivity even if the worker is paid nothing.) This explains why the sweatshop is not present in most industries, even in the earliest stages of economic development, and, since development usually involves a shift to increasingly capital-intensive forms of production, why it tends to decline over time in those industries where it can be found. The garment industry, however, has experienced less pressure from growing capital intensity.

A major reason for this has been the difficulty of mechanizing garment manufacture. The difficulties are twofold. The first lies in the nature of cloth. Unlike wood or metal, fabrics are pliant, twisting and bending in the process of production. The second factor deterring mechanization is fashion. Because styles are so unpredictable and change so rapidly, it is not generally profitable to produce in the long runs that justify investment in dedicated machinery. Instead, garments tend to be produced in short runs, using a combination of general-purpose tools and equipment—especially the sewing machine—manned by an operator who can switch easily from one style to another. Considerable progress has been made, with the help of information technology, in overcoming the problems created by short runs and in automating some of the preparatory stages of garment manufacture, especially marker making and cutting. But the technology of sewing has changed little over the last hundred years.

The garment production which has been moved offshore to developing countries like Mexico and China is differentiated from the production that remains behind by precisely those characteristics affecting fixed costs. Garments with a high fashion content are difficult to produce at a distance from the market because by the time the goods arrive, the season is likely to be over. At best, the fashion segment of the industry is able to use foreign producers to make the initial stocks in relatively long runs with a certain degree of mechanized special-purpose equipment. If the item sells well, it is then reordered from local factories that produce a much shorter run quickly to restock the retail outlets before the season ends. For the most part, however, the foreign producers are making the items which lend themselves to long runs like

blue jeans and underwear and, as a result, also permit more mechanization. They thus involve a larger capital investment and hence the kinds of fixed costs which deter the sweatshop. The capital investment combines with additional fixed hourly costs imposed by the heavy inventory involved in production at long distances from the market, plus the premium which distant production in a fashion industry places on time. The employer's attempt to maximize productivity explains the orderly layout of factories producing for the U.S. market abroad. Their layout is in fact very similar to that of domestic producers operating outside the major garment centers like New York and Los Angeles, and it is with these producers, rather than the urban centers, that the foreign manufacturers are most competitive.

In the garment centers themselves, the main force reducing the sweatshop over time has not been fixed capital investment, but unionization and government regulation. Probably the most important development in this regard, moreover, is the imposition of a minimum hourly wage. If that wage is set somewhere above the average level of output in the sweatshop, the employer is forced to carry a certain cost of production regardless of the worker's level of productivity. The employer, then, has an incentive to ensure that the worker's productivity exceeds the hourly minimum, which is generally sufficient inducement to move young children out of the shop and to observe health and safety codes. But even when this cost does not in itself promote health and safety, the reorganization of the shop which it prompts increases the employer's span of control over the production process, making compliance with regulations relatively easy—if these regulations are enforced. On the other hand, in the constricted space

140 of the sweatshop, it is almost impossible to police production. Indeed, the employer seldom concerns himself or herself with what the workers do; the piecework system acts as a kind of self-supervision.

The return of the sweatshop in recent years thus appears to be primarily the product of the decline of government regulation and diminishing union strength. Actually, we have no hard evidence that the sweatshop has seen a revival in the last decade and, in fact, it never entirely disappeared. There has always been a fringe of producers who operate outside the regulatory framework. Since these shops exist in an underground economy, they are almost by definition uncountable. Perhaps fashion or politics have led the press to rediscover something that has always been there. But given the economic logic of the sweatshop, trends in government regulation and in deunionization would predict a resurgence, and in that sense the press reports are credible.

The extensive subcontracting chains in the garment industry—especially in sweating, where the attempt to minimize fixed costs leads to small shops operating either as distribution centers to homeworkers or in remote, low-rent locations—pose serious problems for enforcement of both government and union regulations. The difficulty of enforcement led to rules barring homework in the 1940s, since abridged by the pressures of deregulation under the Reagan administration. To effectively control homework and underground shops, government inspectors must search door-to-door in suspect neighborhoods, an extremely labor-intensive and expensive strategy made virtually impossible by budget cutbacks. In addition, the most powerful of the regulatory agencies, the Wages and Hours Division of the U.S. Department of Labor, has assumed responsibility for an increasing array of regulations, including equal pay provisions, which have distracted inspectors from sweatshop issues and turned their attention toward sex discrimination in higher paying employment.

Moreover, the penalty for minimum-wage violators involves little beyond compensating workers for back wages due under the law, a relatively weak enforcement device. Historically, the most effective way to curb sweatshops has been to gain control of the supply chain at the center by compelling the retailer or the chief contractor to take responsibility for the labor conditions of its subcontractors. In the past, this obligation was routinely stipulated in union

*Sweatshop, Oakland California, 1989.*
*The blocked aisles are a fire hazard.*

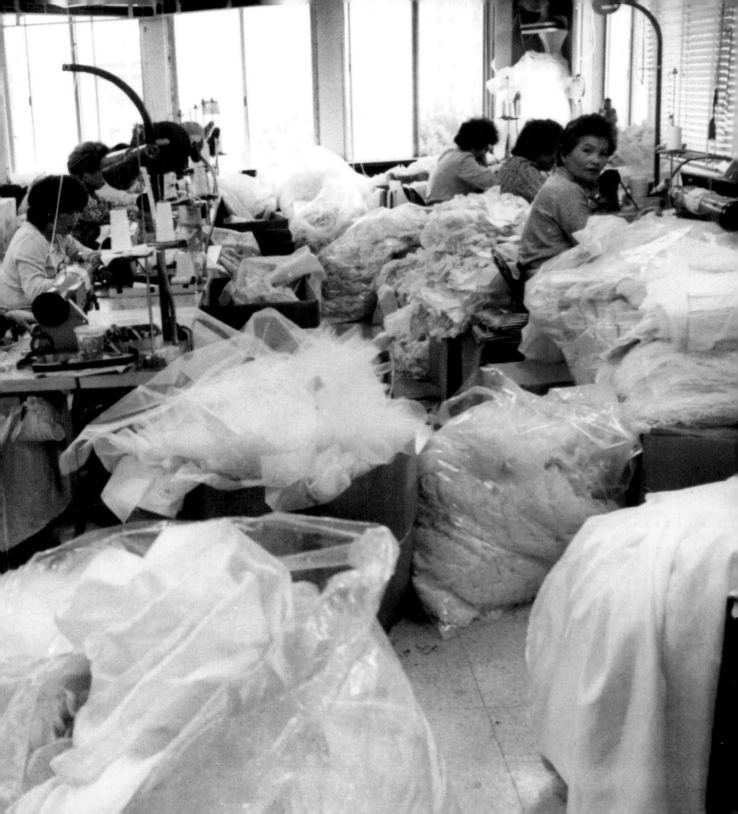

contracts with manufacturers. But these checks on the industry have deteriorated over time as the unionized sector has dwindled and the locus of control has shifted from manufacturers to retailers, since the latter are not generally organized by the union. Government regulators could exact more stringent penalties, for instance, confiscating work-in-progress (in the same way that the DEA appropriates the material possessions of drug dealers). Because manufacturers and retailers typically provide sweatshops with materials, this tactic might persuade them to monitor their subcontractors. But the responsible agencies have been very reluctant to wield this power.

Workers in the late twentieth-century sweatshop are victims of fashion in a very strict sense: the sweatshop is a production strategy that is viable only in industries with very low levels of capital. Elsewhere in the industrial world, the sweatshop has been eliminated by the high levels of mechanization and automation fostered by modern technology. But this kind of investment is discouraged in garment manufacture by the short production runs and rapid turnaround times which fashion dictates. A less fashion-driven industry, however, is likely to do little for the victims of the sweatshop, since it is fashion above all which holds production close to the market in large cities like New York and Los Angeles. The more stable parts of the industry, which lend themselves to long runs and standardized products, long ago moved out of urban centers to rural areas, first to the American South, and today more and more abroad.

But we long ago learned how to maintain a fashion industry in New York without the sweatshop, through unionization and government regulation, and the deterioration of these structures has engendered the revival of the sweating system today. Sweatshops might not exist without fashion, but they are hardly its inevitable byproduct. The people who suffer these deplorable working conditions are more accurately the victims of the reaction against unions and "big government" of the last two decades. We could rescue them if only we could overcome the callousness and indifference which blinds us to their plight.

# El Monte Thai garment workers:
## slave sweatshops

Julie Su

On August 2, 1995, the American public was horrified by press reports about the discovery at an apartment complex in El Monte, California, of seventy-two Thai garment workers who had been held in slavery for up to seven years, sewing clothes for some of the nation's top manufacturers and retailers. The workers labored over eighteen hours a day in a compound enclosed by barbed wire. Armed guards imposed discipline. Crowded eight or ten into bedrooms built for two, rats crawled over them during their few precious hours of sleep. From their homes in impoverished rural Thailand, these women and men had dared to dream the immigrant's dream—a better life for themselves, hard work with just pay, and decent living conditions. What they found instead was an immigrant's nightmare—a garment industry that reaps exorbitant profit from its workers, organized to disclaim any responsibility for the inhumane consequences.

Starvation wages, long hours, and illegal working conditions are standard business practices in the industry, and the El Monte story has helped to dramatize public awareness of these crimes. But the story told here is about how workers have endured, and have mobilized to bring about change.

The Thai workers were industrial homeworkers, forced to eat, sleep, live, and work in the place they called "home." The slave labor compound where they were confined was a two-story apartment with seven units, surrounded by a ring of razor wire and iron guardrails with sharp ends pointing inward. Their captors, who supervised garment production and enforced manufacturer specifications and deadlines, ruled through fear and intimidation. Workers were forbidden to make unmonitored phone calls or write uncensored letters, and were forced to purchase goods from their captors, who charged four or five times the market price for food, toiletries, and other daily necessities. Living under the constant threat of harm to themselves and to their families in Thailand, they labored over sewing machines in dark garages and poorly lit rooms, making clothes for brand-name manufacturers sold in some of the biggest retail stores in America: labels like Tomato, Clio, B.U.M., High Sierra, Axle, Cheetah, Anchor Blue, and Airtime. Many of these labels are privately owned and sold by well-known retailers—Mervyn's, Miller's Outpost, and Montgomery Ward. Others are sold on the racks of May department stores, Nordstrom, Sears, Target, and elsewhere.

**no sweat**

Immediately following the disclosure of conditions at El Monte, Sweatshop Watch, a coalition of organizations, attorneys, and community members, mobilized to bring support and social and legal services to the Thai workers with the aim of securing their release from further detention at the hands of the Immigration and Naturalization Service (INS). Formerly known as the Coalition to Eliminate Sweatshop Conditions, Sweatshop Watch was formed in 1992 as a statewide network. Southern California members include the Asian Pacific American Labor Alliance, Asian Pacific American Legal Center, Coalition for Humane Immigrant Rights in Los Angeles, Korean Immigrant Workers Advocates, Thai Community Development Center, and UNITE. Northern California members include the Asian Immigrant Women Advocates, Asian Law Caucus, and Equal Rights Advocates, among others.

Working around the clock, members of Sweatshop Watch demanded to meet with the Thai workers in INS detention to advise them of their legal rights and to advocate for their

*left: Thai workers released from captivity in
El Monte, California sweatshop.*

release. In detention, the workers were frightened and bewildered. Forced to wear drab yellow prison uniforms, they were shackled by the INS each time they were transported from federal detention at Terminal Island in San Pedro to the downtown Los Angeles facility. Using a makeshift office consisting of the pay phones in the INS basement waiting room, Sweatshop Watch broadcast the message that continued imprisonment of the workers was not only inhumane, but also conveyed the wrong impression of justice in the United States: that workers who have been exploited and abused will be punished further and sent to the INS if they come forward. This practice discourages workers from reporting labor and human rights abuses, and pushes operations like the El Monte slaveshop even further underground.

With the help of the news media, which focused public scrutiny on the inaction of federal agencies, Sweatshop Watch held the INS office open into the wee hours of the morning and refused to accept any bureaucratic excuses for denying the workers their freedom. After meeting with federal prosecutors and public defenders to obtain bail reduction for each worker from $5,000 to $500, an appeal was sent out to the community that bonds were needed. Sweatshop Watch members themselves posted over fifty bonds. Churches, shelters, supermarkets, and hospitals stepped forward to help provide transitional housing, emergency food and clothing, and medical care. One worker, whose teeth had rotted from long neglect and who had extracted eight of his own teeth while confined in El Monte, received a brand new set from a generous dentist. Taking the lead from the Thai Community Development Center, Sweatshop Watch conducted a job search on behalf of the workers. This was no mean task in the garment industry, since it meant locating jobs that pay the minimum wage and overtime in shops that comply with health and safety laws. All of the Thai workers were re-employed within two months, a testament to the efforts of community-based organizations working in coalition.

After the August 2 raid, eight of the immediate operators of the slave sweatshop were taken into federal custody, charged with involuntary servitude, kidnapping, conspiracy, smuggling, and harboring of the Thai workers. In February 1996, they pled guilty to—among other charges—criminal counts of involuntary servitude and conspiracy. The courageous testimony of the Thai workers made this criminal case possible, but their legal struggle has not ended there. As heinous as the conduct of the sweatshop operators was, it represents only the

# no sweat

outward continuum of abuse in the garment industry. The true culprits responsible for slave labor in California are the retailers and manufacturers.

The El Monte compound was just one unit of a slave sweatshop operation which, as early as 1988, ran various locations in downtown Los Angeles, where Latina and Latino workers toiled long hours seven days a week for subminimum wages in unsanitary and degrading conditions. Each location performed a different role in the garment manufacturing process, together constituting one business operation sharing common ownership, control, coordination, and assets. The Latina workers downtown sewed buttons and buttonholes and performed ironing, finishing, checking, and packaging. The El Monte site was one of the locations where cut cloth was actually sewn into garments. The garment manufacturers employed the Thai and Latino workers' services through enterprises supervised by the sweatshop owners, operating as SK Fashions, S&P Fashions, and D&R Fashions. Their downtown facilities, with fewer than ten sewing machines between them during all of 1995, could not possibly have produced the volume of garments, to the quality and specifications, with the turnaround time demanded by manufacturers. In fact, clothes were sent from these front shops to El Monte and another unregistered production site to be sewn to manufacturers' specifications and patterns. The manufacturers' quality-control inspectors either knew or should have known that the orders they were giving to the sweatshop operators could not possibly have been filled at the downtown front shops. Had manufacturers taken their legal responsibilities seriously, the El Monte slave site would have been discovered and the workers' suffering ended much sooner.

*Ken Cheung of the Labor Commissioner's office inspects the property at the El Monte, California, apartment complex Friday, August 4, 1995, two days after state and federal agents raided the building upon discovering slave labor conditions at an illegal sweatshop there. At right is an umbrella under which neighborhood residents said they frequently saw a person keeping watch over the premises and shooing away curious onlookers and pets.*

The example of El Monte demonstrates how easily illegal conditions in the garment industry can deteriorate from sweatshop to slaveshop under the existing industrial system. In response to this system, the Thai and Latino workers have filed a landmark civil rights lawsuit in Federal District Court in Los Angeles. Peonage and involuntary servitude violate the U.S. Constitution and many other laws: the Racketeering Influenced and Corrupt Organizations Act (RICO), the minimum wage and overtime compensation requirements of the Fair Labor Standards Act and the California Labor Code, federal and state prohibitions on industrial homework, false imprisonment, extortion, and unfair business practices. The lawsuit holds responsible not only individual operators of the slave sweatshop but also the manufacturers and retailers whose profits were secured on the backs of slave labor. In addition to their immediate captors, the Thai and Latino workers have named Mervyn's, Miller's Outpost, B.U.M. International, Montgomery Ward, Tomato, L.F. Sportswear, New Boys, and Bigin in their suit.

The lawsuit strikes at the heart of the so-called subcontracting system endemic to the multibillion dollar garment industry, whereby sweatshop operators act, in effect, as supervisors and managers of labor on behalf of manufacturers and retailers, who exercise all meaningful control over the industry. The lawsuit charges that the latter are actually joint employers of garment workers and as such, bound by all the provisions of federal and state labor laws. Manufacturers counterclaim that sweatshop workers are not employees but, rather, independent contractors. However, nominal contracting relationships are routinely ignored under both federal and state law, where an analysis of the factors underlying the relationship belies the independent contractor status. Thus, manufacturers employed these workers in violation of the Fair Labor Standards Act, the California Labor Code, the Industrial Homework Act's prohibitions on homework, and the Garment Manufacturing Registration Act's requirements on wages, hours, safety, and registration. To the response that sweatshop operators were paid the "industry standard" or "fair market value," the lawsuit charges that, in an industry where all prices are substandard and artificially depressed by rampant abuses, the "industry standard" itself is an illegal one. Indeed, this response only highlights workers' points that manufacturers sustain and profit from an industry that operates outside the law.

So far, the workers can claim several victories, including a number of settlements critical in helping them rebuild their lives. In March 1996, the manufacturers and retailers sought to have the case dismissed, claiming the workers had no basis for bringing them to court. The U.S. District Court refused to grant the motion, rejecting the manufacturers' argument that they cannot be deemed joint employers. This decision was a major setback for the manufacturers and retailers, who have hired some of the most upscale law firms in California to defend them, firms that have flooded the workers with endless discovery requests and withheld crucial information on the companies' actual practices. In June 1996, the Latino workers employed at the downtown facilities joined the Thai workers in their legal battle. The inclusion of the Latino workers in this suit sends a broader warning to manufacturers and retailers throughout the industry. In March 1997, the trial judge refused to dismiss the workers' claims that violations of the hot goods provision of the FLSA by retailers constitutes negligence: if sweatshop owners are the agents of retailers, then these violations do fall under the contracting relationship. With this important hurdle crossed, the case proceeded to summary judgment in the summer of 1997.

On trial here are not simply the conditions of involuntary servitude behind barbed wire, but all sweatshop conditions throughout the garment industry. In filing this lawsuit, the workers are suing not only to win back wages, but to put the entire industry on notice that this kind of exploitation must stop. While the Thai workers have come a long way in the last year—they have been studying English, taking the bus to work, paying their own bills, buying their own groceries—they have also entered the unenviable world of immigrant garment workers, who toil long hours and struggle to survive on the minimum wage. Their freedom from enslavement has not meant freedom from poverty or a host of other problems stemming from the long years of neglect to their health, physical exhaustion, and psychological abuse. It is difficult to evaluate the emotional costs of their ordeal, and impossible to place a monetary value on each day of freedom from which they were deprived.

In the face of anti-immigrant hysteria, these Thai and Latina workers are defying attempts to divide them along ethnic lines, and are appealing to U.S. law to remedy the kind of labor abuses that permit powerful forces to blame the victim. When workers face retaliation, intimidation, or deportation for standing up for their rights and pursuing legal redress, garment industry giants will continue to exploit them with impunity. With this lawsuit, the Thai and Latina workers say, "no more."

One-time handouts will not change the structure of an industry explicitly organized to protect profit and privilege and to depress wages and working conditions. Government forums and calls for good corporate consciences are not enough. Manufacturers and retailers will continue to flagrantly disregard the law as long as they can get away with it. The workers' lawsuit is a warning that is long overdue. It is high time these corporate employers invested as much in the basic dignity of the workers who make their clothes as they invest in lawsuits to silence workers, creative advertising, and fancy marketing techniques.

*El Monte Thai garment workers and community activists/volunteers at Griffith Park on their first day of freedom in the U.S., August 13, 1995.*

# labor, history, and sweatshops in the new global economy

Alan Howard

The apparel industry has long been plagued by a noxious creature known as the sweatshop. The word conjures up images of sweltering tenements and dark lofts, of women and children toiling into the night for wages that will barely keep them alive, of that infamous sign on the factory door: *If you don't come in on Sunday, don't come in on Monday*. It is the peculiar nature of this industry that such conditions can be found today more or less as they existed a hundred years ago. The scene of the crime has shifted and spread, the skin color of its victims tends to be darker; but at the end of the twentieth century we are confronted by this man-made plague that at the beginning of the century most Americans considered an insult to human dignity.

Clothing, women's in particular, remains a most unpredictable commodity. Weather and season and the whims of fashion drive apparel merchants to minimize their risks of getting caught with goods they can't sell or without items that are flying off the shelves. The industry has historically dealt with this unpredictability by pushing risk down through the production chain: from retailer to manufacturer to contractor and subcontractor and ultimately into the worker's home. From the retailer's point of view, this broad base of small, readily available, and easily disposable producers is the ideal solution to the inherent volatility of the market. From the point of view of the workers at the bottom of this industrial pyramid, it is a system that subjects them to relentless pressure, and the worst imaginable forms of exploitation and self-exploitation. It creates the sweatshop, which in turn undermines legitimate enterprises and drives standards down even further. "Nice guys go out of business," remarks a union negotiator, reflecting the near impossibility of maintaining decent standards in one shop when the work can be easily moved to a sweatshop down the street or in another country.

This basic dynamic has not changed in a hundred years. But we know how the system works and how to fix it. At various points over the past century the power of the sweatshop to depress the wages and living conditions of workers throughout the industry has been reduced and even neutralized by the power of workers to defend themselves and of government to regulate the industry. It is a struggle profoundly influenced by the prevailing economic and political climate of the times and by the force of public opinion that both shapes and reflects those times.

"The sweatshop is a state of mind as well as a physical fact," writes Leon Stein, in the introduction to his invaluable *Out of the Sweatshop*. "Its work day is of no fixed length; it links

# no sweat

pace of work to endurance. It demeans the spirit by denying to workers any part in determining the conditions of or the pay of their work."

Some scholars trace sweatshops back to the 1840s, when it is recorded that a group of working women in New York, protesting their miserable wages, were told by an employer that "he could obtain girls from Connecticut who would work for even less." Between 1880 and 1900, more than 3 million European immigrants poured into our cities, Jews fleeing the pogroms of Russia, Italians and Slavs and other workers with their own visions of America and freedom. They were drawn into the apparel industry by the tens of thousands, desperate for work at almost any wage. The industry, expanding as the purchasing power of women created a mass market for their clothing, was able to accommodate them. Here is how the economist John R. Commons described the system in 1901:

> The term "sweating," or "sweating system," originally denoted a system of subcontract, wherein the work is let out to contractors to be done in small shops or homes... The system to be contrasted with the sweating system is the "factory system," wherein the manufacturer employs his own workmen, under the management of his own foreman or superintendent, in his own building... In the factory system the workmen are congregated where they can be seen by the factory inspectors and where they can organize or develop a common understanding. In the sweating system they are isolated and unknown.
>
> The position of the contractor or sweater now in the business in American cities is peculiarly that of an organizer and employer of immigrants. The man best fitted to be a contractor is the man who is well acquainted with his neighbors, who is able to speak the language of several classes of immigrants, who can easily persuade his neighbors or their wives and children to work for him, and who in this way can obtain the cheapest help. Enormous changes were taking place in the industry—the use of electric power, the emergence of a mass market for ready-made clothing, economies of scale that concentrated large numbers of workers, even an insurgent labor movement—and yet the sweatshop remained intact and grew even more pernicious.[1]

"Workers toiling in dark, humid, stuffy basements on Division St., children of eight years and women, many of them far from well, sweating their lives away in these hellholes" so shocked State License Superintendent Daniel O'Leary on an inspection of garment shops in

New York City in 1900, according to a contemporaneous account, "that he has asked the union for help and advice."[2]

It would be a few years before the infant International Ladies' Garment Workers' Union (ILGWU) would be able to provide much help, but it had plenty of advice. Outlaw homework. Bring the subcontracting shops under control. Protect the right of workers to strike, organize, and bargain collectively. Improve and enforce health and safety codes. There was more, but that would do for starters.

A decade later, a series of events would mark one of those periodic turning points in the industry—and in this case exert an influence over the course of industrial relations in America for the next fifty years.

In 1909, a walkout of several hundred workers from the Triangle Shirtwaist Company sparked a strike of 20,000 shirtwaist makers throughout the industry. They were mainly young Jewish and Italian immigrant women, their condition as the most viciously exploited workers in the industry long acknowledged but ineffectively addressed by both the male-dominated unions and government authorities. The strike became a cause, as community leaders—particularly socially conscious and socially prominent women—joined the picket lines, raised funds, and galvanized public opinion in support of the strike.

The following year it was the men's turn. In New York, 60,000 cloak makers, inspired by the success of the shirtwaist makers, paralyzed the industry with a general strike. At the same time in Chicago, workers at the Hart, Schaffner, and Marx firm sparked an explosive strike in that city's garment industry that would give birth to the Amalgamated Clothing Workers of America (ACWA), the men's clothing counterpart to the ILGWU.

The cloak makers strike in New York led to the signing of what was called the Protocol of Peace. According to Leon Stein, the Protocol "won universal acclaim. Scholars, journalists, and government experts cited it as a model worth emulating in a time of rising industrial unrest. Out of the turmoil and chaos of the sweatshop a new concept of industrial democracy had emerged." Shaped by the legendary judge Louis D. Brandeis, who had been brought in to mediate the strike, the Protocol required employers to recognize the union and a union shop, set up a grievance procedure and a Joint Board of Sanitary Control to police health conditions in the shops.

# no sweat

Six months after the signing of the Protocol, 146 workers perished in a fire at the Triangle Shirtwaist factory. The tragedy shocked the nation and dispelled any lingering euphoria about how quickly or easily the Protocol would solve the problems it had so hopefully engaged. As Gus Tyler notes in his magisterial history of the ILGWU, *Look for the Union Label*, the Protocol signified the beginning of an uneven progress, fraught with setbacks, that continues to this day.[3]

Over the next quarter century, the struggle against the sweatshop ebbed and flowed with the political and economic tides of the nation and the twists and turns of the industry. It bottomed out in the first years of the Great Depression and then leaped forward with the New Deal. Once again, it became clear that the most effective weapon against the sweatshop and the most reliable indicator of progress in the battle was the organized strength of the workers themselves. Between 1931 and 1933, membership in the ILGWU and ACWA jumped from less than 40,000 to over 300,000. From this dramatically broadened base, contractual demands had an industry-wide impact and fierce debate swirled around the subject of a government-sanctioned code and labeling plan for the industry. The eventual passage of social and labor legislation during this period reinforced the attack on sweatshops, helping to stabilize the industry by setting and enforcing national standards.

Labor Secretary Frances Perkins reflected the tenor of the times in 1933 when she appealed to consumers to think about the human cost of a $4.95 dress she had noticed on display in a store window. The dress was undoubtedly made in one of the hundreds of contractor sweatshops that had moved from New York City's garment district to surrounding states, she noted, where the employer believed the labor laws were less stringent and he could escape attention.

> What is the way out for the conscientious consumer who does not want to buy garments, even at a bargain, made by exploited labor? Common sense will tell the purchaser that someone must pay the price of the well-cut silk dress offered at $4.95. The manufacturer is not producing these frocks for pleasure or for charity. If the purchaser does not pay a price that allows for a subsistence wage and reasonable hours and working conditions, then the cost of the "bargain" must be sweated out of the workers.

> The red silk bargain dress in the shop window is a danger signal. It is a warning of the return of the sweatshop, a challenge to us all to reinforce the gains we have made in our long and difficult progress toward a civilized industrial order.

The sweatshop was never completely eradicated, but over the next thirty years it was steadily pushed to the margins of the industry. A key factor was the union's success in establishing "joint liability" in the women's clothing sector of the industry, making the manufacturer (also known as the jobber) responsible for the wages and conditions of his contractors. This was established in contractual agreements with employers that also required union jobbers to use union contractors. Joint liability strikes at the heart of the sweatshop system by cutting through the fiction of the contractor as an independent entity. This the union learned the hard way. Following the Protocol of Peace, hundreds of manufacturers responded by closing their own "inside" shops and becoming jobbers—contracting out their work to many smaller shops. By the mid-1920s, 75 percent of production workers in the coat and suit industry were employed in contracting shops, a reversal of the ratio a decade earlier.

A commission appointed by New York governor Alfred E. Smith in 1926 documented the way the jobber controlled conditions in its contractor shops and created the pressures that undermined legal standards. The commission recommended the establishment of some form of joint liability, which was rejected by employers. Nevertheless, the union was able to obtain joint liability in contracts in the 1930s and eventually made it a national standard in contracts throughout the industry. Despite numerous legal challenges, the jobber responsibility provisions of garment industry contracts have been upheld in the courts and their protection incorporated into federal labor legislation.

By the mid-1960s, more than half of the 1.2 million workers in the apparel industry were organized and real wages had been rising for decades. The sweatshop had been relegated to a minor nuisance, its very marginality the symbol of an American success story. A new generation of immigrants, primarily from Asia and Latin America, were drawn into the industry and, like their European predecessors, found decent jobs that gave them self-respect and their children an opportunity to do even better. A similar experience was occurring in towns and communities beyond the big city production centers, as employers probed new regions of the country in their continuous search for lower wages.

# no sweat

But this was still a time shaped by the implied social contract of the New Deal and of robust economic growth. The notion that government did not have a responsibility to correct the dislocations and inequities of market-driven decisions was considered the quaint relic of a reckless laissez-faire ideology. While the political convulsions that seized the nation and much of the world during these years were not expressed in the economic terms that characterized previous periods of social crisis, they were nonetheless based on the assumption that democratic governments had an interest in protecting the vulnerable and were accountable to the will of the people. The impact on workers of these social and political upheavals was contradictory, but as the high hopes of the 1960s fractured into the disillusionment and lowered expectations of the 1970s, seismic shifts were underway in the structure of the apparel industry—the consequences of which would not become clear for many years to come.

A human rights group in Honduras recently discovered thirty-three Bangladesh workers in a free trade zone factory, transported there by the contractor. They worked eighty hours a week for 20 cents an hour and could not leave their dormitories without permission from the company. They were sewing shirts that retailed for $12.94 at Wal-Mart.

Why should an employer bring workers from Bangladesh to Honduras to be paid 20 cents an hour when there is an abundant supply of Hondurans ready to work for almost as little? The same question could be asked of the now infamous contractors in El Monte, California, surrounded by thousands of workers toiling for wages not significantly higher than those paid to the imported Thai women. (See the article by Julie Su in this collection.) Why go to all this trouble to save a few cents more? The answer lay in the nature and logic of the sweatshop. Its function is to minimize the cost of labor by whatever means necessary, to appropriate every penny of value. On Clinton Street in 1900 it may have meant charging the worker for the electric power consumed by her machine or for a broken needle. In El Monte and Honduras in 1995 employers rediscovered the advantages of indentured labor. The difference between cheap and cheaper labor, no matter how vile the means of obtaining it, is the organizing principle of the sweatshop.

In 1961, 4 percent of the clothes sold in the U.S. market were imports. Fifteen years later imports accounted for 31 percent. Today it's over 60 percent, and still climbing—about $100 billion a year worth of clothing. The increase has come mainly from Third World countries producing everything from underwear to overcoats. These transactions are commonly referred to as "trade," suggesting the exchange of goods between nations, but that is something of a misnomer.

Some economists describe the industry as being organized along global "commodity chains" dominated by a handful of large retailers. When one retailer, for example, accounts for 25 percent of all the underwear sold in the United States, that corporation virtually sets the price at which underwear must be produced by manufacturers and contractors and ultimately, of course, the workers. The movement of commodities up the chain from producers to market, with the retailer setting not only the price but specifications of design and quality as well, is more like activity within a single transnational enterprise than it is the act of one country selling its goods to another.

These pricing pressures have driven the shift of production to lower wage sectors of the global economy, whether they be located in another country like China or in one of the thousands of sweatshops in the United States. Corporations have been allowed and even encouraged to do this by government policies, virtually unimpeded by the enforcement of minimal standards and laws. The transnational corporations of the 1990s are direct descendants of the New York firms that closed their own factories in the 1920s and became jobbers, contracting out work to the "foreign zones" (as they were called then) of New Jersey, Pennsylvania, and other nearby states. In the fifties and sixties, they extended production into the low-wage and right-to-work South, and then kept right on going across the seas. In effect, employers have succeeded in extending the sweatshop system on an international scale, and just as occurred within this country earlier in the century, it has driven down standards throughout the industry worldwide.

These market pressures were aided, abetted, and to a lesser degree created by cold war political policies of the U.S. government. Alfred E. Eckes, former chairman of the U.S. International Trade Commission, has documented how government tariff and trade policies were designed to favor particular countries, in accordance with their strategic value in containing communism, at the expense of domestic producers. Eckes argued that however you care to measure the success of these policies, they are no longer relevant to the post–cold war economy, and they have done significant damage to domestic industries.[4]

# no sweat

If you believe the apologists for these policies, all is well in the best of all possible worlds. The United States will eventually shed itself of a low-tech, low-skill industry, poor countries will develop an industrial base capable of launching their workers into middle-class prosperity, and the American consumer will have cheap clothes to buy.

The facts tell another story. There are still 860,000 apparel workers in the United States, earning less in real wages than they did in 1955, even though their productivity has more than doubled. In three out of four of those countries to which production shifted, real wages in the industry also declined. It is no coincidence that in the few Asian countries that have raised the living standards of working people, we also find the growth of unions or government income and trade policies that encouraged a more equitable distribution of wealth than unregulated markets would allow. And while there are plenty of relatively inexpensive goods in the stores, take a look at the labels: a lot of those $9.95 blouses are made in the U.S.A. The labels might reveal something else: identical items, one made overseas and one domestically, both selling for the same price. The labels tell us two things. For some goods, the cost of sweatshop labor in the U.S. has been driven so low that it is competitive to produce them here. In other instances, the difference in the labor costs offshore and the unionized U.S. worker, a ratio that averages about 1:15, reflects the vast fortunes that have been made by the middlemen, manufacturers, retailers, and their bankers who have succeeded in globalizing the sweatshop.

The system is out of control, its cruelties and absurdities crying out for reform. In many of the countries that produce shoes and clothing primarily for export, half the people walk around barefoot and in rags. In Africa, entire national industries have been wiped out. In Asia, companies that had abandoned production in Japan, Korea, Hong Kong, and Taiwan for the lower wages of the Philippines, Thailand, Bangladesh, and China are now moving on to Vietnam, Cambodia, and Laos, and even to the Pacific Islands like Saipan and American Samoa, where—shades of El Monte and Honduras—Chinese workers have been transported to live and toil as virtual slaves. In India and Pakistan, 1.5 million children are hard at work sewing and stitching products sold in the U.S. market. In China, now the world's largest producer of clothes, textiles, shoes, and leather, some cities have more productive capacity in these industries than all of Europe combined. The European apparel industry is in free-fall, as firms shift production to Central and Eastern Europe where wages are as low as any in the world and where you will find at least one former bomb factory filled with sewing machines operated by nuclear scientists.

Perhaps the biggest "beneficiaries" of this new global production system have been Mexico and the Caribbean region, where half a million workers now account for more than a quarter of U.S. apparel imports. This is the fastest growing area of apparel production in the world, fueled by tariff and other financial incentives from the U.S. government and by proximity to the U.S. market. The economy of countries like the Dominican Republic, now the fourth largest exporter of apparel to the United States, have been transformed but not necessarily improved. "We are not developing a country," observed Jorge Sierra, a human rights leader from the region. "We are destroying a generation."

Where once peasants labored from dawn to dusk cutting sugar cane that enriched local oligarchs and built the Fifth Avenue mansions and Manhattan skyscrapers of the American sugar barons, now the children and grandchildren of those peasants sit at sewing machines from dawn to dusk, and sometimes well into the night, making bras and jeans and blouses that through the magic of the market are transmuted into multimillion dollar CEO compensation packages and handsome profits for the privileged few. The average wage in the Dominican assembly plants known as maquilas does not come close to the country's official poverty line, but apparently some of the wealth is bubbling up. Not far from one of the largest free trade zones in the country, merger mogul Henry Kravis has put the finishing touches on his new $24 million Greco-Roman estate, financed from his various leveraged buy-outs that included at least one big retail chain, a monument so outrageously ostentatious, suggests a local newspaper, that the famous American financier has ordered a Stateside media blackout for fear of a public relations backlash.

In addition to the geographical spread of the industry, a change has occurred in its internal structure that has accelerated the return of the sweatshop: the role of the retailer. Many contractors now work directly for retailers, producing what is known in the trade as private labels. In this relationship, the retailer functions as a manufacturer, creating the design, providing the fabric and other raw materials, and setting the price. Even when a big retailer deals with a traditional manufacturer, the retailer by virtue of its dominant market position sets the parameters to such an extent as to often reduce the manufacturer to a virtual contractor.

# no sweat

There is a wide and subtle spectrum to this relationship, but there is no question that the balance of power has shifted decisively to the dozen or so big retailers that have consolidated their control in this bankruptcy-wracked industry, as evidenced by the $9 billion in profits they registered in 1995.

At the same time the U.S. government was opening the domestic market to apparel produced in Third World countries, a more diverse and family-oriented immigration policy increased the number of immigrants coming from many of those same nations. Like earlier generations of new Americans, many found work in the apparel industry. But these new immigrants would be forced to swim against powerful currents. Not only had the U.S. garment industry begun to shrink because of the shift to offshore production, American politics had also entered one of its uglier periods.

It is common to blame "illegal aliens" for the prevalence of sweatshops. It's worth recalling that back in the days when there were no "illegal" immigrants because there were virtually no quantitative restrictions on immigration—with the egregious exception of the discriminatory anti-Chinese laws—the same alarm was raised about the masses of "foreign" and "inferior" European workers who by the millions poured into American cities. It was these same workers, of course, who did so much to organize the unions and propel the great reform movements that shaped America as an industrial democracy. And while you would never know it from the rancid demagoguery that frames this issue in the political arena, those good, hard-working, family-loving immigrants of yore relied on public services in proportionally far greater numbers than the vilified immigrants of today.

What has changed, of course, is the growth in our body politic of an alarming malignancy we have seen before. *Scapegoat* is derived from the old Hebrew name of a demon and refers to a goat on whose head are symbolically placed the sins of the people. When it was the Irish and the Italians, Romanism and Rum were going to ruin the country, and then came the always handy Jews. There has not been a day in the 220 years of the Republic that some citizen has not stood before a gathering of fellow Americans to declare that the end is near due to the presence on our shores of this or that group of foreigners. Most of the time, this ironic ritual is held in check. But in moments like these, when large numbers of people begin to question the legitimacy of the system, the primitive ritual is transmuted into public policy and we are supposed to be convinced that in this way the problem will be solved.

It is essential to focus on the people responsible for the problem. There may be as many as 3 million illegal immigrants in the country, constituting less than 2 percent of the labor force. They are here because there is a market for their labor: thousands of employers who are rewarded for extracting value from workers who cannot defend themselves. These employers are even rewarded by the law designed to punish them, an insidious provision in the 1986 Immigration Reform and Control Act known as "employer sanctions" which requires the federal government to penalize anyone employing an illegal immigrant. Theoretically, it sounds reasonable. In practice, it succeeds only in denying a few day's pay to someone who will find another job down the street under the same wretched conditions, and actually makes it harder to enforce labor laws since employers have learned to use it as a threat against workers who dare to assert their rights. Employer sanctions should be repealed, replaced with sanctions on those much higher up the corporate commodity chain and with international development policies that do not force millions of people across borders that no democracy can ever completely close.

The anti-immigrant fervor is a gigantic and cruel distraction. Our borders are naturally porous and we are close to the limits of how much we can restrict the flow. What we could do, however, is invest some political capital in labor standards that transcend increasingly irrelevant national boundaries. There are virtually none now: the only laws operating in the global labor market are those of supply and demand. One authoritative study projects that in such a market, wages in a global industry will tend to equalize at a level slightly higher than those paid today in Nigeria—a little under $2 an hour.[5] That's the good news, because it suggests that millions of workers in poor countries now making a lot less than that are in for a big raise. The bad news: in the real world, the chronic suppression of workers' rights in many of those countries means that wages will not rise even to what a "free" market should permit. The weakness of laws protecting workers' rights and the lack of international labor standards have generated the infamous "downward spiral" of workers forced to compete with each other on the basis of ever more miserable working conditions.

# no sweat

Perhaps this is what Ronald Reagan had in mind when, shortly after he broke the PATCO strike early in his first term, he tried unsuccessfully to lift the fifty-year ban on homework in the women's apparel industry. He lost that particular battle, but he succeeded in setting into motion the antigovernment hysteria that, among other things, has left the Department of Labor with 800 inspectors to monitor 2 million workplaces—the same number of inspectors, by the way, that Nike claims it employs to assure that its worldwide production facilities are in compliance with the law. If DOL's 800 inspectors did nothing but monitor the 22,000 apparel plants in this country, they would still have their hands full. With these limited resources going to enforcement of labor laws, nobody should be surprised that workplace standards throughout the economy have deteriorated.

Resistance to these policies has mitigated some of their most harmful effects but it has never been able to stop them. Until NAFTA and GATT signaled the apparent triumph of "free trade," the labor movement followed a strategy of alliance with its own domestic industries to limit imports. In the apparel industry, this entailed a series of elaborate quota systems that are now being phased out and are due to expire in 2005, at which time there will be no quotas on any apparel, textiles, or most other goods traded in the world market. This is the point we have actually been moving toward over the past thirty years, based on mountains of learned disputation about the blessings of open trading systems and the evils of protectionism. Official ideologies tend to reflect and promote the interests of dominant economic powers. When nationally based corporations ruled their own countries, trade barriers protecting national industries were official policy. In this era of transnational corporations, about 2,000 of which control half the world's trade and three-quarters of its financial assets and fly no flag but their own, it is their insatiable interest in consolidating access to the entire global market that animates the fashionable economic theories of the late twentieth century.

The purpose of the transnational corporation is to maximize profits for its shareholders, which, it is argued, is the most efficient way for a society to organize its economic system. But what if this "efficiency" marginalizes hundreds of millions of people from the system itself? What if it destroys the environment? What if it tends to equalize wages at less than $2 an hour? What if it reduces mass purchasing power and depresses the economy as a whole? What if it condones and even encourages the proliferation of sweatshops?

Unless we are prepared to accept the notion that corporate profits have now become the final authority of right and wrong, then there must be limits placed on the enormous powers of transnational corporations—limits that direct economic activity toward the values and vision of social justice and political equality. Let us now examine our strategic options for confronting the global sweatshop of the twenty-first century.

We must begin by recognizing what in the apparel industry has changed and what has not over the past half-century. It is an industry still characterized by many small firms competing on slender margins. This is less the case in the men's wear and mass-produced commodity sectors of the industry than in the more fashion-sensitive women's sector, but in the United States alone there are more than 20,000 firms with an average of fifty employees, starting up and shutting down with the seasons and the vagaries of the market. Add to these numbers the new element of globalization, the contractors large and small scattered across the face of the earth, the families in rural villages and the thousands of workers in free trade zone factories, all feeding the flow that terminates in our department stores and malls, and we begin to get a sense of the daunting scope of the challenge.

The first and indispensable order of business is to make the system visible and keep it in the public eye. This has begun to happen, with a peculiar American flavor, the details of which are documented throughout this volume. The shock of El Monte was followed by a campaign that focused on the Gap and one of its contractors in El Salvador, and then came the Kathie Lee Gifford scandal. The coalescing of grass-roots labor and human rights activists brought a crusading spirit to the issue that made it impossible to ignore.

It was a turning point, but it would be foolish to underestimate the resistance to change. Within weeks, the ever-resourceful *New York Times* dispatched reporters to a free trade zone in Honduras and a Nike contractor in Indonesia and published stories with headlines like "Hondurans in 'Sweatshops' See Opportunity" and "For Indonesian Workers at Nike Plant: Just Do It." Passing lightly over references to strikes against abusive conditions and reflecting peculiarly selective interviews, the reports concluded that "sweatshops," their very reality questioned by those deftly placed quotation marks, are better than no jobs at all. Perhaps encouraged by this support for their case by no less an authority than the *New York Times*, the

*Immigrant workers, 1910.*

big retailers and several large manufacturers refused to participate in President Clinton's high-level panel convened to study the problem. They are not keen on the idea of exposing their voluntary and self-policing codes of conduct to independent scrutiny, nor do they seem any more receptive to the notion of organized workers than they have ever been.

But most of the elements of a successful strategy can be found in these hectic few months of 1996: public exposure and pressure, government action, corporate responsibility, and—most critical of all—the empowerment of workers. These are the checks that must be placed on corporate power. A system of industry-wide standards must be rebuilt, almost from the ground up, as was done at the time of the Protocol and then again during the New Deal. The building materials have not changed all that much, but the dramatic changes in the scope and structure of the industry mean that we cannot simply reproduce old formulas.

There are special problems, for example, with the application of offshore codes of conduct and monitoring programs. In most of these countries, regulatory infrastructures are exceedingly weak; employers often wield dictatorial power; massive poverty and unemployment and no tradition of unionization leave workers nearly powerless. Under such circumstances, the typical company monitoring program simply extends the control and concealment that breeds the sweatshop.

If companies really want to know what is happening in their contractors' shops offshore, they need credible independent monitors who have the confidence of the workers. This is the great virtue of the path-breaking programs established by the Bangladesh garment industry or the Gap in El Salvador, or the Rugmark labeling campaign for hand-knotted carpets made in India and Nepal. But these models are important only if they become prototypes for a comprehensive international system, administered by an organization with adequate authority and resources like the International Labor Organization.

Competitive pressures being what they are, however, we have seen that monitoring programs will not work without dramatically enhanced legal enforcement of industrial standards. Governments at the local, state, and national level must enact the necessary laws and provide the resources to enforce them. Legislation is needed that establishes "joint liability" for retailers and manufacturers. When Kathie Lee's blouses were discovered in sweatshops in New York and Honduras, neither Wal-Mart nor the manufacturer who had contracted with the shops had a legal responsibility for the working conditions. The "guilty" parties were the owners of the sweatshops. This defies the logic of the system and lets retailers and manufacturers off the hook. Besides fines and responsibility for unpaid back wages, retailers must be legally required to have monitoring programs, with specified and uniform standards, for their manufacturers and contractors. The Wal-Mart executive who agreed to pay $5 wholesale for the blouses did not have to be a mathematical genius to know that the garment would be made in a sweatshop. Such a decision is irresponsible—and should be illegal. The Department of Labor has developed highly detailed monitoring guidelines that are currently offered to employers on a voluntary basis. If we are serious about eradicating the sweatshop, these standards should carry the force of law. The big corporations that drive the production process must take responsibility for labor standards the same way they are responsible for quality, price, and delivery schedules.

But effective enforcement standards domestically will not solve the problem, for as we have seen, employers have the option of sending the work to shops offshore where workers are often even more vulnerable to abuse. Transnational corporations and the production systems they have developed have outraced the ability of laws to follow them across national borders.

And if the legitimacy and authority of international law is still in its infancy, international labor standards and worker rights are embryonic.

The rules of GATT and its successor, the World Trade Organization, restrict the ability of any single nation to deny entry of goods produced under conditions which the importing country may deem objectionable, from products made with child labor to tuna caught with nets that kill dolphins. The restrictions are legally amorphous, however, subject to fierce debate and geopolitical maneuvers. There are those who say that free trade means exactly that, no restraint on the sale and purchase of goods across national borders; violations of international law and standards should be duly punished but not with trade sanctions, which will only be used by protectionists to undermine the new system. The other side argues that these new WTO rules overturn a half-century of U.S. laws that say the conditions under which goods are produced do matter and matter greatly; that the only effective punishment for such violations are trade sanctions; and that rules can be established for assuring that sanctions are applied for violation of internationally recognized rights and not for protectionist measures.

These are the conflicting principles underlying the great policy debates on China and NAFTA and various other issues in which the banner of basic human and worker rights is carried into battle against what appear to be the far superior forces of the New World Order. But the situation is not hopeless. There is a consensus on the content of "internationally recognized worker rights"—prohibition on child and forced labor, discrimination in employment, the right to organize, bargain collectively, and to strike—but the terrain of how violators should be penalized is still very much contested. The weak labor and environmental "side agreements" in NAFTA implicitly recognize the principle of trade sanctions while rendering them practically inoperative. Several U.S. laws, such as the Generalized System of Preferences (GSP) and the Caribbean Basin Initiative, contain stronger provisions making access to the U.S. market contingent on the enforcement of internationally recognized worker rights. All remain in effect. The European Union recently passed its own version of GSP, and virtually every international organization with any authority pertaining to the issue finds itself entangled in the conflict.

This question of how laws and standards will be extended and applied to the contours of the new international economy will only be resolved over the course of a long struggle, and then never with satisfying finality, just as the process has unfolded within nations. Some view the challenge as utopian, and perhaps it once was. Today it has a practical urgency, and not only because of what happened in the apparel industry. Testifying before a government commission on worker-management relations in 1994, Jay Mazur, president of UNITE, offered some advice:

> Our long history with contracting out contains important lessons for other industries, many of which are following the example of apparel by assigning more and more functions to indirect or contingent workers... I believe the broad principle involved here could be applied across the board to many industries, services, and situations. That principle is that the businesses which control outsourcing, under whatever name you call them—"virtual employers," "core corporations," or simply manufacturers—must be held responsible for the wages, benefits, and working conditions of their "virtual" or contingent employees, who are known as contractors. Much of the poverty and economic disorder in the world today stems from the system we have tragically allowed to develop, in which practical economic power has been allowed to divorce itself from legal responsibility... The history of our century clearly shows the differing results when the controlling manufacturers are or are not held to account for conditions in their contractor shops, including compliance with wage and hour, child labor, and other laws, let alone union contracts.[6]

This advice, perhaps not surprisingly, was ignored, leaving the matter once again in the hands of the workers themselves.

The role of the North American labor movement in this struggle is critical. The late twentieth-century myth surrounding the movement was that it had been rendered obsolete by its own success. We now see this was inaccurate on both counts: its success was momentary and it is still very much needed. The decline of the workers movement, the result of its own complacency and a relentless ideological and political assault by employers, has tipped the balance in our economic system. The evidence of systemic crisis is everywhere, the data almost numbing on the hungry and the poor, the growth of inequality, the anarchy of production. Defenders of the status quo invoke the holy laws of supply and demand and moral precepts of hard work and abstinence. It is too much to take. No wonder the labor movement has rediscovered its vocation of comforting the afflicted and afflicting the comfortable.

# no sweat

In taking on the global sweatshop, unions have had to adjust their vision to the new horizon of the industry. From the time that Inspector O'Leary concluded his tour of the sweatshops on Division Street in 1900 with an appeal to the union for its help and advice, the most efficient mechanism for curbing abuses in the industry was a union strong enough to monitor and enforce standards that had been set either by legislation or contractual agreement. This strength was built over decades of sacrifice and struggle, passing through stages that parallel those of other industries: isolated strikes, rudimentary national organizations, more strikes, and then pivotal moments in which massive uprisings coalesce with reformist political currents and social movements and change becomes structural, rooted in industrial practices and legislation.

But it is always an uneven process, two steps forward, one step backward, offensive and counteroffensive. The pattern in the apparel industry has been for firms to seek new areas of production beyond the union's reach. To maintain standards, the union was forced continually to follow the work. In the 1930s, there were still New York City locals with contracts that defined their jurisdiction as the area within the five-cent fare of the city's mass transit system; beyond that were the hinterlands. As the industry spread to other cities, states, and regions of the country, and then to Puerto Rico, the union kept adjusting its sights and followed. But when the industry began its huge movement offshore in the 1970s, the union did not and perhaps could not follow the work in the same way. Relations were maintained with unions in other countries through international structures of the labor movement. Some assistance was provided to needy affiliates. Meetings and congresses were duly convened. In theory and rhetoric, international solidarity was alive and well. In practice, it was overwhelmed by cold war political considerations and employers' technological and strategic command of the playing field.

Workers and their unions in the apparel industry are now undergoing an historic adjustment of their strategic vision. It has become a matter of their very survival. The industry must be rationalized and humanized and there is no greater force with the interest and capacity to do this than the workers themselves. The sewing machine operators in Honduras and New York City stitching together Kathie Lee blouses work in the same industry, are

*Women workers, 1910.*

employed and similarly exploited by the same firms, and literally speak the same language. Like generations of workers preceding them, they can, must, and will organize—with the active solidarity of a revitalized labor movement that exercises the same freedom of communication and movement across national borders that corporations have long utilized to their exclusive advantage. Enlightened employers will accept this development, as they have in the past, allowing them to compete in a more stable industry, on the basis of technological innovation, superior design, and more effective marketing. Those who resist the establishment of decent standards in the industry must pay a price: fines from stepped-up enforcement, disrupted production by demoralized or angry workers, and the rejection of their goods by consumers increasingly sensitive to the conditions under which goods are produced.

This spells big trouble for many apparel manufacturers and retailers, who in recent years have placed great importance on brand identity and the good image of their labels. Huge investments are made to enhance those images—and information reaching the public that damages them can have serious economic consequences for a firm's bottom line. This vulnerability gives workers and consumers a powerful new weapon in the struggle against sweatshops.

But it would be premature to announce the imminent death of the sweatshop. Too much remains to be done. This optimistic scenario can only be imagined in a radically altered political climate. The historic gains of apparel (and other) workers have coincided with the ascendancy of national political movements, like those of the Progressive era and the New Deal, that redressed the balance between human needs and property rights.

The force required to move an institution as powerful and entrenched as the modern transnational corporation is beyond the capacity of one group of workers or a single strata of the population. Sparks may fly from a strike in one factory or, to invoke the spirit of the kind of movement we need today, a sit-in at one lunch counter, but unless and until they involve the action of masses, reverberate through the structure of the entire society, coalesce with allies, and eventually take political form, our momentary victories will be smothered in a system and culture that regard the sweatshop as inevitable and the suffering of its victims of very slight human consequence.

# New York: defending the union contract

Carl Proper

Chinatown garment workers still remember the great demonstrations of 1982. Chinese factory owners appealed to their workers in the name of ethnic loyalty to abandon the union. Instead, on two occasions, 15,000 immigrant women garment workers marched in the streets in defense of the union contract. A few stunned employers, pressed by customers to meet production schedules, ratified the contract at union rallies or in the street, pleading with their Cantonese-American operators to return to work. The historic victory is still commemorated with a patchwork quilt hanging in union headquarters.

Fourteen years later, May Chen, education director of UNITE Local 23-25, recalls the battle as "the first salvo" by union contractors in management's ongoing effort to weaken the union and eliminate every defense against the "free market" in apparel manufacturing—which has led instead to actual slavery in El Monte, California, and to a widespread resurgence of sweatshop conditions around the country. (By 1982, the jobber/importer assault was already well under way.)

Mei Lin,[1] a sewing machine operator at Good Luck factory on Lafayette Street, is clear about how the challenge has affected her. Her average piecework earnings were about $50 a day at her first American sewing job in 1975. In 1996, she is back to an average of $7 to $8 per hour, less money after inflation than twenty years ago. This kind of wage stagnation results in part from a shift toward more difficult work (small batches and frequent style changes) which largely negates union increases in piecework rates. This is because even experienced piecework operators go through a "learning curve" before achieving peak productivity—and earnings—on each new style. Good earnings result when operators work for a long time on the same style, operating mainly at the top of their learning curve. But "long runs" of the same style are now mostly contracted overseas, or sometimes to domestic sweatshops. Retailers and manufacturers assign small lots, "quick turn" work, and more difficult styles to better paid union shops. As a consequence, workers in these shops rarely have time to master a style and achieve peak productivity and earnings.

Even so, Mei Lin's wages, plus health insurance, vacation time, and other benefits, lift her workplace well above the nonunion, no-benefit standard in Sunset Park, Brooklyn or Ridgewood, Queens, and other urban neighborhoods. "There were not as many garment factories in Chinatown in 1975, and there was more union work to do," she explains. Indeed,

*above: Pattern cutter in a garment factory in Chinatown, New York City, 1976.*

with the union's previously extensive control over the flow of work battered by decades of global and domestic nonunion competition, the number of contractors covered by agreements with the largest New York UNITE local has increased in the 1990s, as the amount of available work from union manufacturers has fallen off.[2] In economic terms, the "excess supply" of labor leads to reduced wages. In fact, loss of union power has resulted in "excess competition," a concept unknown to economists but familiar to garment workers and to many other stressed-out or downsized Americans.

"We were very united" in earlier days, Mei Lin explains. "If we didn't like the piece rate, anyone could shut off their machine and call on everyone else to shut down. We would go shopping, or do anything else until the contractor set a fair rate." This Norma Rae scenario is less common today. While Chinatown garment workers still join the union for the family health benefits (most husbands work in nonunion restaurants, shops, and other small businesses), as well as immigration, education, and child-care programs, they are sometimes too discouraged to raise objections to unfair wages. "My boss tells us the rate before we start to work," says Mei Lin, "but in some shops you don't know the rate until you see your pay."

From the perspective of new UNITE member Rosa Hernandez, a Dominican immigrant employed since 1992 by Corona Fashions[3] in Queens, the union glass is at least half full today. Until her factory was organized by the union in 1994, it was a sweatshop by any definition. The union contract brought with it many important changes—better pay, benefits, more work—and the growth of social communication and a decline in fear. "We're like a family here now," she says. "The boss is a good person, too."

When Corona owner Jose Ramos first opened his factory in a two-family home in a residential area of Queens around 1990 (locating the pressing department in the garage), relationships were less friendly. Ramos paid no benefits, no holidays, no vacation, and all payments were in cash on a straight piecework basis—that is, when a sewer's piecework tickets totaled three dollars an hour, that's how she was paid. There were no taxes, no books. Given the inefficiency of the shop and prevailing market conditions, he would have had difficulty paying much more, while still supporting his own eight children from the labor of twenty-five marginally skilled employees. Like most of his workers, Ramos was an immigrant from the Dominican Republic. At $300 to $400 apiece for ancient Singer single-needle machines,

$1,000 apiece for used multithread overlock machines, $10,000 for a boiler, and a few thousand dollars for electrical wiring, he was in business for $30,000.

Ramos built his factory just ten minutes' walk from the Mets' home at Shea Stadium, and the workers came. With real unemployment in the city at 12 to 15 percent, and unemployment for high school dropouts at 25 to 30 percent,[4] working-class immigrant women, including some (by no means all) without a green card, have no better option.

When a unionized manufacturer on Long Island became Corona's principal source of work, UNITE Local 155 manager Joe Lombardo applied a contract provision requiring placement of union work with union contractors and, with some persuasion, Corona and one other contractor came into the union. The next step necessarily included improving the small firm's performance to the point where Ramos could afford to stay in business.

Lombardo turned to professional staff at the union-initiated Garment Industry Development Corporation (GIDC) to play midwife. Shimmy Cohen, an immigrant from Israel with a degree in textile engineering and an MBA from Philadelphia College of Textiles, spent days tutoring Ramos on the basics of work-flow management, product costing, overhead cost control—and business law. Ana Perez, former garment worker and supervisor, set about training the operators in better sewing methods that led to greater output—and piece-rate earnings—for the same effort. ("She found a way to help them sew easier, faster, and with quality," says Ramos.) Antiquated machines were upgraded with specialized attachments. An experienced production manager, recommended by Perez, briefly took over sewing supervision.

Annual wage increases, health insurance, vacations, and holidays were instituted. Equally important to many of the workers, improved performance led to more work from the manufacturer, in spite of higher labor rates. With steady, year-round work (not always available in the garment industry), annual earnings took a turn for the better.

A decline in fear and the development of labor unity were also part of the union package. The new supervisor, recommended and trained by GIDC, was technically competent but deficient in "people skills," and rubbed the newly unionized workers the wrong way. One day they stopped work altogether, until the supervisor went home, never to return.

Corona employee Rosa Hernandez now earns $60 to $70 on a good day, significantly better than her previous rate. She has also found a reason for hope outside the workplace. Her daughter, in her first year at New York University, hopes to be a psychologist. A merit-based NYU scholarship covers most of the cost—twice Rosa's annual income—and a Local 155 scholarship pays for $1,000 in books and supplies. The American dream, along with harsh economic realities from the turn of the century, is still alive for her.

### Does It Matter?

While the horrors (real enough) of the sweatshop economy have recently begun to receive the attention they merit, the strengths of the legitimate apparel industry—indeed, its reason for existing at all in our developed "first world" economy—are not always perceived. Why, after thirty years of government-backed (ours as well as theirs) competition from every low-wage nation, has this most labor-intensive of all manufacturing industries survived? And would it matter if it disappeared?

One reason for the industry's survival—there are still 800,000 apparel workers nationwide—is often unnoticed outside the industry. Labor costs account for a small part of the price that consumers pay for apparel. As the chart on "your clothing dollar" shows (fig. 1), raw material costs (mainly fabric), manufacturing management overhead and profit, and retail markup all take more of the consumer's dollar than garment workers and contractors. Thus, savings on transportation, inventory, reduced retail markdowns and stock-outs, and other factors can outweigh wage differentials and make domestic production competitive. For instance, strategies such as "quick response" to changing consumer taste focus on reducing *non*labor costs, such as costs for shipping and losses based on not having the right styles, colors, and sizes in the store when the consumer is ready to buy. Virtually all manufacturers, even heavy importers, maintain a share of domestic manufacturing in order to respond quickly to an unpredictable market.

Why the industry matters to New York seems clear enough. The "value added" by New York's apparel industry—the difference between the cost of materials and the selling price— was last measured by the U.S. Bureau of the Census at $4.4 billion in 1992,[5] and presumably approaches $5 billion today. Eighty-four thousand workers are officially employed in 4,000 establishments within the five boroughs in apparel and knitwear manufacturing, with underground operations possibly bringing the total to 100,000 workers.[6] Apparel buyers,

# no sweat

## Where Your Clothing Dollar Goes
Consumer Dollar Shares/Domestic Apparel

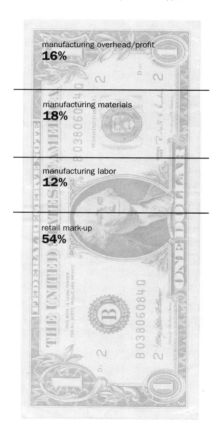

manufacturing overhead/profit
**16%**

manufacturing materials
**18%**

manufacturing labor
**12%**

retail mark-up
**54%**

(estimate: actual shares will vary by
product, wage/efficiency levels etc.)

source: UNITE research department

## NYC Share of US Employment;
## 1958-1992

women's wear

% employment and earnings

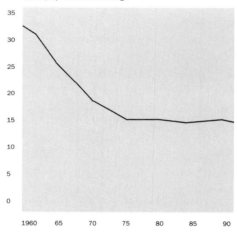

**figure 3**

### New York City
### Garment Manufacturing Network

**Marker-Making Contractor**
- Marking
- Grading

**Fabric Suppliers**
- Converters
- Overseas Textile Makers

**Repair Contractors**

**Contract Warehousing/Distribution Center**

**Jobber**
- Design
- Finance
- Licensing
- Sample-making
- Fabric & Trim Sourcing
- Contract Management
  - Domestic
  - Imported
- Sales
- Shipping

**Contract Duplicate (Sample) Makers**

**Cutting Contractors**

**Trucking Contractors**

**Apparel Service Contractors**
- Pleating
- Embroidery
- Other Services

**Peripheral Sewing Contractors**

Active •
Back-up •

**Trim Suppliers**
- Belts
- Buckles
- Buttons
- Zippers
- Other Items

**Core Sewing Contractors**

*above: The interior of a Chinatown garment factory, New York City, 1976.*

*right: Labor Law rally sponsored by the Chinese Staff and Workers Association, a pro-union immigrant organization in New York City, 1994. The rally took place on The Bowery outside the Silver Palace Restaurant, the only unionized restaurant in Chinatown.*

# no sweat

numbering 125,000, make multiple trips to New York showrooms every year, leaving behind $100 million spent on hotels, restaurants, taxis, and entertainment. Names like Oscar de la Renta and Donna Karan, Calvin Klein and Anne Klein add luster and glamour to New York's cultural scene—and contractors like Good Luck and Corona Fashions provide jobs as they did one hundred years ago to tens of thousands of otherwise unemployable immigrants (more than one-fourth of the city's population), some of whose children and grandchildren, like Colin Powell and Mayor Rudy Giuliani, reach the heights of American society. Major institutions of higher learning, such as the Fashion Institute of Technology and Parsons College, are embedded in the industry, as are New York–based advertising, retailing, and labor unions.

Indeed, the decline of apparel manufacturing in New York—from 350,000 jobs in the 1950s (fig. 2)—has paralleled the loss of power and prestige of the New York economy overall. The world's tallest towers are now in Malaysia, and will soon be in Shanghai, built, no doubt, with income from our imported shirts and blouses. But although the apparel industry has shrunk in New York, it has not been fully displaced, still accounting for one-third of the city's manufacturing base. Importantly, in spite of overall job loss, New York's share of a key "fashion" niche, domestic women's outerwear production, has stabilized and even grown slightly since the mid-1970s.[7] What are the characteristics that have enabled this industry to survive in New York, while more technologically advanced industries, as well as apparel jobs in the more technically advanced and less unionized Southeast, have disappeared or fallen still further behind?

### Virtual Corporations, Corporate Irresponsibility

Figure 3 portrays the manufacturing network maintained by a real New York women's apparel manufacturer doing about $15 million of business. In structure, it is typical of hundreds of other such businesses.[8]

At the core is a small company, the "jobber," with only twenty to thirty direct employees, all earning a middle-class standard of living or better, and none engaged in the actual manufacture of apparel for the market. The pedigree of this player deserves mention. "Outsourcing" or "contracting out" of production functions began around 1915 in the New York garment industry as a way of avoiding the union and playing one legally "independent" contractor (really a glorified labor foreman) against another to get the lowest possible price. A

commission named by then New York governor Al Smith described the origins of the     183
jobbing/outsourcing system as early as 1926:

> A decade ago the industry had risen out of the old sweatshop conditions in which much of
> the actual work had been done in tenement-house homes. Manufacturing had become
> concentrated in large "inside" shops under employers who were directly responsible both
> for manufacturing and for marketing the product. Since that time, however, there has been
> a gradual displacement of inside manufacturers by so-called jobbers. This system has grown
> up partly as a device to escape labor responsibilities and partly as an adaptation to the
> newer methods of retail buying.[9]

# no sweat

Today's jobber develops and markets styles, purchases materials, finances and oversees production. S/he must guess what consumers will buy, commit months in advance to the purchase of fabric, meet contractor expenses and union benefit costs as they come due, ship finished goods to the customers' warehouse/distribution center, and wait sixty to ninety days after shipment for the check from retail customers far more powerful than herself (though not uncommonly facing bankruptcy themselves), with the check typically accompanied by various nonnegotiable discounts and charge-backs for "late" delivery, quality defects, or simple failure to sell in predicted quantities and prices.

As orders flow further down the "commodity chain—from the retailer to the manufacturer/jobber and fabric supplier to the contractors, their suppliers and workers—most players, unless unusually gifted or fortunate, can expect to be paid at best no higher a price for the same volume of work this year than last. Clothing is a deflationary item in an economy run for bondholders.

Under this system, the task of the jobber's production manager is to coordinate the efforts of a remarkable network of contractors and suppliers, relating in particular to "cut and sew" assembly contractors through a team of quality control (QC) managers who visit every production shop on a weekly, sometimes daily basis. (Most jobbers in the women's apparel industry, including the multinational giants, have no "inside shop" where they directly supervise their own production employees.) As in the chart, patterns or "markers" are produced from sketches and samples by one outside business, while another outside contractor may assemble the special "sample" garments displayed in trade shows and marts. Next, one or two other independent businesses cut[10] the goods into collars, sleeves, and other parts for assembly (along with buttons, zippers, sequins, and similar "trim" items) by a variety of sewing contractors—commonly two or three regular sources whom the jobber can count on for quality and special attention, plus a dozen or more contractors with "arm's length" (strictly price-driven) relationships to the jobber, sometimes with an assist from specialized pleating, embroidery, or other subcontractors. A trucking contractor then transports the finished goods through busy streets and usually under the Hudson River to a contract warehouse/distribution center in Secaucus or North Bergen, New Jersey, which provides a final inspection and sends imperfect items out to still other contractors for minor repairs. New York, and to some extent other urban centers, have a competitive advantage in having every necessary good and service readily available in the community.

Dozens of hands may touch the garment, with only the "QC guy" directly employed by the company that designs and owns it.[11] Although carefully controlled to satisfy increasingly demanding customers, the labor system is based on organized irresponsibility. Whatever terms of labor may be applied by the contractors to their workers, the jobber can claim, "They're not my employees. I'm not responsible." Every contractor and supplier to the jobber understands well the almost unlimited supply of alternative sources to which his customer can, and does, go. Thus, while regular ("core") contractors may be able to look forward to a steady supply of work from their jobber, the wages they pay are set at levels little better than the short-term ("peripheral") supplier.[12]

The process by which payments to contractors are most commonly set has changed radically over the past twenty-five years, from a system of calculating and covering the contractors' legitimate costs to a "race to the bottom" in which an oversupply of contractors and of labor bids down prices below levels once considered "American." The old system was largely developed and regulated by the union—then the ILGWU—with a charter from federal legislation beginning with the New Deal that acknowledged the interconnectedness of apparel jobbers and contractors in an "integrated system of production." When the union represented a majority of the garment workers producing for the U.S. market, wage/price competition was consciously limited (although hardly absent, with thousands of independent and competing businesses). Union jobbers were required first to supply work to their "inside" (directly owned) shops, and after that only to agreed-on union contractors. In the union's heyday, a jobber could not take on a new contractor without first clearing it with the union, and showing that his regular contractors were supplied with work. While undoubtedly bureaucratic and frustrating to many employers, the system actually served union jobbers' and contractors' economic interests at the same time that it protected workers from exploitation. Nonunion contractors sought to sign contracts with the union in order to get work, and union contractors dealt with the union as their agent for finding work (many still do). Jobbers turned to the union for references to qualified contractors. The industry was never more profitable, and wages were competitive with other major industries.

*below: Past and present garment workers at a union rally sponsored by ILGWU, Columbus Park, New York City, 1992.*

As industrial development in the South and West and then the globalization of the economy have multiplied the effective labor force many-fold, government-backed union regulation of this inherently "overcompetitive" sweatshop industry has been forced back step by step. The new prevailing system for setting the contractor's price is sometimes referred to as "what's left over." When jobbers put out work, they begin with a retail selling price that they must (or want to) meet, figure in the costs of fabric and sales, plus management salaries and overhead and the target profit margin. "What's left over" is the price offered to contractors. While contractors complain and resist, those that survive working for this kind of jobber (barring extraordinary skills and bargaining power) are driven to standards and methods they might once have found unacceptable. Many more simply leave the business, and new, less scrupulous players take their place. In New York City, a contractor sector once dominated by Jews and Italians who developed in the predominantly union domestic environment was largely taken over in the 1970s and '80s by hungrier Chinese immigrant entrepreneurs. More recently, Korean contractors (employing a mainly Latina work force) who have never considered nor been compelled to work with a union, have become significant players. Taxes and fair labor standards are commonly ignored.

Missing from the chart is the most dominant player, the retailer. The once fragmented retail industry—each major city with its own locally owned department store network—is now dominated by a score of huge nationwide and global corporations. While retailers often present themselves as the marketers of other people's work, a quarter of the manufacturing market is now controlled by "private (retailer) label" garments, and even major brands must reorganize their businesses around the big stores' "matrices" of price and product. Retailers such as Sears or J. C. Penney set quality standards in specific detail, as well as price. Fair labor standards, of course, become matters for inspection and criteria for contractor selection only when public or union pressure compel it.

Apparel labor standards, ultimately, are actually set by the price paid by the retailer to the manufacturer or jobber—typically a little less every year for the same item, despite rising material costs. The wholesale price is then passed through by the jobber to the contractor, and by the contractor to operators like Mei Lin or Rosa Hernandez in the sewing department, and to their families.

*UNITE members from New York turnout in support*
*of Peerless workers in Canada, 1996.*

### The New York Niche

While the typical New York City contractor is hardly at the cutting edge of technological innovation (even a typewriter and a bookkeeper would be steps ahead for Corona Fashions), the city has maintained an important market presence in fashion-driven apparel, particularly in women's dresses and sportswear. New York jobbers typically are on-line with their retail customers (at the retailer's insistence), as well as occasionally with their suppliers and even contractors. But while apparel contractors and manufacturers in rural and small-city America have competed based on investment in new production technology and systems, including "flexible" manufacturing of relatively small batches with greater product variety, New York and other urban immigrant centers have found they can provide far greater flexibility, along with quick response to customer demand, by the old expedient of an excess supply of labor willing to work long hours when available and endure short time or joblessness when work is slow.

The dress industry—the most uncertain market in the business—is New York's specialty, with more than a quarter of all U.S.-made dresses produced in the city.[13] (New York also specializes in more formal apparel than its major U.S. competitor, casual Los Angeles.) New York's share of domestically produced dresses and women's sportswear increased substantially from 1975 to 1990, while declining in more predictable sectors. In addition to union avoidance, the inherent unpredictability of fashion—and the choice to relegate seasonal layoffs outside the corporate walls—has always been a prime motivator for contracting out. (Thus, the more stable and predictable men's wear industry has until recently been built around "inside," manufacturer-owned factories.) Many garment workers have come to accept forty, or even thirty weeks of work each year—or fifty to sixty hours of work in a busy week—as tolerably satisfactory.

For the past sixty years, union women's wear contracts have adapted to the instability of the industry by making benefits portable from one union shop to another, and by issuing vacation and holiday payments from a multi-employer fund. Vacation checks can go out even if the original employer is no longer in business.

While Chrysler can "retool" its Minivan factory once a year, and Levi Strauss can produce Dockers with minor variations year after year, Corona Fashion's jobber must come up with many new styles each season to stay in business. Corona typically completes work on one style—1,000 skirts and 1,000 matching shirt-jackets—each week. Similarly, in the Good Luck garment factory where Mei Lin is employed, three or four styles in a variety of fabrics and colors, for several different union jobbers, are all in process at the same time, with normal delivery in two to three weeks. Production lots are small, only a few dozen or a few hundred tailored jackets apiece, instead of the thousands of similar garments out-of-business manufacturer Evan Picone once provided. By the time the best method for sewing one style is mastered, the style is gone. Women in the shop joke about the difference between the "soy chop suey" (easy and good) work they used to have and the less tasty "pork bones" they work on today.

Aside from sewing machines with electronic needle-positioners and undertrimmers ($1,700 to $2,000 for a new single-needle machine), most advanced technology is of little use in factories like Good Luck or Corona. Better technology is usually too specialized for businesses handling a continuously changing flow of styles. Basic single-needle and "Merrow" or overlock machines are more flexible. The computer-driven "Unit Production Systems" that are common in Pennsylvania at around $5,000 per station, are unknown in New York, and the "modular" or "team" manufacturing systems spreading in other parts of the industry are quite rare. With twenty to fifty multiskilled workers, small work teams sometimes seem beside the point.[14]

The difficult jobs give New York—and America's urban garment workers generally—a reason to come to work. While the big lots and relatively predictable sellers are more often contracted months in advance to overseas factories, the small lots and one- or two-week deliveries must be produced at home.

In the face of ferocious global and domestic competition, however, some New York contractors have still been able to develop a steady flow of work from one or a few regular jobbers. In these favorable circumstances, the union contract is more readily enforced. To cite one example, Tech Sew, with 350 well-paid employees assembling beautifully tailored jackets for Anne Klein and Liz Claiborne, is often cited as the "best" shop in the city. Owner Shunyen Siu, an engineer who spends most of his waking hours in the shop and purchases the best new equipment at trade shows in Germany, likes to say that his shop is "not a Chinatown shop. I'm in Soho." Over the past two years, Siu has developed a completely new line of work, producing 50,000 women's uniform jackets a year for the U.S. Air Force. Normally, contractors are advised to completely segregate military work (built to volumes of specifications instead of sketches) from commercial production, but Siu finds both kinds of work "basically the same. I'm still the contractor. They're the jobber."

At the union's initiative, a Tech Sew executive is now part of a "channel partnership" study team including representatives from Anne Klein, Saks Fifth Avenue, and Burlington Mills, which may lead to a better model for successful domestic production. New York is resistant to, but not totally immune from, modern manufacturing methods.[15]

Traditional good labor-management relations also obtain at Jordan Fashions, where another exceptional businessman, Ned Giordano, has found success as a manufacturer and exporter of bridal and bridesmaid's gowns, produced in his inside shop and by a select network of trusted and well-treated contractors. Though barely known outside the industry, he provides almost as many union jobs in the city as Anne Klein or Donna Karan, who are primarily importers like most large jobbers.

Other contract employers have found a measure of success by expanding their control over a variety of contractors (from two to two dozen), enabling them to fill large and small orders, and even bid directly on private-label work from retailers, going around the usual jobbers. But while this particular type of consolidation brings a degree of business success, it shows little sign of improving the condition of garment workers.

### Standing Against the Tide: The Union in New York City

Once the dominant player in the women's division of the nation's largest manufacturing industry, the International Ladies' Garment Workers' Union was remarkably effective in giving structure to an industry made up of thousands of small, mostly immigrant-owned businesses. Now merged into the Union of Needletrades, Industrial, and Textile Employees (UNITE), the union must find ways to organize the oncoming generation of global jobbers, to extend "best practice" from shops like Tech Sew to less sophisticated contractors, and ultimately to compel the new dominant powers—giant retailers and a few major jobbers—to offer an American standard of living for their indirect as well as direct employees. To achieve this, government at all levels will need to be an ally, not just a neutral party, in the unequal labor-management struggle, or else the long decline to conditions of an earlier century will continue. It is inconceivable that a small number of government inspectors could ever regulate an ethnic, small-business industry including 10,000 contractors with no public reputation to lose—but neither can the union do the job fully without fair judicial enforcement of labor rights.

As for GIDC, it is pushing ahead with a successful export program (Fashion Exports/New York was nominated for a U.S. Department of Commerce export award in 1996) that has brought tens of millions of dollars and a new mindset to previously landlocked New York jobbers. It has also developed a sophisticated package of other useful services for manufacturers and contractors, including its Technology and Training Extension Service, Statistical Process Control, on-line market listings, courses for workers in whole-garment sewing and English as a second language, and courses for contractors in sewing machine maintenance and repair. With a tripartite labor-management-city board of directors, GIDC has relied until now on industry support, through a negotiated labor-management development fund, and on matching city and state funding. Despite broad cutbacks in most state and city assistance programs, GIDC has been able to expand its budget to around $2 million per year. As its capabilities and reputation grow, a potential step up to federal funding and to the provision of services to a truly significant number of New York members and their employers is becoming an active possibility.

Because of New York's prominence as almost the last major urban and unionized apparel industry center, near-term organizing success may be necessary to prevent the unchallenged slide of the fashion end of the industry (not including the larger scale, more advanced technology industry of rural America) into domestic sweatshops and imports. But someone has to take responsibility for paying the benefits and assuring fair wages for contractor employees (provided, under ILGWU/UNITE contracts, by the jobber, not the contractor), and enforcing decent conditions. Only the retailers—and a few very large manufacturers or jobbers—have the full resources to take on this role successfully. Only the workers in the industry, represented by a union that takes away their fear of speaking up, have the knowledge and motivation to identify and fix the problem.

"Why do you allow so much nonunion work?" is the question most asked by Good Luck employees of their union representatives. They may be ready to march again to defend the contract, but as the global economy comes home, only a powerful social movement can give them and their union the strength it needs to restore humane standards for garment workers.

# sweatshop workers speak out

Jo-Ann Mort

Conservatives complain that if immigrants want to live in this country, they should know the language. But for Aracely, who has worked in the sweatshops of Los Angeles' garment industry for thirteen years, language instruction is a luxury. Aracely is a presser, working on her feet more than twelve hours a day, seven days a week, pushing an industrial iron. "I've no time to learn English," she tells me as I sit with her and Leticia in the headquarters of UNITE, the garment union, on MacArthur Park just a few blocks from what has emerged as the nation's largest garment center.

Aracely's kids speak English, but she isn't home enough during their waking hours to learn the language from them. She and her children communicate only in their native Spanish. They live in the heart of South Central, a tough, low-income neighborhood, but even there her average weekly earnings of $80 can't be stretched into a living wage. She shows me the callouses on her palms, and the purple scars on her fingers from burns that weren't treated properly. There is no first aid available in her sewing shop. The bathroom is wretched. "You want to get out of there as quick as possible," she says through a translator, as she describes the stench and filth.

For six years, Aracely worked for the Thai owners of the El Monte slave factories. In one of these shops, the Latino workers were assigned the day shift and the Thai workers sewed and pressed at night. A company driver picked up workers from South Central at 6 a.m. for the trek to El Monte, where they worked until 9 p.m. If the driver was in a foul temper, he would abuse the workers. Sometimes his girlfriend came along and they would fight in front of the workers, in which case he drove like a mad-man. "We had to pay the consequences of his bad mood," Aracely said.

At the end of each week, they were paid in cash for each finished garment by a Salvadoran supervisor who collected the goods for the Thai owners. The supervisor routinely skimmed a cut from their meager earnings.

Holidays are also a luxury in Aracely's world. She works the Fourth of July, Christmas, and Good Friday. The Mexicans are very religious, but under these conditions rarely have time to observe their faith. When Aracely and her co-workers asked for time off on Good Friday to attend church, the owner snapped back: "Does God give you money? If you don't want to work, just tell me. I will find others."

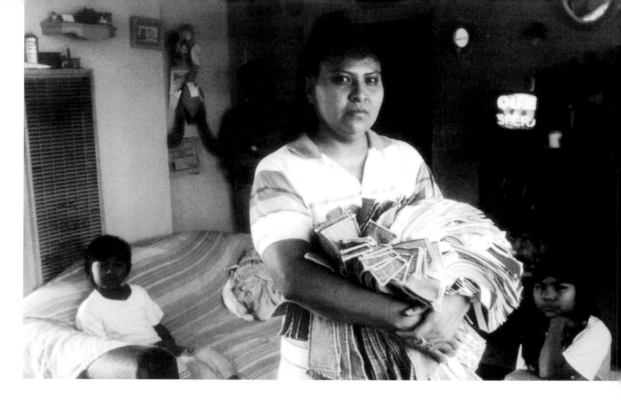

"They tell us, 'You come to this country to work. If you want to live like the rich, go back to your country.'" Aracely has numerous health problems. She underwent a C-section, after which the doctor recommended a six-month hiatus. She returned to work in eight days. She would have been fired otherwise. Another operation was necessary to stop internal bleeding, brought on by lack of rest. The boss called the hospital to make sure that she wasn't lying about her illness. Once again, she was back after eight days—and now, she bleeds often. She is fatigued by her surgery and the purple veins bursting out of her legs make it difficult to stand. A doctor has given her a prescription to ease her sleep. With no health insurance, she is dependent on the profoundly overcrowded L.A. County General Hospital. Her kids have Medicaid because they were born here, though congressional action could jeopardize their coverage in the future.

"I suffer a lot," she says. "I don't know how much longer I can do this." I ask her if she still has hopes and dreams and wonder, as I ask, if this sounds cruel. She tells me that she has nightmares and worries that she is heading for a nervous breakdown. "I don't know," she says again, shaking her head, "if I can make it." She is thirty-five years old. Her husband also works in a sweatshop. The owner of his shop wants the workers to clock in two hours after they actually start working, so that the company can steal two hours of the workers' time. (This way, *left: Aracely and her son.*

when they record that they are paying minimum wage, no one will know that the legal hourly wage has been stretched with all this free labor.) Aracely's husband refused, and the owner, buoyed by his bogus record-keeping, had the police throw him out of the shop. He is now fighting for back wages through the Justice Center.

I ask her what she wants for the future. "I want better treatment from employers to ensure at least the minimum wage. I feel like I'm killing myself. Every day I'm working harder and harder and making less, and it seems to me I'm running out of strength. Everyday I get up at 4 o'clock in the morning. At 6:30, I'm dropping off my kids at school. I pay someone to pick them up in the afternoon. My worst nightmare is when a teacher wants to talk to me or I have to be at school at 3 o'clock and the employer wants his work done."

"We come here and they treat us like dogs. I'm always scared. The supervisor yells and screams at me and I start remembering the others who were worse. I'm traumatized when I see them yelling and screaming. When the woman raises her voice, I immediately start shaking because I am very scared. Sometimes I get very, very desperate, but I know I have to keep up the struggle because I have children. We suffer a lot in this country, too much. We will continue to struggle, see if we can get ahead."

How does she keep herself going day after day? "I keep on struggling so my kids will have a better life and won't end up like me as a presser. That's all I want."

Aracely has two children in the United States, eight and ten years old. Her daughter hopes to be a lawyer, her son a policeman. Another child lives in Mexico and attends high school. She plans to go to college and become a doctor. But Aracely can't afford college for her daughter in Mexico because, even though university is free, all the extras—including books— are beyond her economic means.

Without documents, however, Aracely's job prospects are limited to sweatshop labor. Once she tried to get documents, spending precious time and money in the process, but was eventually rejected. She can't afford to try again. Like thousands of others, Aracely is trapped in a never-never land of economic servitude.

Letitia is a bit luckier. A thirty-three-year-old sewing machine operator, she has been in Los Angeles for nine years. Leticia was a secretary in Mexico, but here has worked only in garment shops because she doesn't speak English.

# no sweat

Why did she come to the U.S. if she had a secretarial job in Mexico City? "Because I'm married and my husband came here," she explains. "He was already here for three years, so I had to follow him. He's a garment worker, like in Mexico—all his family worked in the garment industry." She has three children—two born in Mexico and one here—ages thirteen, ten, and four.

Leticia is documented. "Last year, there was an immigration raid at the place where I work. They arrested us. I asked for a hearing to stop deportation. The union Justice Center helped and now I do have my papers. I live in East L.A., very close to my work."

"They want to kill us for a little money," she says. "We don't have a guarantee even for a minimum wage. It's piecework rate. The owner, a woman, tries to cut the wages. We make reports every day of all the work we did and she'll look at our report and go, 'I already paid for this work,' or 'This isn't finished,' or 'It's not done well.' Sometimes we'll work thirty-five to forty hours and get paid for twenty hours. We give as much as we can, but they always want more."

"I went to a union shop the other day." Her eyes light up. "I couldn't believe it. I would love to work there. The union shop is like a dream shop. Even the bathrooms are so beautiful, you could eat there. We don't even have toilet paper, you have to bring it from home."

"There is no space to walk in the shop. Everything is on top of you. When it rains, you have to cover yourself because the roof has a lot of holes. Rats come out. But the pressure is the worst. They won't even let you go to the bathroom—'I need this work and I need it now,' they say."

Leticia sews clothes for a label called *Little Children*. On the label are the words *Made in USA*. The children's suits, dresses, and tuxedos sell for about $65. They are found in specialty stores where the large Los Angeles Mexican community buy clothes for their children's first communions, baptisms, and Quincianeree (a special Mexican celebration held when a child turns fifteen).

Though she works nine to five, Leticia also brings work home. Her kids don't help, but her husband does homework. Her daughter wants to be a pediatrician and the boy wants to be an engineer. "My kids can make it because they are very smart and we are trying our best—working in the factory and doing homework to have food on the table and pay the bills. We hope we can provide for them because they have the intelligence."

*Aracely and Leticia.*

Leticia goes to school to learn English every day after work from 6 to 8 p.m. After school, she sews her industrial homework until 10 to 11 at night. She has managed to save enough money to buy a car. "Little by little, I have set goals and met them," she explains. "My dream is to learn English and work as a secretary. I hope my kids do well and have their dreams realized."

The Los Angeles garment industry is largely nonunion. It is like a sponge that soaks up all available labor and thrives especially on illegal immigrants who—in this anti-immigrant climate—are more dependent on their bosses. They produce the goods in what has become a $13.3 billion–plus industry in Southern California. Virtually none of the legislation either to tighten or to discourage illegal immigration will do anything for the tens of thousands of illegal immigrants who already work in the Los Angeles area garment shops. About two-thirds of the sewing shops in L.A. are sweatshops, many operating in full view of anyone who cares to look, especially in the downtown garment district in the shadow of the Convention Center.

Aracely explains that she keeps track of garments made in her shop by taking labels home, an increasingly common practice among sweatshop workers. With the assistance of UNITE and KIWA, the Korean Immigrant Workers Advocates, groups of sweatshop workers have begun visiting stores, searching for garments made in their factories. The strategy is to pressure retailers to discontinue goods made under illegal conditions. These workers know that only when the stores insist that goods be made in legal shops will their misery end.

As I say goodbye, Aracely tells me that workers must unite to stop the abuse. But in the present climate, it will take more courage than even these two brave women can muster. It requires increased unionization, government intervention, and a change in public attitudes which demonize immigrant workers who have made and continue to make a contribution to the economy of this country. It will also take outraged consumers to hold the garment industry accountable for the economic servitude upon which many retailers and manufacturers make their profits.

# the structure and growth of the Los Angeles garment industry

## Steve Nutter

Poised on the Pacific Rim, close to Mexico's maquilas, and blessed with an infinite supply of immigrant labor, the Greater Los Angeles area is home to the largest and most dynamic concentration of garment production in North America. The L.A. industry has become a powerhouse combining twentieth-century technology and glamour with nineteenth-century sweatshops and unbridled greed, and these stark contrasts have regularly thrust it before the public eye as the literal embodiment of the growing wage gap and social divide haunting U.S. workers. The scandal involving more than seventy Thai nationals held in virtual slavery behind barbed wire in an El Monte apartment building represents only the latest chapter in a long, dismal story of exploitation.

Los Angeles is the production center for a region that includes the San Francisco/Oakland area and a number of urban Southern California counties. The region has so far largely overcome the threat of imports and retailer consolidation, which have devastated the garment industry elsewhere. Instead, L.A. and regional manufacturers have prospered, for three reasons.

First, manufacturers created a casual sportswear niche market of low- and moderately priced clothing for young women. Second, manufacturers meet retailer demands for reliable fashion delivered close to season, thereby reducing inventory carrying costs, cutting costly closeouts and markdowns caused by mistakes in forecasting consumer preferences, and allowing retailers to reorder as sales dictate. Third, retailers and manufacturers produce garments under a subcontracting system that promotes the abuse of labor: retailers squeeze manufacturer margins, manufacturers cut the prices they pay for sewing assembly to their contract sewing shops, and sewing shops impose illegal and dangerous conditions on the seamstresses who actually make the clothing.

More than 120,000 workers cut, sew, press, and trim garments daily in over 5,000 factories and in thousands of garment workers' homes, in order to satisfy the appetite of L.A.'s spot market for garment production. About 80 percent of these workers—some 96,000—work in mostly small factories that are nominally "above ground" and usually counted in official records. Another 20 percent or so work in factories that are located wholly within the underground economy. Thousands more are employed in industrial homework, where child labor is rampant. Another 12,000 workers are employed in L.A.'s related textile sector, some 4,000 in knitting mills and 2,000 in textile finishing (dye houses). Apparel is now a big fish in an

# no sweat

even bigger pond—the largest manufacturing industry in the leading manufacturing county in the United States.

L.A.'s apparel industry is not only holding steady, it is growing. Employment expanded here by more than a third from 1982 to 1992, almost doubling since 1972, when the industry claimed about 60,000 workers. During the same period, industry employment dropped 35 percent in New York, 43 percent in Pennsylvania, and 12 percent nationally. Today, the fastest growing manufacturing job in Los Angeles is "sewing machine operator." California's garment industry overall has grown as well, with about 20,000 employed in the San Francisco/Oakland area and almost 10,000 working in Orange County. Not including jobs in the underground economy, California claims over 145,000 garment workers.

California firms have succeeded in part by creating and exploiting consumer demand for casual sportswear and life-style–oriented fashions, including the development of a popular "California style" in women's outerwear. While apparel sales overall increase at about 2 percent annually, women's sportswear sales have gained at twice that rate. California firms are concentrated in two of the most fashion-forward segments of the apparel market: young contemporaries (ages twenty-five to thirty-five) and juniors (twenty-five and under), with trendy young men's clothing becoming an important new sector.

L.A. has followed the California pattern. More than 80 percent of the apparel made in Los Angeles County is classified as "women's outerwear" (blouses, jackets, pants, skirts, and dresses), compared to about 27 percent of the clothing made in the United States. This clothing typically has "fashion content," a value added because its fabric and design meet the demands of the current season, and must be delivered on time to claim that value. But it also has a limited shelf life once delivered: if sales are poor, retailers must mark it down or unload it to discounters.

The extremely skewed distribution of power among the industry's players is reflected in the division of the spoils on a $100 garment: $50 to the retailer, $35 to the manufacturer, $10 to the contractor, and $5 to the seamstress. Using a pyramid to show the power relationships: 120,000 workers form the base, about 4,000 contractors are positioned almost mid-level, 1,000 manufacturers sit above them, and a handful of retailers perch very comfortably at the top.

Retailer power in the L.A. garment industry is dominant and expanding. Each year, retailers buy about $9 billion wholesale in clothing made in L.A. and sell it retail for twice that amount. With the merger and acquisitions among department stores in the 1980s, the emergence of large discount and off-price retailers (T. J. Maxx, Ross), the ascendancy of mass merchants (Wal-Mart, Kmart, Target), and the closing of more than a third of the department and small specialty stores, retail power has become concentrated nationwide in a few hands. L.A.'s manufacturers have fewer and fewer outlets for their products, and often argue that they cannot afford to refuse a retailer's proposal. The result is retail control over product mix, delivery, terms, and price. As retailers source "narrower and deeper"—that is, buy more from a shrinking circle of manufacturers (or "vendors")—small manufacturers are pushed out of the market and survivors must grow to stay in the game.

Retailers also squeeze L.A.'s manufacturers through "backward integration"—taking on many of the functions of garment manufacturers. Retailers compete directly with manufacturer brands by developing their own private labels, using in-house design and merchandising departments. Consumers learn to rely on private labels for fashion content, quality, and status, just as they do manufacturers' brands. Retailers may produce private-label merchandise offshore, dealing directly with foreign contractors, or they may turn to domestic sources. In Los Angeles, retailers sometimes use local manufacturers to make private-label goods, paying them a lower price than they would for a manufacturer's own proprietary label. In other cases, retailers turn to larger, more capitalized contractors to make their goods, bypassing manufacturers altogether.

L.A. manufacturers often make contacts with retailers at the California Mart, the hub of the Southern California fashion industry. This thirty-year-old complex houses showrooms for nearly 1,500 tenants who court primarily women's wear buyers from national and regional department and specialty store chains. Smaller L.A. manufacturers use independent representatives at regional marts to sell to retailers, while the larger manufacturers use their own sales staff to meet with retailers in the marts or to travel to the home offices of the mass merchants, big discounters, or department stores.

More than a thousand manufacturers are based in L.A., directly employing over 30,000 workers. They tend to produce locally, contract out production, and rely on quick turnaround of women's casual sportswear as their niche. Although most firms are small, averaging about thirty-five workers, a few big ones account for most of the production. A third of the firms sell less than $1 million wholesale each year and employ fewer than ten workers. Eighty percent sell less than $10 million, 90 percent less than $20 million. Only about 10 percent of the firms—about 110 manufacturers total—sell over $20 million wholesale each year. This 10 percent accounts for about two-thirds of the garments made in the Los Angeles area, giving them considerable bargaining leverage in the industry.

Fashion-oriented manufacturers have an edge when they produce in L.A.'s factories, where unlimited space in numerous small contract shops allows them to make short runs with frequent style changes and short lead times, expanding and contracting production as business dictates. Production in Los Angeles usually involves a five to seven week "turn" from the date of order, and even shorter times are possible. The city's dye houses permit manufacturers to dye stock textiles locally and deliver to their contractors within hours. Risk is greatly reduced by delaying decisions, on how to dye fabric and what styles to produce, until two months closer to season than is possible for imported goods. Local domestic contractors typically require no commitments prior to the actual delivery of the fabric to be cut and sewn. Manufacturers can finance their fabric purchases, dyeing, and other production costs with short-term loans from local factories and banks, secured by pledging receivables on retail orders. In this way, manufacturers produce with other people's money, maintain little or no inventory, operate with limited overhead, and are less likely to face retailer charge-backs for poor margins and high closeouts. If a product sells well in the stores, they can move quickly to fill reorders on hot items before season's end.

The location of contract sewing shops within blocks or a short drive from the manufacturer's office allows firms to minimize the risk of contracting by closely monitoring production. Manufacturers send their staff into the factories, on a daily or weekly basis, to check quality and progress and ensure timely delivery. Proximity of these factories to warehousing and distribution centers set up by retailers to handle imports cuts down on delivery times and enables retailers to supervise private-label production.

These natural advantages of Los Angeles production have been augmented by new retailer low-inventory strategies, called Quick Response (QR) or Just-In-Time (JIT), based on new information technologies. Retailers stock more variety on their racks, monitor what sells, and replenish their inventory with fast-moving items. Monitoring has become possible with the bar code on each clothing tag, which allows retailers to collect data on each garment sold. Product information, including vendor, style, color, and size, can be sent instantly to the retailer's main office. Retailers can then use so-called EDI (Electronic Data Information) systems to transmit the information with reorders to the manufacturer. In this way, retailers cut financing costs, reduce closeouts, and capitalize on the sale of popular merchandise. This program began with commodity products but is now being adopted by fashion producers and retailers, and works best with vendors (manufacturers) who can restock quickly using domestic sources. Even large garment firms, which import most of their products, are striving to develop local L.A. resources for domestic production in order to make later adjustments in product (fabric, color, size, style), to meet rapidly changing retailer orders, and to fill retail reorders.

As a result of the neat fit between women's outerwear and L.A.'s ability to turn units quickly, most manufacturers there produce domestically. Only about a third of all L.A. manufacturers import garments for sale; 15 percent cut some of their garments locally and consign sewing assembly to foreign contractors. While most of the larger firms produce some of their garments offshore, only a few (like the huge Bugle Boy firm) are primarily importers.

With Mexico just a few hours from L.A., area manufacturers are well situated to take advantage of NAFTA's protection of foreign investment and its tariff and quota breaks. (Mexico's role in the U.S. apparel industry is increasing, having recently surpassed China as the largest exporter of garments to the United States.) Consequently, some L.A. manufacturers have moved production to Mexico. For instance, in 1996, California Connection, a firm selling $70 million wholesale per year, announced it was closing its 1,000-worker Orange County factory and shifting operations below the border, claiming a labor shortage. Like most area manufacturers, L.A.'s largest firm, Guess, has adopted a mixed approach to sourcing, importing most of its nondenim items from the Pacific Rim, while making 90 percent of its fashion-sensitive denim products in the L.A. area and 10 to 20 percent in Mexico.

Manufacturers are growing in size in Los Angeles in order to meet the needs of larger retailers. Subcontracting allows them to expand productive capacity quickly, without adding to their own overhead, by simply adding contractors. According to *Bobbin* magazine, fourteen of

# no sweat

the top hundred garment firms are based in California (eight in Southern California), including Guess ($491 million in sales), Bugle Boy ($414 million), Carole Little ($368 million), Chorus Line ($206 million), St. John Knits ($127 million), Quicksilver ($126 million), and Cherokee ($114 million). Other major manufacturers are B.U.M., Ocean Pacific, Introspect, Z Cavaricci, Francine Browner, Rampage, and Karen Kane. The top twenty-five firms sell about $4 billion per year wholesale to U.S. retailers. Domestic women's swimwear has long been an important L.A. sector, with such firms as Authentic Fitness (Speedo, Cole, and Catalina), Apparel Ventures (Sassafras), Sirena, Beach Patrol, Lunada Bay, and DeWeese (Jag). Hip hop clothing is a new L.A. sector, with Cross Colors and Tag Rag as key firms.

Manufacturers in Los Angeles are also employing "forward integration" to survive, assuming some of the functions of retailers. Firms like Guess have opened their own stores to market their products, either as boutiques or outlets. Guess brings in 35 percent of its sales from its own stores. Just as retailers using private labels become manufacturers, manufacturers using their own stores become retailers. The lines are blurring.

Most contractors in Los Angeles are small, employing less than fifty workers. The average shop has about twenty-five workers and performs sewing assembly and finishing only. It receives from the manufacturer "bundles" of cut fabric which must be sewn into garments, trimmed, pressed, inspected, and sometimes packed. Cutting contractors employ fewer workers and pay hourly rather than piece rates. One cutting shop can provide cut goods to numerous sewing shops.

*Graciela Morales, a teenager who would not give her age – the photographer visited with an official from the Department of Labor. The company Graciela worked for had been issued with many citations for breaking various labor laws.*

Today, as many as 4,000 contractors are chasing work from a shrinking pool of manufacturers, in which the largest hundred firms control most of the production. The constant influx of new immigrant entrepreneurs has created a surplus of contractors in Los Angeles. A recent study found that most shop owners, like their workers, are immigrants: 36 percent Latino, 19 percent Korean, 13 percent Vietnamese, 9 percent Chinese, and 10 percent other Asian.[1] Armenians are an important growing contractor group. Chinese contractors, who employ only Chinese workers, are the only group not increasing. Vietnamese contractors employ many Southeast Asians. All other contractors employ mostly Latino workers, primarily Mexicans.

Start-up costs in L.A. are low, perhaps $5,000 to $10,000 to buy used machines and a few supplies for a shop with ten to twenty sewing machine operators. Industrial space for contractors is plentiful in L.A.'s garment district, where a few landlords own most of the fifty or so multistoried, aging industrial and office buildings. They charge low entry fees, carry contractors through seasonal swings, and demand a premium in return. In the last ten years, many sewing shops have abandoned the downtown area in search of cheaper labor, better space, or anonymity, settling in immigrant communities like El Monte, Huntington Park, East Los Angeles, and Orange County's Little Saigon, or in industrial areas like Vernon or the City of Commerce.

Contractors in L.A. often seek to reduce the cost of renting factory space and equipment by using industrial homeworkers, who make the clothing in their own crowded apartments or

garages. The homeworker is invisible to wage and hour inspectors and immigrant agents. She rents the machine, pays for supplies, and is paid in cash for a fraction of factory rates.

Price cutting, low capitalization, and the instability of contracting relationships all serve to ensure that equipment and methods will not be upgraded. Manufacturers show little loyalty to their contractors. Work orders are verbal, long-term commitments rare. Competition for work boils down to doing it faster and for less. Failure to pay overtime and the minimum wage, paying cash off the books, and sending out homework are all predictable consequences. This low-wage strategy adopted by contractors, who have little incentive to invest in labor–saving equipment or methods, has a limited future. But contractors in Los Angeles have been unable (or unwilling) to organize themselves to improve their bargaining position. Although protective associations do exist (for instance, the Garment Contractors Association of Southern California or similar Korean and Chinese groups), less than a quarter of L.A.'s sewing contractors belong. These associations assist their members in getting business, reducing workers' compensation costs, fighting wage and hour complaints, and lobbying against sweatshop legislation.

The typical garment worker is a young, non-English-speaking immigrant woman with no prior sewing skills. L.A. offers the comfort of an ethnic enclave, where she may have a family, and the chance to work without learning the language or having any experience in garment making. Once here, she joins the working poor, earning low wages when work is available and paying the equivalent of two weeks' wages on the monthly rent of a tiny apartment. She is probably from Mexico, perhaps stopping to work in a border maquila before crossing over. Like Alicia Sotelo, beaten by police alongside an L.A. freeway following an INS chase, she might have worked in a Mexican factory that closed down.

*A 9 year old boy works in a garment factory in September 1992.*

Mexicans comprise 75 percent of workers in L.A.'s apparel industry, and continue to migrate north for jobs in increasing numbers. NAFTA has spurred rather than slowed immigration, with rebellion in Chiapas, plant closures by trade losers, and the huge devaluation of the peso which effectively cut Mexican wages by more than a third. About 10 percent of the immigrant work force in Los Angeles comes from Central America, the first groups fleeing civil war and now entering as economic refugees. Salvadorans and Guatemalans come to the city in hopes of making ten or twenty times the wages offered in garment factories back home, where jobs are scarce. Another 15 percent come from Asia, primarily China and Vietnam. Asians play a greater role elsewhere in the region. Most garment workers in the San Francisco/Oakland area are Chinese immigrants, and in Orange County there are high concentrations of Southeast Asians.

The majority of immigrants working in L.A.'s industry today arrived in the last fifteen years, and are undocumented. Contractors have largely avoided being fined under federal immigration law for hiring undocumented workers by filling out the forms required by law and asking workers to produce proof of their status. The INS occasionally investigates the larger

# no sweat

manufacturers, demanding that they fire workers who lack the right to work, and from time to time factories are raided and workers deported. But the INS lacks the resources to detain and deport the hundreds of thousands of undocumented workers laboring in L.A. factories. On balance, employer sanctions contained in the 1986 Immigration Reform and Control Act (IRCA) have failed to stop immigration and have aggravated already deplorable working conditions by driving more factories underground. In fact, IRCA has become such a handy weapon for employers, wielded against desperate and vulnerable immigrants, that some shops now prefer to hire undocumented workers.

Work is frequently assigned on the basis of gender. Cutting is almost exclusively performed by men, as is heavy pressing. While most sewing machine operators are women, increasing numbers of men are now working as operators, especially on denim, which requires greater physical strength to handle the fabric. Almost all training is done on the job, paid at straight piece rates, and subminimum wages are the norm.

Nearly eradicated by union organizing, sweatshops began to reappear in Los Angeles with the growth of the industry in the 1960s. The efforts of workers to fight the problem through union organization have continually met with stiff resistance. Accelerating waves of immigration, the growth of casual sportswear, ineffective government regulation, and the increasing use of subcontracting have encouraged sweatshop growth.

While the El Monte Thai slavery case shocked the nation, what is most startling about labor and human rights abuses in Los Angeles is just how routine they are. Often located in high-rise buildings that do not meet current codes, L.A.'s garment shops are typically fire traps: blocked or locked exits, aisles jammed with bundled fabric or finished goods, electrical wiring violations, and defunct fire extinguishers are common. A few years ago, garment workers narrowly escaped a fire in their shop when they were rescued by helicopter from the roof. Numerous other safety violations abound, including lack of handguards on machines, poor ventilation, excessive heat, and filth. Medical attention is rare; seamstresses putting needles through their fingers have been forced to apply a band-aid and keep working. Workers are habitually subjected to physical and verbal abuse and other indignities. Sexual harassment of women is an everyday event in many shops.

With few exceptions, workers are paid by the piece and not by the hour. Although such an incentive system can force the pace of work to extreme limits, it is legal provided the workers are guaranteed payment of at least the minimum hourly wage. Factory owners circumvent this law by manipulating time cards, adjusting the time worked to the wages earned under the piece-rate system—using computers to assist with calculations. Constant style changes make it difficult for workers in most shops to build up speed by learning shortcuts. Frequent factory closings leave workers stranded, owed weeks of wages. It is not uncommon to find that the same factory has reopened in another neighborhood under a different name, doing work for the same manufacturer. For workers, getting paid can be a shell game.

Long shifts are routine, as retailers demand fast delivery. Some shops will work all night to finish a job, and overtime is not voluntary. Many shops have workers who labor all day in a factory, then take work home to finish with their children at night. Although California mandates payment of overtime premiums after eight hours per day in manufacturing, and federal law requires payment after forty hours per week, most factories continue to pay only piece-rate earnings with nothing extra for overtime.

Unfair competition and abuses by sweatshops take other forms as well. Many factories fail to carry workers' compensation coverage, or underreport the work force. Workers are often threatened to prevent them from applying for unemployment benefits. Payment for work after an eight-hour day is frequently made in cash to conceal the overtime and avoid payroll taxes. In many cases, employers will deduct the payroll taxes and pocket them.

Garment workers also cannot depend on regular work because production is seasonal. Employment peaks in March of each year, declining in the summer (July and August), picking up in early winter (September to December), falling off again in January, and accelerating in February. With different seasons for different garments, workers often must switch shops to stay employed.

In 1994, the U.S. Department of Labor (DOL) and California state labor officials conducted a survey of conditions in garment shops, randomly selecting for inspection sixty-nine factories from a list of thousands of California garment firms that had paid state payroll taxes. Of course, by neglecting to include factories that did *not* pay taxes (which may comprise 20 percent of the total), the survey understated the problems checked. Even so, the results were shocking. Violations of law were found in 98 percent of the sample firms, including health and safety infractions (92.8 percent), deficient or false records (72.5 percent), failure to pay overtime (68.1 percent) or the minimum wage (50.7 percent), cash payments (30.4 percent), failure to register with the state (11 percent), and illegal homework (14.5 percent).

A second state-federal survey was undertaken in 1996, this time focusing on five counties in Southern California, including Los Angeles. As before, only factories paying state payroll taxes were examined. This time seventy-six were drawn from the list and inspected. This time 99 percent of the shops surveyed had violations. Health and safety violations were found in 96 percent of the firms; in 72 percent of these, conditions were dangerous enough that an accident could lead to a "substantial probability of death or serious physical harm." These included blocked fire exits, electrical problems, equipment lacking protective guards, and violations involving guns used to attach tags to clothing which can cause the spread of diseases like AIDS and hepatitis. Other common violations included failure to pay overtime (55 percent) and the minimum wage (43 percent), cash payments (33 percent), and failure to register with the state (33 percent). Declining rates in some categories may not be significant, given the small size of the sample, increased efforts to conceal violations, and the failure to include underground shops in the survey.

The low rate of compliance found by government inspectors reflects ineffective enforcement tools, inadequate staffing, and the need for organized worker participation. While the industry in California grew by a third from 1980 to 1992, state field enforcement staff declined by a third in the same period. Annual factory inspections have dropped from more than 2,000 to about 600. The state enforcement strategy has been to conduct periodic "sweeps" of the industry, checking many factories in a single area over a few days and imposing fines on violators. In this way, the state hopes to terrorize the industry into compliance. But since state agents only inspect about 10 percent of the factories in any year, contractors treat penalties as a cost of doing business, and often cheat their employees further to pay off fines and the cost of fighting them. Workers cheated typically do not complain until they have been fired or quit, and then must beat their boss and his "cooked books" with only their memories of hours worked and wages not paid.

The DOL Wage and Hour Division has for years suffered cutbacks in inspectors nationally for all investigations. Additional cuts were imposed by Congress in 1996. Beginning in 1989, the DOL in L.A. began to use an old "top down" enforcement weapon: the New Deal era "hot goods" provision of the Fair Labor Standards Act (FLSA), which bars interstate shipment of goods made in violation of the FLSA minimum wage and overtime laws. By threatening to get court orders blocking manufacturers from shipping their finished products to retailers, the Los Angeles DOL began to secure new settlement agreements from manufacturers caught breaking the law. These agreements, first signed by Guess and later by Chorus Line, Carole Little, Z Cavaricci, and others (about forty in all), obligate manufacturers to monitor their contractors' wage and hour compliance and to assume responsibility for any such violations by their contractors committed while working on their garments. Recent surveys conducted by the DOL suggest that manufacturer monitoring of contractors improves compliance somewhat, but still leaves violations at very high rates. The summer 1996 discovery of Guess clothing being made in a string of illegal industrial homework operations, a lawsuit filed by employees of Guess contractors alleging FLSA violations in many sewing shops used by the firm, and the DOL removal of Guess from its "Trendsetter list" of sweatshop busters, highlight the importance of active worker involvement in exposing violators and of independent monitoring by community organizations.

For more than twenty years, there have been attempts to organize the various sectors in the Los Angeles market, including swimwear, sportswear, denim, lingerie, knitting, embroidery, finishing, dyeing, and warehousing, with limited success. Employers have retaliated by browbeating or firing employees, reporting undocumented workers to the INS, engaging in bad-faith bargaining, provoking strikes, and even closing down. Seldom has the National Labor Relations Board moved swiftly enough or with much effect to vindicate workers' rights in such cases.

Guess responded to UNITE's recent campaign by holding captive-audience meetings of its workers, threatening to close or move its operations, and shutting off work to the factories of contractors where workers dared to voice complaints about sweatshop conditions. Guess had promised the DOL, in a 1992 sweatshop agreement, to work with its contractors to correct abuses. In 1996, at Kelly Sportswear in El Monte, a Guess contractor for years, factory workers blew the whistle on an illegal homework operation and wage violations in their own shop, and found themselves on the street when Guess stopped sending Kelly new work and their boss removed the machines and closed the factory. In January 1997, Guess announced that it was moving 70 percent of its production to Mexico (see postscript). The message: stand up for your rights and lose your job.

UNITE has established Worker Centers in the L.A. garment district and San Francisco's Chinatown to educate, assist, organize, and activate nonunion workers in the fight against sweatshops. Center staff have attended teach-ins, testified at public hearings, picketed shops to demand unpaid wages, and brought legal actions. As a result, millions in back wages have been collected. UNITE also fought sweatshops on the legislative front, winning a state ban on industrial homework in 1975 and a mandatory state licensing system in 1980. Following a new round of sweatshop exposés in 1990, a labor-community coalition drafted legislation, introduced by state assemblyman Tom Hayden, which would make manufacturers jointly liable for wage and hour violations committed by their contractors while making their clothes. The bill cleared the state legislature and was vetoed by Republican governor George Deukmejian. In 1992, the same legislation passed both houses of the legislature and was again vetoed by Republican governor Pete Wilson. Finally, in 1994 three separate pieces of antisweatshop legislation, including the joint liability bill (carried by Assemblywoman Hilda Solis), were passed by the legislature with the backing of a labor-community coalition. All three were vetoed by Governor Wilson. When the El Monte scandal raised public awareness, Hilda Solis, now a state senator, reintroduced the joint liability legislation, but it was blocked by the Republican-controlled Assembly.

Los Angeles and its surrounding region are now the battleground where community, religious, civil rights, feminist, and labor activists are mobilizing on many fronts to force manufacturers and retailers to clean up the sweatshops and share enough of the wealth that workers can live in dignity. The obstacles are formidable. The current prosperity of L.A.'s garment industry rests in large part on the vicious exploitation of workers and the successful evasion of regulatory mechanisms. It is not likely that the system's beneficiaries will submit voluntarily to measures that curb their profiteering. It will take massive union organizing, mandated retailer and manufacturer responsibility, and public support to bring this monster to its knees.

*Leafletting shoppers about the clean clothes campaign in Amsterdam.*

# the labor behind the label: clean clothes campaigns in Europe

## Linda Shaw

On September 20, 1989, the British-owned IGMC factory in the Philippines closed its doors. The 1,000 workers of IGMC, which produced women's raincoats for the U.K. market, had been given a half day's notice before they were rudely ejected from the premises. The workers protested the lockout, picketing the factory for over a year in an attempt to pressure IGMC to reopen the plant. The workers' union issued an appeal for support, galvanizing a campaign of solidarity actions in Britain by labor and women's activists, and creating a coalition of NGOs such as the Philippines Resource Center, the journal *International Labor Reports*, and the Manchester-based Women Working Worldwide, together with trade unionists from Region Six of the Transport and General Workers Union.

As Philippine workers turned up the heat at home, the IGMC Union president, Lucy Salao, toured Britain in March 1990. Her presentations on the working and living conditions of garment workers received national media attention: "Ms Salao said she feels angry when she sees the price of raincoats and compares them to her wages. 'The company think we are nothing. They just think of us as little ants even though many of us have worked for them for 15 years.'"

Ants with some bite, however. Salao's visit and the campaign were clandestinely monitored and libel writs issued. The media turned the spotlight on garment retailers. Under this scrutiny, a major British company, Littlewoods, drafted a code of conduct citing compliance with recognized minimum labor standards as essential for its suppliers. This was one of the first codes of its kind created by a British company.

Salao's visit also brought together groups which would later collaborate in the Clean Clothes Campaigns. In the Netherlands, the work done by SOMO on garment retailers provided the European link. An independently funded research group based in Amsterdam, SOMO collects and distributes information on multinational corporations. In 1988, SOMO published a book on a major European retailer, *C&A: The Silent Giant*, which revealed the company's extensive use of homeworkers and sweatshops, and named its suppliers. One of these suppliers was IGMC. Some joint campaign work was undertaken around Salao's visit and a significant network established.

Interest in garment workers was fueled more generally by academic research on production patterns and dynamics of change in the textile and garment industries, especially

*"Nike Fair Play?" Tennis match on Dam Square, Amsterdam between Agassi and an Indonesian worker from a Nike factory. Phil Knight, Nike's CEO, is the referee.*

the growth of international subcontracting chains. Women Working Worldwide tapped this research to compile a resource package on women workers in the garment sector which has been used extensively by community groups in Britain and throughout Europe.

Thanks as well to the fair trade movement, an increasing number of organizations have begun to include the rights of garment workers in their activist agendas. Aid agencies such as Christian Aid and Oxfam established alternative trading operations guaranteeing market outlets for a range of fairly produced goods from the South, including garments. In 1992, the World Development Movement organized the Stop the Stitch Up campaign, demanding more equitable terms for Third World garment workers under the Multi Fiber Arrangement. Magazines such as *Ethical Consumer* ran exposés on the garment industry, and the book *Global Consumer* (1991) provided guidelines for ethical purchasing in both environmental and labor rights contexts. Initiatives aimed at raising consumer consciousness culminated in 1992 in the establishment of the Fairtrade Foundation, which promotes the purchase of "clean" goods by issuing a Fairtrade Mark. The mark was first issued to Maya Gold Chocolate, then Café Direct coffee, which proved relatively successful in establishing a mainstream market niche.

Britain's garment worker unions have been noticeably absent from these campaigns. However, homeworker associations have joined the international effort to curb corporate abuse. The garment industry provides much of the work contracted out to homeworkers, including approximately half of the one million–plus homebased workers in Britain. Homebased work is not actually illegal in most European countries, but in deregulated environments such as Britain, homeworkers are afforded almost no protection by labor legislation. Many British Asian women are to be found in garment outwork and many of the most committed activists also come from this community. In Britain, most Asian homeworkers hold full citizenship, unlike black homeworkers in other European countries.

Homeworkers organized first in Britain and the Netherlands, exposing working conditions and establishing support centers. They also mobilized legislative initiatives which specifically addressed the employment needs of homebased workers rather than calling for a ban on homework altogether. The inclusion of homeworker perspectives in garment campaigns has proved vital in emphasizing that it is not simply poor oppressed women in the South who need "our" help, but that there are many women workers in the "rich" countries of Europe who are also being grossly exploited by garment multinationals. Homeworker activists contribute a directness of experience as laborers and considerable expertise in building international coalitions. These coalitions include organizations in Canada, Portugal, Thailand, Australia, and India. The adoption of a new International Labor Organization (ILO) Convention in June 1996 for homebased workers was due to the effectiveness of this international homeworking coalition. The convention provides campaigners on the garment industry with benchmarks not only for factory-based workers but for the millions of homebased garment workers throughout the world. Of course, the more difficult task of enforcement has only just begun, but for many involved in the Clean Clothes Campaigns, the achievement of this convention has been an inspiration.

The involvement of homeworkers is also important strategically, since many European companies now exploit a mix of domestic-based homeworkers for orders requiring fast turnaround and the factories/sweatshops of Asia in particular for the long runs. Eastern Europe is increasingly being brought into the chains as garment retailers are utilizing the huge untapped pools of skilled and relatively cheap labor in countries such as Poland. Many formerly state-owned garment factories are "adapting" to Western markets and production schedules by shifting to outwork. A recent celebratory article in London's *Financial Times*, entitled "Outworkers to the Rescue," contains no mention of working conditions. But to imagine that,

# no sweat

in this brave new world of entrepreneurship, Polish workers endure anything but the same low-wage and exploitive conditions as their Western counterparts would require foolish optimism. Eastern Europe is fast becoming competitive with Asia, the other main source of mass-produced cheap clothing for the European and especially British market.

The clothing industry remains a significant source of factory-based employment in Europe, especially for women. The industry is dominated by retailers, and most of the European garment campaigns have been directed at the largest firms. In the Netherlands, for instance, the Clean Clothes Campaign (CCC), launched in 1990 using SOMO's research, initially targeted C&A. Demonstrations were staged outside C&A stores (accompanied by a heavy presence of mounted police), and customers were asked to support laborers by signing petitions and questioning retailers' subcontracting practices.

Subsequently, CCC broadened its focus to include all the major garment retailers and developed a Fair Trade Charter for Garments, a cross between a code of conduct and a Fairtrade Mark. By signing the Charter, retailers agree to abide by fair labor standards as established by the International Labor Organization, and to protest noncompliance among suppliers. These standards include the right to organize and bargain collectively; the right to a living wage and overtime pay; maximum working hours; safety and health provisions; and equal opportunity. The Charter also stipulates that retailers must contribute a percentage of their annual turnover toward the maintenance of an independent monitoring system. In return, retailers obtain a trademark signifying that they are sellers of clean clothes.

By 1994, the CCC coalition had expanded to include the garment industry union and the services union of the largest Dutch trade union federation, FNV, as well as the Dutch development agency, NOVIB. Long negotiations with the Dutch Federation of Garment Retailers over the Fair Trade Charter culminated in the Federation's adoption of its own unmonitored code on goods produced by child labor. Currently, talks are continuing with several other garment sector organizations.

The CCC has kept the issue alive in the Netherlands with a series of imaginative street actions, for instance, alternative fashion shows and shop window displays. In 1995, with funding from the European Union, the CCC launched a new project aimed at forming a European network of organizations concerned with labor conditions in the garment industry in

Europe as well as in the developing world. CCC sponsored a series of meetings and workshops in Germany, France, Belgium, and the U.K. over the last two years, and established contacts with several Asian garment workers' organizations. As a result, activists from India, Sri Lanka, Bangladesh, Indonesia, Hong Kong, and the Philippines visited Europe in 1996 to speak out about conditions for garment workers and to strategize with European activists on the future development of garment campaigns. The speakers revealed the appalling conditions in which many garment workers live and work in Asia—from the unheated and unsanitary dormitory accommodations in China to sexual harassment of women as they travel to work in Sri Lanka—all producing goods for sale in Europe.

In the U.K., Women Working Worldwide acted as a catalyst for bringing together a range of groups concerned with the garment industry: homeworker associations, development agencies, environmentalists, education organizations. Calling itself Labour Behind the Label, the network has produced publicity materials but has been hampered by a lack of resources. In April 1996, Labour Behind the Label organized a U.K. program for the CCC European tour. A stronger campaign will be launched in 1997 following on the precedent established by Oxfam, a leading member of the network. Oxfam has orchestrated extensive media and press coverage of their campaign, Sweat Shirt Sweat Shop, the aim of which is to pressure retailers to adopt codes of conduct, although Oxfam prefers to take a "supportive" rather than adversarial stance toward retailers.

# no sweat

Campaigns are now flourishing throughout Europe. In France, Libére tes Fringues consists of twenty-seven organizations, including trade unions and NGOs, which have organized street actions and a program for the Asian workers tour, and are developing a code of conduct. The Kampagne für Saubere Kleidung in Germany is a coalition of fifteen organizations including unions, church groups, and Third World associations, which sponsored a speaking tour of the Asian garment workers. Two campaigns in Belgium—Schone Kleren Campagne and Vêtements Propres—include women's and consumer organizations and trade unions. Schone Kleren is similar to the Dutch campaign and concentrates on educational initiatives. And CCC has been approached by groups from Norway, Japan, Australia, Ireland, Spain, and Denmark interested in establishing their own clean clothes campaigns. Most recently, clothing campaigners have entered into dialogue with international trade unions over codes of conduct and the establishment of closer links.

Although these campaigns are marked by very different perspectives on tactics, there is general agreement that the establishment of a coordinating body, perhaps in the form of a garment campaign Secretariat, is necessary to increase momentum throughout Europe and to generate dialogue with garment workers from the South. The progress of campaigns from country to country has been very uneven, especially with regard to trade union involvement, funding levels, and the commitment to representing homeworker perspectives. Many crucial questions have yet to be articulated and positions formulated. For instance, is it possible or desirable for campaigners to speak with one voice? Should there be a single, uniform code of conduct? How do we create genuinely effective systems of independent monitoring? How can we be more responsive and accountable to Southern garment workers—and not cause job loss by our actions in the North?

The Clean Clothes Campaigns must continue to be attentive to the voices of Southern workers such as Lucy Salao, the IGMC workers, and many others dependent for a livelihood on the garment industry both in the South and in Europe. The IGMC workers eventually lost their struggle to keep the factory open, but union president Salao remains adamant about the importance of such solidarity actions: "Our struggle is your struggle too."

# sweatshopping

Eyal Press

In April 1996, shortly after news broke that Kathie Lee Gifford's clothing line was being produced in sweatshops, the media flocked to cover a story it had until then quite happily ignored. On television and radio, in newspapers and magazines, dozens of articles suddenly appeared on sweatshops, exploring the subject from the perspective of immigrant workers in U.S. factories, foreign laborers, Korean factory managers, labor unions, pressure groups, politicians, and celebrities.

For all the attention that sweatshops have received, however, little effort has been made to examine how the issue plays out among shoppers, salesworkers, and store managers at the consumer end of the fashion chain. There is, perhaps, an obvious reason for this, which is that consumers and salesworkers are so far removed from the abuses being uncovered. Many Americans may genuinely care that companies are using child labor and exploiting workers, but it's difficult to raise serious questions about all of this within the confines of shopping malls and retail stores. It's not as though the merchandise in these stores is labeled "made in a sweatshop," nor are salesworkers and store managers exactly eager to address the subject.

Still, there are signs that, while most shoppers go about their business in the usual manner, more and more would like to know what they can do. In 1995, when *New York Times* columnist Bob Herbert wrote a series of articles linking companies such as Eddie Bauer, the Gap, and Banana Republic to Latin American sweatshops, he received a flood of mail from readers asking how consumers can change things. A recent poll by the University of Marymount found that three in four Americans say they would prefer not to shop in stores that sell sweatshop goods. Even if the number who would act upon such convictions is far smaller, the level of public concern is growing, something industry leaders are aware of. At a 1996 conference on sweatshops convened by Labor Secretary Robert Reich, held shortly after the revelations about Kathie Lee, retail executives from across the country issued urgent calls for "an end to scapegoating" of stores caught selling tainted garments, claiming the retail chains are just as shocked by the revelations as their customers. Clearly, the industry is concerned that customers really do care, and for good reason. As Herbert explains, "Most people do not want to buy clothing made by workers who are treated like slaves ... The best thing [they] can do is let American companies know ... Speak to clerks and store managers. Write to company executives. Ask if garments were manufactured under humane conditions."

# no sweat

Unfortunately, as this reporter discovered on a recent tour of dozens of New York City's most popular fashion outlets, such advice is easier to give than to follow. It's no simple task to get a straight answer about sweatshops as a consumer, especially not at a time when so many companies are feeling anxious and defensive. The day before my excursion began, the garment union UNITE happened to release a report accusing Macy's, Bloomingdales, and Lord & Taylor, three of New York's most chic and elegant fashion outlets, of selling garments made in sweatshops. A union activist dressed as Santa Claus was handcuffed and arrested in front of Macy's, a hint of the barriers that go up to protect the retail world's inner chambers.

My attempt to explore the sweatshop issue at the retail level began at the popular Disney theme store on 42nd Street and Broadway. Within a brightly lit room that seemed more like a playground than a clothing store, customers and salesclerks navigated between piles of stuffed Dalmations and Donald Ducks, Mickey Mouse pajamas and sweatshirts featuring Pocahontas and the Hunchback of Notre Dame. These cartoon icons, cross-promoted in Disney film, television, children's books, and theme parks, are also featured in a recent report by the New York–based National Labor Committee (NLC), which found Mickey Mouse and Pocahontas etched onto clothing produced in Haitian sweatshops where women toil under abysmal conditions, earning a mere 28 cents per hour.

"Can I help you?" I was asked by a saleswoman, or "cast member" as Disney refers to its store employees. Identifying myself as a reporter and potential customer, I told her what I had heard regarding Disney's Haitian subcontractors. Was the clothing in this store made in sweatshops?

"You'll have to ask the manager," she explained politely, dashing through a door labeled "cast members only" to get help. While waiting, I engaged another salesperson. "It wouldn't surprise me," he confided, checking over his shoulder to see who was around. "All these big companies are the same—they'll do anything for that extra dollar." Our conversation seemed to hold promise, but stopped abruptly when the store manager appeared. "Disney doesn't make anything in Haiti," she assured me, saying I would have to contact the company's PR department to get the details. Why were people making allegations? "I can't comment," she replied.

*The retail environment.*

Seeking a more substantive exchange, I ventured to the three-story, 40,000-square-foot House of Disney megacomplex further uptown. "Welcome to the House of Disney!" boomed a cast member holding a Goofy doll at the entrance, which is crowned by life-size steel statues of Mickey, Minny, and Goofy, evoking what William Severini Kowinski aptly terms "Mousekatecture." Again I identified myself as a journalist and posed the sweatshop question to the nearest salesperson/cast member. As before, she directed me to the manager, who again explained that I would have to contact corporate headquarters.

Now somewhat frustrated, I approached a pair of customers near a stack of pajamas: had *they* heard anything about Disney's clothing being produced in sweatshops? "No, I have not," said Per Ekvall, from Sweden, "but I would appreciate knowing if these clothes are made under exploitative conditions." Tom Downs, a customer from Hershey, Pennsylvania, expressed similar curiosity. At that point, as I turned to engage a woman shopping with her daughter, the store manager reappeared, this time flanked by a security guard and a secret-service type with an electronic headset. "I'm sorry, but you cannot ask questions of our customers on private property," she said, whisking me away as though I had been plotting to commit an act of sabotage.

Of course, given the hidden protocols governing behavior within such enclosures, in a fundamental sense I *had* committed such an act. Despite appearances to the contrary, what

transpires on the floors of the retail world is scrupulously regulated and monitored. Cameras and security guards hover from all angles, muzak and aromatics bathe the atmosphere, and retail workers appear on all sides.

The retail workers policing the interiors of such stores themselves constitute one of the fashion industry's exploited classes, albeit in a less extreme form than on the production end of things. Like the factory workers who stitch and sew the clothing in sweatshops, these hamburger-flippers of the fashion world are confined to the bottom rungs of the industry, earning $13,971 a year on average, often with long hours, no benefits, and little prospect of promotion or a raise. Few of these workers belong to a union. The Gap has hundreds of outlets across America, employing thousands of workers, but not a single organized shop. Meanwhile, retail workers must rigorously adhere to the behaviorist precepts set by their employers, which usually means dress, appearance, even speech patterns are standardized. One worker I met explained that he had to shave his sideburns and cut his hair upon moving into sales. *All* the workers I interviewed exuded that saccharine exuberance ("How may I help you?" "That looks wonderful") which is no doubt a prerequisite for the job.

Not surprisingly, most retail workers have no idea what to say when asked about sweatshops. At Aeropostale, a hip specialty store catering to urban youth, my questions about how clothing was made were met with blank stares. Eventually a store manager appeared to explain that, "after the Kathie Lee thing," she and other employees did receive a memo from the company detailing its subcontracting policy. The store did not use sweatshops, she assured me. Pointing to a sweater made in Indonesia, I asked how I could be certain, given the rampant labor abuses in that country. Again, the question elicited blank stares.

"You're never told anything about sweatshops or anything like that," says Benjamin Yost, who worked two years as a salesclerk and then assistant store manager at Abercrombie & Fitch, a retail specialty store owned by the Limited that caters to preppie outdoorsmen. Yost does recall a range of elaborate training instructions he received on how to deal with customers, for example: "learning how to greet them so they cannot answer 'yes' or 'no' to a question. You should ask, 'What size are you looking for?' rather than 'Can I help you find a size?'"

But Yost was taught nothing about sweatshops—indeed, he was actively encouraged to remain ignorant. One day during his lunch break at the Atrium mall in Boston, he was handed a flier which accused the Limited of complicity in sweatshop abuses (this was just after the store had been one of many retail chains linked to the El Monte sweatshop in Los Angeles, where women from Thailand had been locked up and forced to work as virtual slaves). When he showed the pamphlet to another assistant manager, he received a cold response. "You know Ben, we need to make a living too," he was told. Later, the district manager in charge of Abercrombie outlets across the East Coast stopped in for a spot-check and found the pamphlet. "She immediately made it clear that it did not belong there or anywhere near the store," Yost recalls.

While brushing the issue under the rug is clearly the preferred tactic, the effort can sometimes reveal more than is intended. At Bloomingdales, the sales staff was clearly on red alert for needling questions, no doubt because the previous day the labor union UNITE had released *Misery by Design*, a report which catalogues the numerous sweatshops, both foreign and domestic, servicing Federated, Bloomingdales' parent company. An article in the *New York*

# no sweat

*Times* detailed the charges, including use of factories that strip-search workers daily and employ thirteen-year-olds for fourteen-hour days, all vigilantly denied by corporate spokespersons.

"Sorry, I don't want to answer anything from a journalist, and don't ask questions of my sales staff," the store manager told me brusquely before I could even formulate a question. But my friend, Toby Beach, received a very different response when he pressed the same issues, only as a shopper. Selecting an East Island shirt made in Indonesia, Beach told a salesclerk he was interested, but had read the story in the *Times,* and did not want to purchase a tainted garment. "We employ our own people and don't use sweatshops," he was promptly assured. When Beach refused to buy the shirt, the salesman scrawled himself a note indicating the reason for the lost sale: "N.Y. Times, p. 26—Bad Publicity." The same scenario unfolded at Eddie Bauer, the rugged outdoorsman's shop where canoes and fishing gear adorn the walls but the sales staff are electronically hooked up with Star Trek–style headsets. Asked about sweatshops, David Lindell, the manager, told me that he thought the store had a sound policy, but could not offer any details. "I'll have to defer to the corporate office on that." Beach again selected several items and posed the same questions as a shopper. "We're one of the two best companies around…We check very regularly [on factory conditions]," Lindell assured him. Hoping to close the sale, he suggested, "Why don't you buy the shirt, then call this 800 number. If you're not happy, you can always return it."

A few managers were more forthcoming, though they refused to be identified for fear of retribution. At the Manhattan Mall, the store manager of a chain store selling Levi's and other name brands, explained, "Yes, we get questions about sweatshops and where the clothing was made quite a lot." Did it concern her? "Sure. I know we exploit workers over there, and we have sweatshops here too." So what should a shopper do? "I can't really advise—I work for a corporation… This is my job."

At another chain, the manager explained that, "yes, as a personal thing," how the clothing is produced concerned him. Did he share his feelings with customers and employees? "No—it's a personal thing. In here, I'm a performer."

# fashion as a culture industry

McKenzie Wark

Dateline: Geneva, July 25, 1996: *Poorer Nations Plan Attack on Textile Barriers* reads the headline. Clothing and textile importers from the developing world, frustrated by the slow progress of trade liberalization under the Multi Fiber Arrangement (MFA) that regulates these industries, decide they have had enough and take their complaints to the World Trade Organization (WTO). Pakistan leads the charge, on behalf of ten Asian textile-exporting countries, in a paper prepared for the WTO's Council for Trade in Goods. It appears to be a preemptive move, putting issues on the table ahead of the WTO's ministerial meeting in Singapore, scheduled for December 1996. The paper calls for a full review of the MFA, before the December meeting. The Pakistani paper has the backing of the Association of South East Asian Nations (ASEAN), Hong Kong, India, and South Korea. It argues that procrastination runs counter to the arrangement, which urges a continuous process of adjustment, allowing domestic industry to accommodate increased competition.[1]

Welcome to the politics of international trade. Clothing and textiles are a frequent feature in trade disputes between the developing world and what Paul Gilroy calls the "overdeveloped" world. Clothing and textiles have historically played a key role in the development strategies of industrializing countries. Most nations that have successfully developed their economies and living standards passed through an early and crucial phase of specialization in key parts of the industrial processes involved in clothing and textiles, particularly those processes that are intensive in the use of unskilled labor, can be developed through the gradual addition of capital resources, and require relatively low levels of technical skill.[2]

For this development process to succeed, the developing country needs an export outlet. In the case of the development of the British economy in the early nineteenth century, this took the form of colonial possessions, such as India. As Marx wrote in 1853: "It was the British intruder who broke up the Indian hand-loom and destroyed the spinning wheel. England began with driving the Indian cottons from the European market; it then introduced twist into Hindustan and in the end inundated the very mother country of cottons with cottons." Marx goes on to write of the consequences in India, where the "decline of Indian towns celebrated for their fabrics was by no means the worst consequence. British steam and science uprooted, over the whole surface of Hindustan, the union between agriculture and manufacturing industry." By which he means the village system, where families combined

hand-weaving of cloth with the hand-tilling of the soil in one social and economic practice. British interference " placed the spinner in Lancashire and the weaver in Bengal" or supplanted "both Hindu spinner and weaver... blowing up their economical basis... "[3]

Marx thought the destruction of the "semi-civilized" economic and social structure of the subcontinent necessary for the reorganization of the productive resources of the East, although he was well aware that the English sought such an end "for the vilest of motives." I mention this because it is surely an irony of history that clothing and textile producers in the East now seek the destruction of the remnants of these industries in the overdeveloped world, in the name of much the same ideology of progress and development. They have as little interest in the culture and traditions of European garment workers as the English had in that of the cotton spinners of the subcontinent nearly two centuries ago.

Without the dubious advantage of colonial regimes of force, developing countries today are obliged to seek openings in the overdeveloped world for their clothing and textile goods through the baroque weave of bilateral agreements that make up the Multi Fiber Arrangement. The MFA began as a temporary measure aimed at halting the penetration of clothing goods into the overdeveloped world to allow for an orderly adjustment of the industry. That was twenty-seven years ago. The arrangement has been renewed many times, and is not due to conclude until the year 2005.

Some thirty-three countries are party to the MFA. They see a predictable and orderly regime of barriers to the free export of their goods as at least preferable to arbitrary and capricious changes in policy. What Pakistan and other developing countries complain about is that the overdeveloped countries defer liberalization as far into the future as the rules allow. To date, only the U.S. has actually announced its plans for phasing out the MFA by 2005, and its officials intend to leave half of its existing quotas in place to the very end.

It seems unlikely that even as durable a temporary measure as the MFA can last forever. Developing countries, with their strong price advantage, have increased their penetration of the markets of the overdeveloped world in spite of it. The newly industrialized countries of the Asia-Pacific region are gradually increasing their bargaining power, now that the EC and the U.S. want trade concessions to allow goods from the overdeveloped world into these rapidly growing economies.

# no sweat

Perhaps one might also ask whether the overdeveloped world *ought* to have the right to protect the domestic markets and employment for its "sunset" industries from competitors. Labor movement leaders often claim that the competition is unfair because the wages paid in developing countries are miserably low, the working conditions are barbaric, and the goods may very well be dumped on the market at prices below cost as part of a strategy of acquiring market share. Many workers in the developing world do labor in sweatshops. But while unionists are correct to oppose such abusive conditions wherever they occur, trade officials in developing countries are suspicious of this opposition when it appears to them to be a convenient way of justifying the existence in perpetuity of low-skill and labor-intensive work in the overdeveloped world (where work is theoretically regulated) at the expense of the developing world. After all, one must first have work before one can begin to improve the wages and conditions of that work.

The First World campaign against Third World sweatshops would have more credibility if it were combined with a frank recognition that the adjustment of clothing and textile industries in the overdeveloped world is not something that can be put off forever. Low-skill, labor-intensive, and low value-added industrial employment does not have a future in high-wage countries. But there is an alternative to the reactive policy of postponing adjustment. This involves capturing as much of the value-added end of the production process as possible and retaining the overdeveloped world's edge in production processes that require high levels of technical skill and new or expensive forms of capital equipment. It also means recognizing the extent to which clothing and textile industries are not only *manufacturing* industries but *culture* industries. As such, the enormous concentration of media, design, and cultural skill and capital in the overdeveloped world can act as an anchor for adding value of a creative and cultural kind to the garment industry. A piece of cloth, like a sheet of paper, can be a mass-produced commodity of little value, or it can be a rare and highly sought after product—depending on what is written on it.

Fashion can be thought of as a social rhythm that is both cultural and industrial. Since the 1950s, there has been a pronounced growth in the complexity of the consumption side of fashion culture—markets, taste, and style are much more variable and affect many more people. This in turn has produced problems for the system of clothing manufacture attuned to regular, seasonal shifts in style. The relationship between these rhythms connects what is often regarded as the "postmodern" aspect of culture (where social identity is frequently expressed through consumption choices), and the possibilities of post-Fordist forms of work organization, production, and industry policy (where manufacturing is governed by decentralized, flexible, just-in-time production, and niche marketing). In the postwar period, both of these rhythms have become more global, internally complex, and abstract, in the sense that both kinds of movement are less and less tied to inherited place, taste, and tradition.

In the 1950s, the pulse of fashion emanated directly from Paris. Haute couture set the pace in a game where the only options were novelty and status—the baroque and the classical. As one fashion editor commented, "In those days we were reporting one look, *the* look. That was what fashion was about—and it was news."[4] The role of high-fashion couturiers—the famous houses such as Dior—in setting the pace was uncontested. As the 1960s got underway, the postwar economic boom in the overdeveloped countries quickened the tempo of fashion and broadened the base for mass-produced, ready-to-wear clothing, seizing hold of the new middle-class and affluent working-class segments of the market. Yet postwar prosperity also brought qualitative changes to the fashion game in the form of new rules and moves. The rise of pop culture created whole new rhythms based on new modes of fashionability in the information landscape.

This began among young consumers with disposable income who flocked to the great "teenage ball" celebrated by chronicler Colin McInnes: "Yes I tell you, it had real savage splendour in the days when we found that no one couldn't sit on our faces any more because we'd loot to spend at last, and our world was to be our world, the one we wanted, and not standing on the doorstep of somebody else's waiting for honey, perhaps."[5] These young pop consumers created unpredictable, instant, almost impossible demands. Yet the sheer volume of total sales that could be made in the teenage segment of the market led manufacturers to try to produce under these rather uncertain conditions.

The volatile styles of English youth subculture of the '60s are key examples here, throwing up such still famous examples as Biba. "The first Biba shop opened in London's

# no sweat

Abingdon Road in 1963. With its navy blue walls and William Morris print curtains, it made an instant impact. A shade cheaper than Mary Quant, Biba democratized fashion, making it accessible to the young and low-paid."[6] Or at least that is how a journalist enthused over the Biba legend in a recent newspaper story, the occasion for which was the relaunch of the Biba name.

Thus began a period of high commercial risk, which has only intensified as youth fashion has exercised more and more of an influence upon other sectors of the market—to the extent that style now bubbles up the fashion chain more forcefully than it trickles down. Increasingly, fashion has become a culture industry which cannot entirely subordinate its cultural product to the patterns of industrialization and the international division of labor. Indeed, fashion and clothing present a real problem for matching the rhythms of consumption with those of the production cycle.

The relationship of fashion to Fordist mass production has always been precarious.[7] Mass production requires long runs of standardized products in order to generate returns of a large enough scale to cover the high costs of capitalizing a factory with machinery and to cover the wage bill until the receipts come in. Unless mass production can count on a very long run for a standard item, it cannot effectively compete with small-scale or craft-based production, where the overheads are often lower even if the cost per garment tends to be higher. The degree of mechanization and the level of labor intensity vary enormously from one section of the garment production process to another. So the effects of a rising volume of demand on the one hand, and the rapid increase in the rhythm of fashion on the other, are felt in different degrees and in different ways.[8] The manufacture of synthetic fibers, spinning, and weaving are all capital-intensive industries, and fiber making and spinning are also dominated by relatively big firms. Weaving, though highly mechanized, is an industry dominated for the most part by small firms, and is thus more flexible and competitive. Garment cutting is mechanized, but the sewing and finishing of garments is almost entirely a labor-intensive operation.

The design of high-fashion garments is a highly skilled, craft-based industry, once dominated by the couture houses. These latter like to think they still have a monopoly on the cultural capital necessary to create fashion, as was the case in the 1950s. Yet few couture houses can consistently make a profit year after year, given the high costs of staging the elaborate shows that place couture firmly on the map of the information landscape, not to mention the escalating costs of skilled craft labor. On the other hand, the whims of fashion pose a potential threat to the whole manufacturing chain, even to the big fiber and fabric manufacturers who boast the most secure revenue and capital base.

Not surprisingly, an alliance of sorts formed over the years between couture houses and the fabric manufacturing industry, a movement led in France by textile magnate Marcel Boussac and later in Italy by Franco Marinotti.[9] Through this alliance, couturiers hoped to find a secure financial base, and fabric makers hoped to annex the cultural capital of fashion to their sales drive. If couture could create a stable demand for its fabrics, mass manufacturers would come calling to order these same fabrics, or else the fabric firm could set up in the ready-to-wear business itself. Hence, elite, pacesetting craft production based on the cultural capital of the designers made common cause with the slower moving mass producers of textiles or ready-to-wear garments with their fixed capital assets, production schedules, and liquid capital resources.

The Italian industry tried in 1971 to institute a similar arrangement via the High-Fashion Industry Accord, signed by textile and ready-to-wear manufacturers, haute couture houses, and boutique designers. The agreement tried to define common trends in fashion some fourteen months in advance of the release of the collections onto the market. Its purpose was to transfer a little of the glamour of the couture houses onto the mass-market producers, and a little of the latter's wealth onto the cash-strapped couturiers. The latter received a subsidy from a common fund set up by the ministries of commerce and industry and the ready-to-wear and textile manufacturers, on condition that at least 40 percent of the models offered in the couture collections conformed to specifications on line, color, and fabric established in the agreement.[10]

These compromises within the industry were unstable, and in any event depended on couture's absolute control of the general rhythm of fashion. But the new youth market, tuned to a different beat, challenged couture's centrality and shifted the industry off axis. The kind of demand created by pop culture was quite different from that of couture: it did not conform to seasonal rhythms and was not based on a total "new look," lasting only for the duration of a given season. In effect, pop culture created a demand for change and stylistic difference on an

VERSACE

expanded scale, and redefined the game of fashion into more complex subsets and syncopations. In displacing couture as the centerpiece of the game, it also threatened to disrupt the orderly mass production of couture copies and derivatives.

As such, the pop culture explosion of the 1960s was a shot in the arm for craft production and boutique distribution. The couture-manufacturer alliance had been linked to the department store distribution system, particularly in the United States, which formed the biggest single retail market. The new demand for alternative youth clothing benefited craft producers who could run up small batches at short notice, as well as boutique distributors, who could set up shop with minimal capital investment. Hence, the short-term effect of 1960s pop culture was to declare an alternative to the mass production of fashion by giving a temporary advantage to small craft producers.

However, the very same rise in incomes that expanded the consumption pool, especially for youth, also placed cost pressures on clothing manufacture, particularly at its most labor-intensive stages. The temporary advantage gained by craft production was quickly eroded by escalating costs, yet it affected mass producers too. Garment production in industrialized countries went into a steep decline, while the level of imports into these countries began to rise sharply. This trend, which began in the 1960s, accelerated with the big wage hikes of the late '60s, the recession of the '70s, and the economic globalization of the 1980s.[11] In short, the benefits of proximity and the value added through the mingling of the garment trade with pop style were not enough to offset the price advantage of exporters from the developing world.

Given that clothing and textiles accounted for 10 million jobs and 17 percent of manufacturing employment in OECD countries as late as 1963, the rapid erosion of these industries was cause for alarm for employers, workers, and governments alike.[12] Several courses

of action were possible, depending on the perceived interests and alliances of the class fractions involved in each country. In what follows, I sketch out the different paths pursued by capital investors and policy makers in accord with the respective cultures of productivity in the six leading nations in this industry: the United States, Britain, France, Germany, Japan, and Italy. These sketches present what Keynes would call the "stylized facts" of each case.

**United States.** The clothing and textile industries are a perfect illustration of the point made by Robert Reich, before he became secretary of labor: governments cannot avoid having policies on industry, and if no effort is made to shape useful ones, contradictory or counterproductive policies will result by default.[13]

Since the New Deal, American policies in this sector have been disastrously ad hoc. Antitrust legislation, aimed at fostering "competition," and artificially high prices set for U.S. cotton, aimed at bolstering farm incomes, led to a fragmented, disorganized, undercapitalized industry. Since the war, American aid and trade policies have been mixed with cold war strategic objectives. In Japan, viewed as a "bulwark" against "Red China" in the 1950s, American policy helped build a textile and clothing industry that directly competed with American markets—often using American cotton bought at lower prices than were available to

U.S. manufacturers. Quotas and "voluntary agreements" were put in place to stop Japanese competition.[14]

In 1959, textile unions proposed policy initiatives such as a development agency for structural adjustment in the industry and a tripartite labor dispute settlement board. Both were resisted successfully by employers, and no progressive policy organs were created. As competition increased and more jobs were threatened, the unions had little choice but to fall in line behind the merely defensive protectionist policies advocated by employers.[15] The main tool used was the restrictive quota, which limits the quantity of garments that can be imported and has a built-in incentive for importers to bring in high-cost, high value-added goods. Unfortunately, American manufacturers were thereby encouraged to concentrate on low-cost, low value-added goods where the foreign competitive pressure is lower.[16]

As a country with both relatively high incomes and high levels of consumption, American industry policy should have been promoting high value-added domestic production and low value-added imports. Ultimately, what the quota system achieved was company flight: American clothing manufacturers moved the labor-intensive sectors offshore, to Mexico, the Caribbean, and Asia, to reduce costs and shed jobs at home. In part, this process was actively encouraged as an anticommunist strategy in the Caribbean Basin and Central America.

The runaway shop is not unique to the garment industry, and indeed parts of the industry were protected from this for some time by the need for fast turnaround times in clothing makeup. But there is a general pattern of growing import penetration, lack of competitive and high value-added imports, job loss, and declining incomes, which in turn leads to stagnant demand and consumption levels.

New York's once famous garment industry has been particularly hard hit by these changes, and the summer of 1995 was an especially bitter season. The Plaid Clothing Group, the second largest maker of men's tailored clothes in the U.S., filed for Chapter 11 bankruptcy status, followed by Bidermann Industries USA, which once made clothing for Ralph Lauren and another leading firm, Forstmann & Co. In 1995, the industry shed about 1,000 jobs, on top of the 6,000 lost in 1994. There are about 77,000 apparel jobs left in New York City, down from 100,000 in 1988.[17] Some in the industry would rather join the developing world on its own terms than compete with it at higher levels of skill formation and capital concentration. The

Fashion Center Business Improvement District reportedly wanted to set up a foreign trade zone in Midtown Manhattan. The zone would reduce and in some cases eliminate import duties, and would effectively become a cell of the global economy, disconnected from the national trade regime.[18] The proposal highlights the contradiction in relying on tariff or quota regimes as a means to curb adjustment in mature industries. These bump up the cost of imported intermediate goods, making it impossible to base a value-adding industry onto the production chain in the tariff-levying country.

This is unfortunate, since New York is an ideal site for a culture industry with a global focus, if not for manufacturing with a national focus. Calvin Klein, Ralph Lauren, and Donna Karan are identifiable as products of a New York aesthetic and business model, yet all have significant global markets. Klein and Karan were also beneficiaries of the concentration of media industries in New York, which propagated images of both as celebrities with currency in a now global pop aesthetic. Perhaps even more emblematic of New York fashion as a matrix of culture industries is Isaac Mizrahi. Influenced by the Hollywood screen glamour of the '50s, Mizrahi recently starred in his own movie biography, *Unzipped*, directed by his former partner Douglas Keeve.[19] Mizrahi's style ends up stamped on yards of fake fur—and yards of celluloid. The film sells the clothes; the clothes sell the film.

Jay Mazur, president of UNITE, has quite rightly pointed out that the globalizing strategies of Klein and Karan are not going to generate enough jobs to arrest the decline of the garment trade in New York.[20] But what about the jobs sustained by New York's concentration of overlapping culture industries, all tapping into the city's unique creativity to service a wide range of media, from fabric to celluloid to paper to the magnetic surfaces of discs and tapes? Is there not a viable culture industry "center" to be supported in New York? And what industry assistance policies, educational institutions, and kinds of high-profile media concentration might best facilitate the marketing of such a culture to its particular niches in the domestic and global market?

These might seem like strange questions, and not the most optimistic ones at that. But they are aimed at addressing certain obstinate realities. For the once vast, affluent, working and middle classes, whose extended consumption of luxury goods was the whole basis of Fordist production and regulation in the economy, a vicious cycle is in effect. The decline of Fordist

# no sweat

mass production under the impact of import penetration leads to a decline in mass luxury consumption, and in turn to a further slackening of demand. Hence the tempo of elite fashion pulls away from that of mass consumption. It seems unlikely that there could ever be a return to the Fordist era, in which mass production and mass consumption went hand-in-hand within the borders of national or regional economies. This would involve the reversal of a well-entrenched economic pattern, and the replacement of a set of cultural habits.

**Britain.** The U.K. presents a similar situation on a smaller scale, with a highly protected fabric industry which is basically stagnant in terms of employment and levels of technology. British manufacturers survived in the 1960s by lowering labor costs and by an unusual degree of integration on the part of big firms like Marks and Spencers. When the crunch came, the Labour government responded in 1975 with emergency bailout measures such as employment subsidies, which gradually became permanent props. It tried to revive tripartite bodies for industry development and negotiation and instituted rationalization and export facilitation plans, but it was all too little and too late. This strategy was designed to slow up cheap imports to allow an orderly adjustment of the industry based on capital replacement and technological innovation. But little effort was made to link rationalization to the design process, and opportunities for domestic production of higher value-added products were missed. In recent years, the Thatcher and Major governments have continued the policy of ineffectual protectionist measures with even weaker efforts to progressively rationalize the industry.[21]

Britain was the pioneer of the pop mode, but never matched up to the challenge on the production side.[22] Hence the innovative pop styles ended up being put through an unusual feedback loop, back into elite fashion culture. The British art school system[23] turns out a never-ending succession of brilliant pop artists and designers in the wake of Vivienne Westwood, John Galliano, Alexander McQueen, and the like, most of whom look for overseas financing or attempt to survive by utilizing the domestic craft production system.[24] The latter is heavily based on the exploitation of migrant labor and is not known for quality work.[25]

In 1996, the Coats Viyela Group, the U.K.'s largest textile and clothing producer, announced a £50 million restructuring program, accelerating the move to offshore production. Other firms are expected to follow.[26] Meanwhile, star designers such as Westwood and Galliano end up with Italian or French backing. Half of Westwood's clothing production is currently based in Parma.[27] What has always been lacking are the kind of mutually reinforcing business links between design and production that in the Italian and French cases have fostered the formation of a design-based, value-added industry.

In the neoliberal production and consumption cycle of contemporary Britain, fashion has become an elite rhythm, tuned to innovative retail methods based on computerized inventory and stock control. The diversity of the product ranges and rapid tempo of turnover possible in this industrial milieu have favored a return to craft production of stylish objects for the elite consumer.[28] No wonder Biba has been revived. Meanwhile, mass unemployment results in a burgeoning of micro-mass subcultures with time to kill, producing "streetstyles," such as those famously tapped by Westwood, Malcolm McLaren, and their successors.[29]

**France.** Traditionally an exporter of high-fashion goods, France did not feel the crisis caused by rising costs until much later than Britain and the U.S. French manufacturers rode out the inflation of the late 1960s and the recession of the early '70s on the strength of their reputation and prominence as purveyors of style. No attempts were made to increase the value-added content of goods for the domestic market.

The incoming Socialist government inherited the task of providing emergency relief and a restructuring program, and produced a plan as early as 1981. This included capital investment subsidies and the establishment of the Maison de la Mode, intended to bolster the image of Paris as the center of fashion on the global information landscape. From the start, this industry policy was a mixture of featherbedding for inefficient firms and a genuine attempt at rationalization and adjustment. The former appeared to win out in the end. An interesting

"LE MALE"

Jean Paul GAULTIER

aspect of the policy were the "solidarity" agreements signed by firms who received subsidies in return for a promise to restructure without shedding jobs. These agreements became increasingly difficult to uphold as import penetration intensified and, as with British assistance schemes, other countries cried foul through international and EC bodies.

A novel feature of French policy is that apparel is considered an "infant" industry, like electronics.[30] Policy makers assert that it never experienced technological innovation in its labor processes, and hence should be protected along with other nascent industries undergoing technical change. Like Britain, France imposes quotas and other forms of protection, which slow the trend toward moving clothing makeup offshore to cheap labor processing zones.

Paris may still be the center of the fashion information landscape, but is under mounting competition from Milan, New York, and on occasion, London. Haute couture has been feeling the pinch of rising costs for some time. Most of the great houses depend on the licensing of their names for boutique products such as perfume and accessories for the bulk of their income, treating clothing as a promotional expense which sustains the elite point of entry of the label into the information landscape.[31] Meanwhile, ready-to-wear designers such as Jean-Paul Gaultier have been hugely successful in turning the pop ideas of London streetstyle into marketable products.[32]

In October 1996, after Gaultier had turned down the job, John Galliano was brought in as head designer at Christian Dior, replacing Gianfranco Ferre, while another English designer, Alexander McQueen, replaced Galliano at Givenchy. Both companies are owned by LVMH (Louis Vuitton–Moet Hennessy). As one fashion reporter commented, "John Galliano's eccentricity and refusal to compromise has created more publicity for Givenchy than the house has seen since Audrey Hepburn wore its clothes in *Funny Face*. And publicity is what it is all about; perfume sales are the key to haute couture, while jeans lines, accessories, sunglasses and hosiery licences are increasingly the key to ready to wear. LVMH is in the market for a designer who will not so much make beautiful, wearable clothes, as a designer who will generate as much publicity as possible."[33] No surprise that the other rumored appointee at Dior was England's most famous designer, and the only one with her own TV show—Vivienne Westwood. What these events point to is the ability of the French industry to exploit the ongoing allure of Paris as a site of style, and integrate various aspects of fashion and clothing with other culture industries.

**Germany.** Rejecting both U.S.-style protectionism and French and British attempts at arm's-length interventionism, German policy has always favored competitive adjustment. Levels of protection are relatively low and the government offers little in the way of subsidies. The clothing industry has seen a dramatic rise in productivity and a simultaneous decline in employment. Fortunately, in the context of tight labor markets, workers have for the most part found employment in less mature, expanding industries, although now that unemployment is rising, the state may be pressured to step in.

German firms have been much more active than their French and British counterparts in moving labor-intensive clothing makeup offshore.[34] Trade policy encourages this practice in that these goods are partially exempt from import duties if they are made from German textiles, in which case they are considered essentially domestic goods. Trade policy also aims at maintaining high value-added exports and promoting low value-added imports, and offshore production supports the policy.

Clothing produced by German firms with German fabric that is made in cheap labor countries can also enter other EC markets such as Britain or France via Germany, and so there is periodic conflict over these differing industry policies. The British and the French try to conserve employment in existing industries while the Germans try to progressively phase out mature industries. Since reunification, the former East Germany has become a somewhat closer source of low-cost, low-quality labor, subject to forms of economic colonization, not unlike the pattern in Italy.

**Japan.** Here we find a very different picture. Manufacturers responded to the paradox of rising demand and rising costs at home by increasing capital investment in fiber making, spinning, and weaving. Japan happens to make many of these capital goods, and the Japanese Ministry of International Trade and Industry encouraged firms to scrap obsolete machinery through a variety of incentive schemes.[35] In the weaving industry, for example, the ministry persuaded firms to limit output and invest in new air- and water-jet machines. Limiting output kept the price of cloth from falling and putting firms out of business, while the new machines were faster, enabling Japanese weavers to stay in business despite the higher labor costs.

At the same time, tariffs and other trade restrictions have been lowered, so that cheaper Korean, Hong Kong, Chinese, and Pakistani yarn, fabric, and finished clothing found their way onto the market and pushed out the less competitive firms. Japanese firms and policy makers have tried to hold on to as much of the industry as is feasible at prevailing domestic wage and price levels, through recapitalization and the management of output. At the same time, the cost of basic clothing to Japanese consumers has been kept down by allowing cheap imports in more freely.[36]

As a Japanese weaver said somewhat stoically to Ronald Dore, "We haven't got all that much time. What we did to Lancashire, Korea and China will do to us."[37] Meanwhile, in the more capital-intensive fiber business, Japanese firms are holding their own. Recognizing the limits to their own markets, giant chemical firms like Toray diversified into carbon fibers, and also bought into the Japanese fashion design firm Issey Miyake.[38] As a result of this dynamism in industrial policy and practice, Japan is a net exporter and real incomes were continually rising through the late 1980s. This has been accompanied by an explosive growth in the complexity of the rhythms of fashion and in the volume of fashion imports. A rapid proliferation into a complex, polyrhythmic system has lately taken the place of the more straightforward, status-driven consumption patterns of the postwar period of growth. This development is discussed in Japan in the sociological terms of the "rise of the micro-masses" or of the spread of postmodernism, which is often conceptualized as a form of postindustrial, information-intensive consumption.[39]

The fashion industry has been subject to the same innovative principles by which Japanese manufacturers have transformed the inflexible large-batch production techniques of Fordism into flexible yet efficient small-batch production, a system sometimes called "Sonyism."[40] This was achieved largely through the application of information technology and automation. Goods as diverse as stationary, vacuum cleaners, and pocket calculators now appear in seasonal ranges of distinct colors and shapes, manufactured with a flexible system combining advanced robotics and automation with highly competitive, low-tech sub-contracting.[41] The success of the Japanese economy in exporting high value-added goods and importing low value-added goods created a trade surplus, pushing up the value of the yen. So while the fashion system has developed very rapidly in a postmodern direction, and Japanese designers such as Issey Miyake, Yoji Yamamoto, and Rei Kawakubo have captured a slice of the local market, they have been less successful in exporting fashion garments than in exporting cars and consumer electronics. The very success of export industries where Japanese firms have a production advantage prevents the export of fashion goods.[42] This is partly because, unlike in Italy or Britain, there was much less investment in the development of cultural capital and its promotion on the global information landscape.

**Italy**. By trial and error, the Italians have managed to work out a coherent industry policy for fashion, clothing, and textiles, and have been the most successful at coming up from behind in exports. Where Japanese success in reinvigorating fiber and fabric making was based on coordinated policies of fixed capital investment, the Italian situation combined both fixed capital improvements and cultural capital development.

Italian fashion had a strong, if rather outmoded, center in Rome, dominated by craft-based high couture which imitated Parisian design for a local elite. With the development of Cinecitta as a film production base for American movies, Roman designers were able to find a promotional outlet for their quality craft product through the cinema. This helped attract American department stores, looking for alternatives to an increasingly idiosyncratic Paris couture. But the Rome-based scene remained an elite affair, slavishly imitating Paris, and as such, could not sustain an integrated fashion and clothing export industry. Northern fabric manufacturers launched a coordinated PR campaign for a native Italian design sensibility, applying strong political pressure to implement government schemes such as design schools. Fabric and ready-to-wear manufacturers also sought out promising designers to increase the cultural value-added content of their clothing products. Some new internationally famous designers such as Armani and Versace benefited from initial backing by textile manufacturers.

By the early 1960s, these various strategies were beginning to pay off. A distinctively Italian look based on Renaissance styles attracted media attention, giving Italian design a place in the information landscape.[43] Italian couturiers and manufacturers began receiving orders from American department stores. The basis of the industry was shifted from skilled craft production to industrial manufacturing and, after the explosive growth of the 1960s, to a combination of the two.

EMPORIO ARMANI

Firms such as Fiorucci[44] and later Benetton learned how to integrate the forms of demand stemming from pop consumption into their production and distribution systems. Benetton achieved a mix of high-quality, high-design content with low-cost and small batches by investing in a sophisticated, computerized dyeing plant, combined with the exploitation of unorganized Neapolitan pieceworkers to run up the garments. Like Chanel before him, Armani provided wardrobes for films to increase the visibility of his wares on the information landscape. The textile, clothing, and fashion industries succeeded in putting Milan on the map as a fashion center, while continuing to provide employment and export earnings—a rare achievement for an industrialized country. This was due in part to the availability of cheap, skilled native labor, and the fact that as a country with a trade deficit, Italian currency is undervalued and hence its exports are comparatively inexpensive. All the same, credit must be given to creative state policies, design innovation, and productive investment. A less charitable view would stress the role of tax evasion in the viability of Italian fashion and clothing firms. Gianfranco Ferre, Santo Versace, and Giorgio Armani have all had the kind of publicity money can't prevent for allegedly attempting to subvert the tax system.[45]

Finally, mention must be made of the strength of regional strategies in Northern Italy, based on regional chambers of commerce and patterns of alliance between local government, groups of mostly family-owned companies, and organized labor. Wool processing in Biella, the silk industry of Como, and the textile district of Prato are examples of regions that have reputations for innovative, high-quality, and highly flexible production. Maintaining a stable pool of highly skilled workers, high levels of capital investment, and strong trade associations and educational institutions, as well as concentrating related parts of the production process in close proximity, are key features of these regional industrial strategies.[46]

As these "stylized facts" indicate, the relation between forms of structural adjustment in industry and modes of consumption can vary widely from country to country. Due to the low-skill, labor-intensive operations endemic to garment production, clothing is one of the first industries to emerge in the industrializing process—and one of the first to decline if and when that process succeeds in generating capital accumulation, development of technique, and rising productivity and wages. These problems have been compounded by the cultural rhythms of pop, which make increasing standardization and scale in manufacturing unworkable.

The shift away from Fordist production techniques now occurring in the overdeveloped countries is necessitated in part by the postwar rise of living standards that Fordism itself created. While the growing affluence of many workers in the industrialized world created the conditions for participation of working people in the temporal culture of fashion, and in particular, of youth in pop culture, it has also necessitated massive adjustments in industrial organization. This in turn threatens the organized power of workers to maintain their share of income and their participation in the consumption of the surplus product.

The challenge for organized labor and policy makers within existing industries is to identify where the value-added components of the emerging industrial processes are likely to be. A related goal is to identify new industries that might grow out of a comparative advantage in skill associated with an existing but threatened industry. The aim in both cases is to create new jobs further up the skill, value-added, and technical sophistication hierarchies from new and emergent combinations of industrial and cultural capital.

# Tommy Hilfiger in the age of mass customization

## Paul Smith

The June 1995 issue of *Bobbin*, a garment industry trade journal, contained interviews with a number of high-ranking executives from the top forty apparel companies in the U.S. Each was asked to make some predictions about the industry and the challenges facing it in the run-up to the millennium. Of the primary concerns these industry leaders expressed, the first related to the organization of labor: they were clear about the need for continued downsizing, particularly within the domestic side of manufacturing. The second related to product development—they saw the need, in essence, to speed up the industry's process of product design, manufacture, and distribution in order to satisfy the ever changing and accelerating demands of retail outlets and their customers.[1]

These two areas of concern reflect the bipolar nature of the industry in the 1990s and in the era of the so-called globalization of economic processes. On the one hand, the "global" economy, dominated by Northern nations, is in the process of shifting the place of production to the South or the Third World, with the aim of reducing the costs of variable capital; in other words, core labor is being located on the periphery. On the other hand, or simultaneously, the place of consumption—and, of course, capital concentration—becomes ever more centralized in the North itself, opening up new channels of product distribution, marketing, and retailing.

In terms of the disposition of world labor power, then, this is a moment of redefinition, or of the search for a renewed vitality in capitalist rates of profit, and it is coincident with the tendency to abandon the old liberal productivist economic order and move toward the ideal, or the fantasy, of global capitalism. For the Northern "developed" nations, this shift has already subvented the rapid expansion and intensification of the means of consumption in the 1980s and '90s, provoking cultural changes and challenges as well as political and economic ones. The economic shape of the last two decades, especially here in the U.S., has been relatively clear in that respect: a downward turn in productive capital and a rise in the importance of financial capital have had the cultural effect of installing what can only be called a revolution in consumerism. For the garment industry, this revolution has had special relevance. The industry has responded by developing mass designer fashion, extending and expanding the role of mass-produced clothing, affecting all kinds of cultural arenas and encouraging the construction of cultural identifies by way of apparel choices. However, it is open to question whether the industry is in fact responding to cultural demand or whether it is producing that demand as a

**no sweat**

way of itself responding to the changing conditions of global capitalism. Much of the pressure on apparel companies to refunction their production, to contract it out and offshore it, or simply to sweat it in the domestic workplace, derives from a perceived functioning of the domestic market which is said to be more highly competitive than ever and to be driven by the demands of retail companies—especially department stores—which are themselves responding to straitened domestic circumstances.

Apparel manufacturers have argued that this cranking up is driven by retailers alone. The fact that the tendency is equally bound up with the manufacturers' own continual offshoring of labor, in response to globalization trends, is too often downplayed. Northern apparel producers have to compete with Southern labor, but they can scarcely do so in terms of simple cost—the social conditions and the consumerist nature of Northern societies cannot countenance a drop in wages sufficient to compete. Thus, other modes or areas of competitive advantage have to be found, and these tend to concentrate around the acceleration of sales and, therefore, the speeding up of product development and change. So, for example, the California project Garment 2000, a corporation and union cooperative exercise, specifically suggests that, "We can't compete with the foreign market on labor rates, so we're going for another niche—an accelerated turn-around time for garment production."[2] The possibility of such accelerated turnaround and delivery, provoked by the international labor conditions of the industry, has its effect then in the consumer markets of the North. The retail industry and the apparel companies themselves adjust to this acceleration with speedier fashion cycles and merchandise availability. In any case, apparel companies find themselves in a position where they have to create a demand for the ever more transient commodities in the retail space.

The companies themselves call this process "mass customization," according to a recent lengthy survey of industry practice in the *Daily News Record*.[3] Mass customization entails a number of components that are, if not relatively new for the industry, at least of increasingly central importance. The imperatives of mass customization boil down to three essentials: greater product variety in stores, higher turnover, and lower and better managed inventories. Success in each area depends upon increased cooperation between apparel companies and their retailing outlets. As one executive notes, "Retail partnership is more critical than ever before. We have to share information about the consumer." Such sharing is by now heavily dependent on the use of new information technologies, or what the industry calls "data mining." "We're heavily into Electronic Data Interchange," another executive explains. EDI helps increase the speed and flexibility of merchandise sourcing, the flow and distribution of goods, and their replenishment and inventorization. In general the industry is now seeking to cut down the time between retailers' orders and warehouse shipment. Some manufacturers now accelerate these processes even more by shipping pre-priced goods, which can be put on display with minimal checking by in-store workers.

EDI has a second essential function, that of enabling research into the habits of consumers—both groups and individuals. One company claims that, as a result of data mining, "On a daily basis, we know 75 percent of what is sold, down to the lot and size." Such statistics are used to "anticipate" consumer trends and to fine-tune inventory control, but also to contribute to what the industry euphemistically calls "consumer communications," a term that exceeds the traditional sense of advertising. Companies now expect to engage in "an ongoing dialog with the consumer"—a "dialog" encouraged by means of a whole array of mechanisms, from 800 phonelines, Internet communications and Web sites, to in-store surveys and special event sponsorship (both in and out of stores), in addition to the more familiar use of visual and print media advertising.

Tommy Hilfiger's clothing company, TOM Inc., has been among the leading exponents in this intensified process of mass customization over the last few years. Indeed, Hilfiger

# no sweat

clothing can be seen as an extreme case of how the idea of mass designer fashion operates. Mass designer fashion is a specific formation within the industry; it is not equivalent to traditional haute couture (which is often dependent upon highly artisanal means of production and is still somewhat outside the circuits of globalizing capital that nurture the mass clothing industry). Nor is mass designer fashion equivalent to standard garment production (which relies on reordering of staple and relatively stable goods season after season). Mass designer fashion is that peculiar formation which occurs within this nexus of the globalizing economy and the concomitant expansion of the means of consumption. Almost by definition it demands the capture of ever wider segments of the mass market at the same time as it needs to maintain familiar standards of product differentiation between brands, and offer frequent variation. Thus Hilfiger's relative importance and visibility in this context is in part a result of an ongoing strategy which has put his company in a position to cover just about all segments of the clothing market, but which also marks the products as identifiable and unique (the familiar Hilfiger logo and red-white-and-blue designs), offering appreciably variable "looks" or themes from season to season and year to year. While older companies like Levi Strauss, Timberland, or even Ralph Lauren have been slow in entering the mass designer fashion stakes—some being particularly wary of attempting to enter ethnically or racially identified areas of consumer culture—and while many other companies have been content with their long established market niches and hierarchies of market segmentation, the story of Hilfiger's company is just the opposite.

Beginning with a line of preppie-looking, clean-cut, and conservative sportswear (similar to that offered by the Gap, but somewhat more expensive), Hilfiger set out in the early 1990s to compete against department store staple lines like Ralph Lauren and Liz Claiborne with essentially Young Republican clothing. In the course of only a few years, this basically khaki, crew, and button-down WASP style, while remaining a constant theme in Hilfiger collections, has been submitted to variations which were intended to bring the product closer to hip hop style: bolder colors, bigger and baggier styles, more hoods and cords, and more prominence for logos and the Hilfiger name. These variations on a house-in-the-Hamptons theme opened up the doorway to black consumers, and Hilfiger's status is often closely linked to his popularity among African Americans. But at the same time, that market has clearly been only one focus for Hilfiger's ambitions, set on maintaining and expanding markets among nonblack consumers, and continually multiplying the range of products offered. In addition to hip hop styles, Hilfiger now sells golf wear, casual sportswear, jeans, sleepwear, underwear, spectacles, fragrances, and even telephone beepers. Tommy has recently moved into women's wear, and offers a women's cologne to go with the popular men's line. Not content with crossing all these areas of the mass market, Hilfiger seems currently to be conducting a foray into more classic designer markets with high-fashion shows, marked by his appearance at the British fashion shows in 1996 and by the introduction of a line of brightly colored men's wear that was clearly his attempt to become more of a haute couture designer.

Hilfiger's success has been quite astounding since the initial public offering of TOM in 1992. The company now has over 850 in-store department store sales points in the U.S. In addition, there are now almost fifty Hilfiger specialty stores across the country, a figure that has almost doubled in the course of two years. The company's annual report in early 1996 showed that revenue in the last quarter of 1995 was over $130 million, a 47 percent increase over the previous year. The company's cost for goods sold was less than $72 million, leaving more than $58 million in gross profits—a rate of more than 80 percent. The sound financial health of the company ensures its regular appearance on stockbrokers' to-buy lists, even though share prices keep rising. Early in 1995, the small consortium of TOM's original investors—which had bought the company from Mohan Murjani in the late 1980s—sold their remaining TOM stock for over $50 million, after a year in which the value of the stock had increased by 106 percent. Hilfiger

# no sweat

himself was one of this small group, of course, and after his profit-taking he remained as an employee of the company, drawing more than $6 million a year in salary.

The economic success of TOM is explicable largely because the company has led the way in many aspects of mass customization. Hilfiger still does not have (so far as I'm aware) a Web site, or other of the mechanisms that apparel companies now routinely use. But TOM's corporate strategies have been ahead of those of many of its competitors, stressing the acceleration of product delivery, new forms of retailing partnership, innovative EDI usage for inventories and customer tracking, and of course, the speedy and timely introduction of new lines and redesigned goods, assuring consumers a wide range of product choices (something which Hilfiger himself sees as crucial in provoking and expanding demand).

TOM has been especially willing—again, leading the field—to engage in what is now the standard industry practice of licensing. TOM has licensing agreements with some of the world's major clothing companies. This network of links has been methodically and aggressively built up in just the last few years: Pepe plc for jeans, Stride Rite for shoes, Liberty Optical for eyewear, Estée Lauder for fragrance, Russell-Newman for shirts, Jockey for underwear, and so on. While licensing agreements probably have little impact on consumer consciousness, one advantage they have for a company like TOM is that they offer the borrowed cachet of known and respected manufacturers. This is all-important in negotiating sales points with department stores and generally in testifying to the quality of TOM products. Most of TOM's retailing partnerships are with department stores, and in 1995 about 70 percent of Hilfiger's products were sold at those venues. Added to TOM's strategies for speeding up product design, delivery, and turnover, licensing helps ensure access to what is still the principal channel for clothing sales in the U.S., where 65 percent of all clothing is sold by only thirty-five companies, the majority of which are chain retailers with department stores in malls and urban spaces all across the country.

One reason why the department stores are crucial for mass designer fashion is that many of them are located in the very malls where teenagers proverbially hang out. But perhaps a more important reason is that most big department stores offer their own credit cards which are relatively easy to obtain even if the consumer has low income or a bad credit rating. The industry standard is to offer such cards on the spot with only minimal credit checking and with an initial credit line (usually somewhere between $250 and $750, a relatively low risk for stores) that would encourage the purchase of, say, one complete outfit which would then be paid off over a period of about a year. Naturally, consumers pay heavily for this privilege, since interest rates on department store cards are typically about 21 percent per annum, almost 5 percent higher than the average U.S. credit card rate. However, this cost does not seem to deter those who can access these credit lines. In both Britain and the U.S., clothing purchases constitute a huge part of consumer credit spending. A measure of the importance of this phenomenon is that the all-time record monthly credit spending in Britain — £6.9 billion in June 1996—"was due in large part to clothing purchases."[4] U.S. credit card debt in this era of the expansion of the means of consumption passed the $1 trillion mark late in 1995 and has continued to climb ever since. The peak production of this sea of debt occurs not at the Christmas holiday season, but rather at the "back-to-school" season when, according to the American Express Retail Index, a majority of U.S. parents expect to spend an average of $363 per child, and a goodly proportion of that spending will be done on credit cards. The same report suggests that Hilfiger clothing would account for 5 percent of all back-to-school purchases.[5] In this respect, it's quite clear how TOM's strategies intersect with the expansion of the means of consumption.

Where the nexus of consumer-retailer-manufacturer is always most apparent, however, is in the area of advertising. Although TOM, as I've already said, has not explored the area of "consumer communications" quite so thoroughly as companies like Levi Strauss or retailers like Carson Pirie Scott, Hilfiger's exploitation of advertising media has been both thorough and path-

# no sweat

breaking. Perhaps the most prominent feature of Hilfiger's strategy in this realm has been the use of high-visibility consumers. In a way that has still not been copied by many other apparel companies (Nike being an important exception), Hilfiger has always ensured that his clothing is found on celebrity bodies. In the last few year his clothing has been publicly displayed by sports figures like Don Nelson, coach of the New York Knicks, popular musicians such as Michael Jackson and the women of TLC, and by black male models like Tyson Beckford. In a series of 1994 spots on the music cable channel, VH1, Hilfiger tried to keep tabs on a more mainstream audience too, featuring performers like Tori Amos and Phil Collins. Any of these celebrities is, of course, a trendsetter, whose mostly urban image is intended to then become desirable in the shopping meccas of suburban malls.

Most important, Hilfiger clothes have been sported by a whole succession of African-American rap musicians. The story of Hilfiger seeing Grand Puba in the street wearing his clothes and inviting him to wear Hilfiger in public appearances is perhaps apocryphal, but it does speak to the general strategy that Hilfiger has adopted in relation to garnering a huge clientele among African Americans. Frequently donated Hilfiger outfits for use in performances and music videos, rappers have functioned as conduits of approval and authorization—authenticity, perhaps—for this white business attempting to sell what are essentially white styles to black consumers. In that sense, Hilfiger has used prominent African Americans in ways that, while they are often less formalized and contractual than the relationship between, say, Nike and Michael Jordan or PepsiCo and Michael Jackson, essentially serve the same purpose.

A certain rank of black sportspeople and entertainment figures (usually men) act as what I call a "regulatory elite" in U.S. black culture. These are people who, earning millions of dollars a year in the face of the chronic and systematic immiseration and devastation of black communities in the U.S., are elevated to the status of cultural icons and are taken to bear virtually the whole burden of representing blackness in the culture. Even though the bill for the rewards collected by this regulatory elite are footed by predominantly white capital, their cultural significance stems from being venerated as bearers of black identity (by both blacks and whites, most likely—by whites wishfully thinking that racial divisions could be elided by their presence; by blacks, wishfully thinking that the status and spoils of someone like Michael Jordan are not eccentric).

Some of the force of this mechanism of regulation could be seen on display, of course, after the O. J. Simpson trial in 1995, when the not-guilty verdict was greeted by African Americans as a triumph for their race. A less spectacular or public instance, narrated by Darcy Frey in his book about black basketball hopefuls, *The Last Shot*, gives another insight into the workings of this system. Frey tells a story of trying to interview some promising young basketball players in the Coney Island projects, only to be told by their parents that he must pay large sums of money for the privilege.[6] The point, of course (and indeed, the point of Frey's whole book), is that within this one black community, the system whereby the regulatory elite is established is known and used as one of few possible ways of escaping the projects. Frey goes on to tell how the superstar elite is formed, beginning with the injection into the black community of money and inducements by sportswear manufacturers like Nike and by the white-run National Basketball Association (NBA), while the majority of the community remains in poverty, bound by totally limited expectations and possibilities. It is in this sense that the strange system of tokenizing black stardom can be described as regulatory.

And yet it is no simple matter in U.S. culture to criticize this black regulatory elite, since it carries such a burden of African-American identity. It does, of course, become easier to criticize when someone so prominent as Michael Jordan shrugs off the ethical and political problems in his sponsorship relation with Nike and its Third World labor practices. Called to answer for the contradiction of his position, Jordan simply suggested that he could trust Nike "to do the right thing."[7] But for the most part, and as Jordan in fact demonstrates, the system

does its work, and the African-American stars can count on there being little concern about the cultural and financial gap between them and the African Americans who are called upon to be their loyal and admiring audience.

For Hilfiger's company, the deployment of rappers like Grand Puba and Snoop Doggy Dogg in extended "consumer communications" has constituted a crucial part of the process of mass customization and has enabled a deliberate and thoroughgoing entry into the black youth market. It is, however, just one such component, and its efficacy depends absolutely on Hilfiger's coordinated effort in other areas of mass customization. The effectiveness of TOM's assault on this particular segment of the market is a function of the successful implementation of industry-wide strategies which have to be seen in conjunction with capital's tendency to outsource labor, to cut the costs of variable capital, and to expand the means of consumption in Northern markets. According to TOM's 1995 annual report, the five places where most Hilfiger clothing is made are Hong Kong, Sri Lanka, Macao, Indonesia, and Montebello, California. In that light, when Hilfiger gives away clothes to rappers, or establishes a loose professional alliance with African Americans like Def Jam boss Russell Simmons (also the owner of Phat Farm clothing company), or hires Kidada Jones (daughter of record tycoon Quincey Jones) to appear in his ads, these are in a sense epiphenomenal activities. What is crucial is the political and economic circuits in which they have their effects. Similarly, when black kids wear TOM merchandise, adopting the clothes and accessories and the Tommy logo as signs not just of fashionability but even of racial authenticity, they are doing more than just establishing a cultural identity and communality. Equally, they are placing themselves in a particular relation to political-economic circuits for which the possibility of their consuming in this way is one of capitalism's central desiderata or imperatives at this juncture when capital is dreaming of globalizing itself.

Of course, not all of Hilfiger's desired consumer audience and clientele is necessarily content with the spectacle of so many black males devotedly sporting Hilfiger clothing and willy-nilly directing African-American dollars into the Hilfiger coffers. One of the most vibrant forums on the Internet where the issues of fashion consumption are discussed is the "chat-room" of Streetsound,[8] a wildly energetic and mind-boggling torrent of opinion, most of which seems to be submitted by African-American men. Hilfiger's clothing and the operations

**no sweat**

of his company are perennial topics—a testament in itself to the central role his fashions play right now in black culture. But even though Hilfiger merchandise appears to enjoy support and patronage in towns from coast to coast, there are some dissenting voices.

The most common opposition to Hilfiger on this site appears to be an objection to the very principle of black patronage of white business. One such posting will give the flavor of many similar ones:

> Y'all are nothing but Tommy's wench. Some of you do not even have enough money to support the people who put on the jams (the place where you show how real you are and get your new bitch). Yet you spend your last fucking dollar to support some yout' in New York who doesn't give a fuck about give a flying fuck about you. Y'all are real stupid!!!

Such objections are both common and powerful—especially when seen as versions of how black identity might be safeguarded while rejecting the regulatory means put into place by white capitalism, and they echo longstanding debates within black culture. But obviously, they fall short of making connections between cultural and economic processes in the era of global capitalism and the age of mass customization.

This can be seen in an even starker light if we consider the nature of many of the advertisements for Hilfiger merchandise that appear in popular magazines. The principal motif in nearly all of them is the American flag. For instance, in Hilfiger's 1996 campaign for his new line of jeans, the American flag is spread out behind the figure of Kidada Jones, or is apparently the pillow for Ivanka Trump's pouting face. The American theme is even more overt—in the sense that it is verbal as much as visual—in ads for Hilfiger fragrances. The men's fragrance, Tommy, is now advertised under the slogan, "the real american fragrance" (after the first few advertising rounds, when it was called "the new american fragrance"), while the ads for the women's perfume, Tommy Girl, call it "a declaration of independence."

In the double context of, on the one hand, increasingly internationalized economic processes (where core labor is zoned to the periphery), and on the other hand, rampant mass customization (with its production of regulated subcultural identities in the North), TOM's use of this American-national motif is utterly symptomatic. The display of the U.S. flag and the appeal to American identity obscure both the international and the subnational processes that are at stake in the political-economic and cultural formations of this our new world order. Another way of putting this is to say that the U.S. national motif precisely names the power which presides over a division between the zoned labor of the South and massified consumption in the North and confirms that division as an opposition of interests.

These U.S. nationalist emblems in TOM do have the unintended consequence of highlighting some of the complexities and difficult issues that are involved in thinking through the politics of the present situation. What we might call "production activists" in the North sometimes have a limited view of the way labor issues relate to the processes of consumption in the North, and often seem reluctant to address the fact that capitalism deliberately sets off the Northern consumer's "right" to forge cultural identity through consumption against the economic and social rights of core labor. But it is in everyone's interest to challenge such an imposed opposition between the interests of core labor and the interests of massified consumers.

There are, that is, potential benefits in stressing the fact that international labor issues are inextricably tied to the current expansion of the means of consumption in the North. A sharper understanding of the cultural consequences of mass customization might allow production activists to more effectively address those cultural constituencies whose interests are routinely represented as disjunct from the interests of laborers in the periphery. By the same token, cultural activists and organizers, especially within minority communities in the North, might perhaps be able to intensify their opposition to the international aspect of economic processes in the recognition that these are what underpin—indeed, regulate—contemporary forms of cultural identity.

Not that anyone would claim that such recognitions would immediately bring to a halt capital's double-headed movement—the international reorganization of labor power and the expansion of the means of consumption. But they might help produce a bit more anger.

# the problem with ugly chic

Robin Givhan

Ugly has become fashionable. The secondhand, mix-and-match style of the world's poor is now chic. The design industry has found inspiration in the global recycling bin.

The clothes that we discard and ship to distant countries are coming back to us. Returned by some downtown designer searching the past for the next new thing. He may find his inspiration on an exotic vacation, on the evening news, in a music video, or in the depths of a used-clothing bin. Rich Americans are beginning to dress like poor Africans who are dressing like well-to-do Americans did some twenty or thirty years ago.

One wonders who is getting the better deal.

Models are looking more like famine victims than raging beauties, slouching down the runways of Europe and New York with sadness and desperation scripted across their scrawny, childish faces. These wan mannequins appear dazed, sullen, uninspired. They stare out at the audience with vacant eyes. Their shocking looks, evoking poverty and disenfranchisement, represent the latest Seventh Avenue styling brilliance. Impoverishment—or at least the appearance of it—has become an artistic accessory.

Following the meteoric rise of the supermodels in the 1980s, models became younger, thinner, and blander. Gone were the statuesque women with impossibly long limbs and runway struts full of confidence and bravura. The glorification of Kate Moss was the beginning. The British waif, who was discovered in New York's Kennedy Airport, was so slim that vandals took to scrawling the phrase "feed me" underneath her emaciated image in Calvin Klein ads that decorated bus stops.

In contrast to the toned Naomi Campbell and curvaceous Cindy Crawford came a legion of girls, like aristocrats Stella Tennant and Jodie Kidd, prized for their gangly bodies and appalling posture. Their hollow-cheeked look is that of the poor and hungry, not of the rich and superthin. Hip bones protrude from beneath clingy jersey dresses, the '90s version of the beauty mark. Models are hardly sex symbols anymore. They are burdened souls. Pretty is passé.

Recently, British *Vogue* was threatened with a boycott by an advertiser publicly objecting to the painfully thin models that dominate the pages of the fashion publication. In response to the aborted protest, the magazine promised readers a "fat issue," which the editor plans to fill with models who look well fed, healthy… but in the fashion world, abnormal. At about the same time, *Allure* ran a story about the inner workings of a live-in clinic for anorexics. Readers

angrily pointed out that the clinic's residents actually looked healthier than the models on the magazine's accompanying fashion spreads.

All of these skeletal models are decked out in clothes that most Americans associate with thrift stores, secondhand shops, and back-of-the-closet rejects. The colors in these shirts and trousers are murky, dull, and seemingly faded from a lifetime of wear. There are depressing shades of institutional green and odd hues of yellow—not cheerful sunshine or lemon, but the color of dull straw or sunbaked grass. Murky brown has replaced black as the ubiquitous neutral. The patterns are dizzying and confusing, suggesting antiquated, rusted pipes or ducts, at times recalling the pattern of static on an old television set. These crazy, crisscrossing designs are intended to jar the aesthetic sensibilities.

The bulk of this latest high fashion looks cheap, made of fabrics reminiscent of the piling, oft-derided polyester of the 1970s. Occasionally, hemlines don't fall as smoothly as the discerning shopper might want. But the prices are far from bargain basement. Antifreeze-green evening gowns cost $3,500, mud-brown trousers go for $900. It looks as if the embarrassing mistakes that even the best designer sometimes falls prey to are making their way not only to the runway but also into the stores, in exclusive lines and knockoffs.

Nor is the trend confined to women's wear. The men's wear market has been inundated by a resuscitated disco style. Guys dressed à la pimp stroll down the runway of New York designer John Bartlett. Audiences are treated to bulked-up models whose sculpted muscles strain against too-tight trousers or shiny polyester shirts. The leisure suit is back, an extravagant mix of Euro-trash, New York porn star, Superfly, and ungainly American tourist. In short, a style born of every '70s and '80s cliché formerly lost to the secondhand clothes house.

The leader of this stampede of poor-boy and poor-girl chic is Miuccia Prada, whose grandfather founded the family's leather goods company in 1913. Prada the younger is well educated both politically and culturally. And in spite of (or perhaps because of) her immersion in good taste and social consciousness, she introduced the aesthetically shocking ready-to-wear lines that have transformed the family's rather staid business into one of the hottest fashion houses in the industry. Annual sales of her women's ready-to-wear collection are reportedly $100 million, and the company is branching out into the beauty business with a line of cosmetics. (Will there be dark powders to create under eye shadows? Odd hues of yellow foundation to give the skin a touch of jaundice?)

No sooner had this strange new fashion hit the runways than celebrities began turning up in influential and popular magazines styled to look, if not unattractive, at least not quite so prosperous. Starlets used pomade to make their hair look as if it hadn't touched water in weeks. It was a mark of prestige to look a little rough around the edges, a bit unpolished. Ugly was officially a trend in both Europe and the United States.

"There's a certain bad taste, but it looks so charming," Prada told the *Washington Post* after one of her fashion shows in 1995. "When we do the fittings, we say, 'How awful—and how charming.'"

Ugly and its purveyors like Prada rose to the top in part because they are so extreme, so startling, and so lucky. Ugly arrived on the heels of school-girl chic, the revival of Jackie Kennedy style, and the umpteenth return of glamour. Politics was particularly divisive, youthful malaise the story of the moment. It was time for something new, different, and controversial.

Embraced by fashion's most elite players, ugly has been endorsed by top designers like Italian Gianni Versace, Frenchwoman Martine Sitbon, Austrian Helmut Lang, and a host of American and European manufacturers. "With every collection Prada does, she makes a change and she does it before the others," says Polly Mellen, creative director of *Allure*, to the *Washington Post*. "I admire everything she does."

Mellen, renowned for her aesthetic sensibility and a soothsayer-like ability to predict trends, loaded *Allure* with scowling models and chintzy-looking clothes. She has been spotted along the New York runways cheering on young models who look so hungry that it is difficult to imagine how they stand upright let alone strut convincingly down a catwalk.

There is a fragile beauty to be found in some of these ugly clothes. Sometimes customers claim they can see in their faded colors the same elegance that antique hunters often find in a chair or vase. And in some cases, the clothes are *so* ugly, *so* strange, *so* ridiculous, they become amusing. Not fashion, but a joke. Campy. Delightful.

Mostly, though, customers aren't really supposed to *like* these clothes. This is fashion with a message, a point of view. There are plenty of pretty frocks already in the stores. These clothes are intended to make folks rethink their notion of beauty, reassess their idea of fashion (and, of course, give them something completely different to buy).

Perhaps this is why ugly has passed muster as *intellectual* fashion. Here are clothes for folks too wise, too intense to be bothered with silliness like frills and flattering colors. The look of poverty is rendered chic, honorable, and cool. The fact that so many people don't get it or have such a negative reaction only makes the jarring style that much more alluringly exclusive.

"I hope [people] don't understand completely because I want to be different," Prada explains to the *Washington Post*. "They can't understand completely because it's very personal."

The rich are dressing like the poor, and some experts have commended them for it. The upper classes are expressing their empathy with those less fortunate, or so the argument goes. In reality, fashionable folk are selective about the "style" of poverty they appropriate. The new chic does not include, for instance, old T-shirts, torn jeans, camouflage painter's pants, Starter jackets, or overstuffed duffel bags. And of course, the rich have the option of rejecting the downtrodden style, unlike the homeless men and women they pass on the streets.

In many ways, the new poverty chic is directly related to the prevailing obsession with decades-old fashions. Not every castoff trend finds its way back to the designer's sketchpad. Sometimes a rejected style does fade into oblivion. Often, though, styles are resurrected under the rubric "retro chic." Ugly is retro gone wild, a revival that occurs in defiance of taste, beauty, or acceptability.

Retro chic was born of the flea markets and secondhand clothing stores frequented by New York downtown designers and the young kids on the street who inspire them. But in a broader sense, the look also reflects the styles of the struggling. Sometimes, during the large catwalk shows held in New York's Bryant Park, it's difficult to discern the fashion elite from the part-time clerk who lives from paycheck to paycheck, so often is their dress similar. Junior editors from magazines have gushing fashion moments at the sight of some designer's vinyl maxi-coat, artificially hardened with lacquer, coming down a runway. A few blocks away, a street peddler may be selling, for a few bucks, a similar item scavenged from the dumpster

# no sweat

behind an upper-crust apartment building. The former reeks of creativity. The latter is about necessity. But they are inextricably linked in design and appearance.

Designers love rescuing silhouettes and fabrics from the same used-clothes bins where the disenfranchised are forced to pull their daily wardrobes. Shabby chic no longer refers just to overstuffed sofas and slipcovered chairs but also to the wardrobes of the well heeled. Everyday, in all design formats, our castoffs are being reborn as high fashion.

Designers often spend their weekends rummaging the flea markets and junk shops of downtown New York. Designers such as Todd Oldham and Anna Sui are renowned for their ability to stay close to the "street" even as their businesses become ever more successful and hightone. When Sui was in her Victorian period, critics marveled at her talent for conjuring such an eccentric style, but one only need dig through the nearest antique clothing store to find the authentic versions of Sui's artistry.

No one has benefited more from junk store sojourns than downtown designer Marc Jacobs, the darling of the fashion press for his luxurious variations on thrift-store cheapies. Jacobs has offered women ill-fitting sweaters knitted out of cashmere. His dowdy, below-the-knee skirts might be sewn out of silk, but they have the look of a charitable contribution to Goodwill or the Salvation Army. While Jacobs isn't exactly recycling clothes, he is recycling the *idea* of them, the look and the style.

Paris-based designer Martin Margiela, however, *does* recycle clothes. Why stitch up a 1920s-style opera coat when one can pop down to the nearest thrift shop and pick up the real thing? It is a rhetorical question that Margiela poses with each collection. He operates a factory-style showroom in which workers take used denim jeans, paint them or cut them off. Margiela calls the result a new design. He stitches antique silk scarves into skirts. He puts no labels in his garments. He has staged shows in an old Salvation Army quarter. And he has gone so far as to present a "new" collection of his greatest hits.

Belgian designer Dries Van Noten is also known for his slightly oversized silhouettes and delicate, antique-style fabrics, hailed for his ability to delve into the flea markets and emerge with a lost style that is marketable. Consider the garments and fabrics that fill the pages of fashion magazines: maxi-coats, long cardigan coats, safari jackets, jersey dresses, bootleg pants, Hush Puppies, flat-front trousers, Ultrasuede, velour, polyester.

# no sweat

As a term, retro chic is redundant. It goes without saying that if it's chic, it must be retro. There is little else.

The remarkable thing is not that designers play fast and loose with the notions of originality and newness. What is amazing is that *we* buy the stuff. Designer reputations blossom, and we wind up dressing in ways that mimic the citizens of Third World nations.

"The only place people naturally are wearing this look is in Third World countries and African countries where we offload clothes after their life cycle," according to fashion and retail consultant David Wolfe in the *Washington Post*. We spend thousands of dollars to dress like those who spend a few cents to wear our castoffs. Exotic poverty is in vogue.

Consider this scenario. A woman decides to do a bit of spring cleaning and flings open her closet doors to rid her home of the piles of clothes she hasn't worn in almost a decade. She begins by tossing out all of those power suits bought during the '80s, then a pair of gauchos, skirts that fall to about mid-calf, jackets with lapels just a tad too wide, jumpsuits that make her feel like one of Charlie's angels. She realizes that her days of wearing bellbottoms and the outlandish disco patterns of the '70s are over, and so she stuffs another Hefty bag with those pieces. She may even turn to her husband's closet and begin a mad cleaning frenzy there. Into more plastic bags go leisure suits, Sansabelt trousers, clingy Quiana shirts, and a seasoned pair of Hush Puppies.

Then she hauls her load down to the local Salvation Army, assuming the clothes will benefit some underprivileged person in her community. Or perhaps they will be sold piece by piece to kids looking to play dress-up, or to a seamstress who can run up a few stitches here and there and make them wearable again.

This process is repeated thousands of times all over the United States by people who envision their clothes somehow being absorbed into a vast, mysterious clothing cycle that benefits the poor. In reality, the secondhand clothes end up with the brand new clothes lining the racks of fashion retailers.

About 70 percent of the clothes donated to the Salvation Army are sold abroad, according to a May 1996 CNN report. These sales generate some $30 million a year to help the organization run its drug and alcohol rehabilitation programs. In 1995 alone, the United States exported $235 million worth of secondhand clothes. About a third of this clothing is imported by countries in Sub-Saharan Africa.

According to a report in the *Dallas Morning News*, the invasion of bundles of American secondhand clothing now threatens Kenya's domestic textile industry. In a country where the gross national product per capita is about $260 a year, most folks, including professionals such as teachers and nurses, cannot afford to buy garments produced domestically, even though these clothes may be considered relatively inexpensive by American standards. So while tourists buy made-in-Africa garb, native shoppers go to open-air markets where they choose garments from the hundreds of pounds of used American clothes bearing the logos of well-known manufacturers and (occasionally) designers. They choose the clothes that we wore— sometimes more than a decade ago—for their durability and cachet.

Designers are not exactly dashing off to Kenya to peruse the flea markets for fashion ideas. Still, industry stars from Ralph Lauren to Romeo Gigli regularly venture—both literally and figuratively—to distant lands in search of inspiration. They go with open minds ready to embrace or appropriate fresh ideas, unusual fabrics, and innovative ways of dressing. They may be reminded of the practicality of the sarong. Or they might be taken with batik prints, mud cloth, or tie-dyed fabric. On occasion, they return ready to dress their clients in a wardrobe inspired by the African diaspora, from dashikis to oversized hip hop jeans.

Ugly style, however, comes with more baggage than its exotic connections. It reflects not only the style of a group of people, but their living conditions as well. Ugly fashion, this conglomeration of retro looks and rejected fabrics and colors, is the look seen on the streets of African nations. It is also the style worn by immigrants for whom money is scarce. It is a look that reflects straitened circumstances. And it is distressing that some designers and consumers are willing to transform an unfortunate state into a style that retail consultants say is being purchased and worn by veritable "trust fund" babies.

For some, the embrace of ugly signifies an underlying desire to shed the accoutrements of wealth and to connect with those less privileged. For others, it is yet another chapter in the book of slumming.

# no sweat

274 Consider that the first segment of the retail industry to show signs of rebounding from years of dismal sales is the high-end luxury market. Names like Gucci, Hermes, Neiman Marcus, and Chanel are the ones separating shoppers from their hundred-dollar bills. In this context, "ugly" must be seen as a callous mockery of global poverty. The rich can don expensive versions of too-tight shirts, skirts with sagging waistlines, and shoes that appear scuffed and scarred. For them it is simply "a look." The poor will continue to line up at the used-clothing bins and buy for a buck or a few cents the rejects of the privileged.

Unlike other consumer products that reach the poor through a trickle-down effect, clothing trends increasingly move from the street to the salon. But as a style travels farther and farther away from its street origins, it is never fully divorced from the circumstances of its birth. It reminds us that wealth, exclusivity, and creativity—three of the basic ingredients of fashion—so often depend on the poor, resourceful masses.

# a *new* kind of rag trade?

Angela McRobbie

If we are to understand fashion as a vigorous cultural phenomenon, we must see it as a series of social processes involving mutual dependencies between each sector, from design and manufacture right through to magazines, advertising, and consumption. Likewise, if feminists want to escape the political paralysis that afflicts any vision of real change and improvement in the industry as a source of work and employment, we need an analysis which gathers together these constitutive parts and brings people involved at each stage into a dialogue. This has tended not to happen because it is assumed, especially among feminists, that there is an unbridgeable gap between, at one end of the spectrum, the women who make the clothes and, at the other end, those who eventually wear them. I will attempt here to describe those points at which political opportunities for dialogue and change do arise. This in turn should demonstrate why it is a mistake to view the fashion sector as the unmanageable thing it appears to be, discouraging close scrutiny of a fundamental area of human activity and employment.

Back in the 1970s, feminists drew attention to the exploitive conditions that prevailed in clothing manufacture and production on a global scale, and especially in the developing countries. Later, attention came to be focused on the realm of fashion representation, resulting in a barrage of assaults on fashion images of women in advertising and in magazines. Through the medium of clothes, it was argued, these images idealized forms of female beauty that are unattainable for most women and girls, giving rise to almost universal anxiety, self-hatred, and possibly eating disorders. This critique was then followed by a wholesale attack on consumer culture and the role fashion played in enslaving women to the imperative to buy. At this point in feminist thinking, fashion could only be seen as a bad thing. But then something happened, and by the mid-1980s fashion became, if not a good thing, at least not such a bad thing. What brought about this feminist revision?

By pushing to one side the difficult and seemingly unsolvable problems of sweatshop economies and child labor, feminist scholars began to reconsider those aspects of fashion that brought pleasure to women (and when they were able to admit it, to many of these feminists themselves). The guilt factor had hindered the feminist left, it was now suggested, by preventing an engagement with and understanding of the small, stubborn enjoyments of everyday life that are such a vital part of women's culture. Feminists ran the risk of political marginality and elitism by appearing to place themselves above ordinary women. It wasn't long before a flood of studies appeared which reclaimed commercial cultures of femininity as more open and disputatious than had previously been imagined. Fashion, romance, and even shopping could give rise to transgressive pleasures and defiant delights that were important to girls and women. There is a host of literature in this vein, including some of my own previous work on girls' and women's magazines.[1]

However, this reconceptualization of fashion often required silence on the question of the point of origin of clothes or the identity and working conditions of those who make them, since this would bring into view the suffering of "other" women. Alternately, knitting and home-dressmaking could be rediscovered as part of a tradition of female leisure culture (like quilting in the U.S.) as long as these activities were done for creative pleasure rather than for pay.[2] In fact, these remained part of the household economies in Britain until the late 1950s, and in some cases into the early '60s. If a mother couldn't knit or sew (and most women could do at least one of these), she would have to pay a local dressmaker or knitter, since ready-to-wear clothing and quality knitwear remained beyond the reach of most family budgets.

In effect, the emphasis on the social meaning of fashion in contemporary culture and in everyday life has often occurred at the expense of thinking seriously about the work that goes into making fashion consumption possible. But the analysis of consumption should not require neglect of the conditions of production. A new starting point for a feminist politics of fashion has to bridge this divide and encompass six major stages in the fashion cycle: manufacture and production; the practices of design; education and training; retailing and distribution; the magazine and image industry; and the practices of consumption. In the pages that follow, I will provide a brief account of the main dynamics of these sectors, drawing on some of the material from my own recent research on this subject. I will argue that fashion can be redefined as a feminist issue in a way that avoids both the deep pessimism of the approach to labor and production and the celebratory zeal of the more recent attention to women's pleasure in consumption. If the former envisages no light at the end of the tunnel, the latter runs the even greater risk of political complacency or indeed the flight from politics itself.

**Garment manufacture and production.** There has been a good deal of interest in these areas within the socialist feminist tradition of scholarship in the U.K. Most recently, Sheila

Rowbotham and Swasti Mitter have looked in depth at patterns of exploitation of women workers in the free trade zones and also at new forms of self-organization, while Jane Tate has developed further the extensive research on British women homeworkers. Annie Phizacklea's *Unpacking the Fashion Industry* offers the most useful account of recent developments in clothing production. In particular, she shows how new flexible units of production have sprung up in large cities, replacing the "sunset" factories of northern England which, for over a hundred years, produced textiles and clothing for both the home market and for export.[3] Some argue that if not for Marks and Spencers' commitment to use U.K. suppliers, most of these factories would have disappeared much sooner. However, Marks and Spencers has now joined the other large fashion chains, including C&A and the Hepworth Group (which together control an astounding 51 percent of the U.K. fashion and clothing market) in outsourcing up to 40 percent of their garments.

Phizacklea shows how, from the early 1980s, under the banner of Thatcher's new "enterprise culture," tiny units of production began to appear in London and the Midlands. Asian men, cashiered by the car factories and their subsidiaries, used their modest redundancy packages to establish themselves as small-scale garment entrepreneurs. This was possible because fashion remained a low-investment sector, requiring minimal space, a few sewing machines, an electronic cutter, and a press. Most important, these men had at their disposal a steady supply of cheap female labor within the immediate Asian community. Patriarchal family relations precluded work for these women outside the community, and financial need forced them to work long hours in tiny workshops or at home. Positioned on the wage floor of the labor market with all the forces of racial disadvantage weighing against them, these women continue to provide extraordinarily cheap labor for the Cut, Make, and Trim chain of production.

In the U.K., then, it helps to see the "return of the sweatshop," ordinarily discussed as a *pure* result of globalization and/or import competition, in the context of Thatcher's own economic policies. Enterprise culture was as much a matter of avoiding unemployment and dependence on benefits as it was about setting up in business. And in the new business environment mandated by Thatcherism, there was no room for trade unionism, let alone any provision for sickness, holiday, or maternity pay. One of the results was the new flexible

# no sweat

sweatshop—a potent example of the intensification of labor which has become almost the norm for those in employment in contemporary British society. For example, in my last home in North London, neighbors on either side participated in the Cut, Make, and Trim economy. On one side, an Asian grandmother worked as a child-minder during the day. All through the night we could hear the whirring of the sewing machine as she assembled fabric parts delivered by her sons and then returned to the wholesaler as finished goods the following morning. Likewise, on the other side, a Greek Cypriot woman received her garment pieces from a local Greek middleman, who would reappear the next day for the completed goods. Each of these women as a matter of course was expected to remain in or around the home rather than enter the world of "real work."

It is women like these who are now producing for the U.K. fashion industry. They manufacture for well-known fashion designers even though the doings and identities of each agent remains quite unknown to the other. The designers farm out their orders to wholesalers or merchandisers who place advertisements in local newsagents or in the trade press and who then subcontract out the various stages of the work through a long, anonymous chain of ethnic producers, each of whom takes a cut. For all the designers I interviewed (most of whom were themselves surviving on a shoestring budget), this was the only way to ensure that orders would be done in time, to cost, and to the standard required by the retailers or stockists. Having suppliers working locally rather than offshore also meant that mistakes could be rectified within the required time frame.

The privatized, nonunionized work carried out by these women, sometimes for less than £1 an hour, has made it difficult for feminists to see any way forward. Reformers and activists have suggested that the most feasible remedy is a revival of trade unionism on a global basis, focused on the self-organization of Third World women workers in the clothing industry and supported by First World consumers in the form of the boycott. But any such alliance has to be more inclusive. It is rarely suggested, for example, that other workers in the fashion sector be involved in these struggles, least of all designers, who are assumed to stand at the opposite end of the political spectrum, on the side of management. Nor is there any real attempt to engage with the politics of consumption outside the boycott (although in the last few months in the U.K. the charity Oxfam has launched a clothes code campaign, asking retailers to display a label

indicating that basic human rights have not been violated in the production of their garments).
But even the most successful boycott can quickly be forgotten when publicity wanes and when hard-pressed consumers return to the cheapest stores in disregard of their suppliers.

There is also an assumption that the women who make these clothes exist only as producers and never as consumers themselves. Some element of style and taste always enters into the small pleasures which the poorest garment workers also derive from items of consumption (TV sets, clothes, cosmetics, for example). If these are ignored, the effect is to "culturally deprive" these women and thus emphasize only their status as victims of capitalism, reducing every aspect of their lives to a matter of, as the title of Rowbotham and Mitter's book indicates, *Dignity and Daily Bread*. However, as Stuart Hall has argued, "everybody, including people in very poor societies whom we in the West frequently speak about as though they inhabit a world outside culture, knows that today's 'goods' double up as social signs and produce meanings as well as energy."[4]

I would like to suggest a less gloomy prognosis. In Britain at the present moment, it is not impossible to envisage higher degrees of self-organization and cooperation among low-paid clothing workers. This has already begun to happen with the appearance of homeworker associations. A New Labour government (committed also to introducing a minimum wage) could encourage local authorities to support such developments with fairly modest grants and funding. Skill levels and qualifications could also be improved by encouraging attendance at local community-based colleges, thus increasing the earning potential of these women. In the longer term, greater business confidence on the part of these women workers could lead to some elimination of the various middlemen who currently skim off most of the profits. This would bring ethnic women workers closer to the designers, who would also benefit from being able to see their work right through to the finished garments. It would give the designers better insight into a production process about which they remain surprisingly ignorant.

**British fashion designers.** The results of my recent study of art school–trained designers shows most of them setting up in business from within a culture of unemployment.[5] Every young designer I interviewed had been enrolled at some point in what was called the Enterprise Allowance Scheme (EAS). To be eligible, applicants technically had to be unemployed for at least three months. With £1,000 of capital (usually borrowed from relatives), they could receive payments of £40 or £50 a week, which could be retained alongside any profits made. The scheme was ended a couple of years ago, but during its existence provided the underpinning of the fashion design boom of the mid-1980s to early '90s. Despite all the publicity garnered by figures like Darlajane Gilroy, Pascal Smets, Pam Hogg, Sonnentag and Mulligan, Workers for Freedom, Pierce Fonda, and two sisters working under the English Eccentrics label, there have been many points in their career when they openly admit that they barely scraped a living. The cost of producing orders for well-known department stores in Britain and the U.S. while awaiting payment for sales from retailers has put too much stress on many of the small design companies. Cash-flow crises in what is a massively undercapitalized sector have made bankruptcies a very normal occurrence. For example, when I visited Sonnentag and Mulligan in 1993, I had high hopes they would survive. Their clothes were featured all across the fashion press, and the big clothing department stores on both sides of the Atlantic were placing regular orders. Even at this stage, however, they were living and working from the same studio space, employed only one machinist, were both on the EAS, and relied on a student intern to handle publicity. Despite their levelheaded approach and market savvy, they had to call in the receivers earlier this year.

What emerges as a career in fashion design is a mixed economy with designers surviving only if they free-lance for bigger, more commercial companies, while reserving time for their "own work" on a one/two-day a week basis. Sometimes they free-lance for up to three different companies, all the while harboring the dream of getting their own label off the ground. As one young woman put it:

> I was doing well and Madonna bought onxit, stitch for stitch, and then mass produce it. Bloomingdales didn't reorder, and with all the overhead, I went under. I was twenty-six, with over £20,000 of debts, so I gave up and went back on the dole.

In this context, it is not surprising that young designers are either silent or else embarrassed by discussions about how much they are able to pay their own in-house sample machinists, pattern cutters, etc.—never mind the women further down the chain who produce the orders. The designers I interviewed were, to some extent, willing victims of self-exploitation for the reason that they considered themselves artists first and entrepreneurs second. Even the most successful labels, like Ally Capellino, Helen Storey (which has since ceased trading), and Pam Hogg (likewise), on my estimate were working with an annual turnover in the range of £1 million to £2 million (figures that are borne out by the British Fashion Council survey of 150 companies in 1990). All fashion designers work a punitive round-the-clock schedule made more palatable by the knowledge that this is what creative people do.

While this might make it difficult to see designers lending support to machinists seeking union recognition and better working hours, it is not inconceivable that those who sketch might find they have quite a lot in common with those who sew. To do so, they would need to find a way of breaking down some of the social barriers that currently make it unlikely their paths ever cross. Nor should we assume that all fashion designers are the direct products of Thatcher's enterprise culture. Many have simply found ways of making enterprise fit with their artistic identities as creative designers. With so many of Britain's most successful designers coming from poor, working-class, or immigrant backgrounds, and with mothers who have worked in the rag trade, they are likely to be more than sympathetic to the idea of a better organized and better paid work force. My research certainly shows them to be angry and frustrated by Tory governments' refusal to take fashion design seriously as a matter for industrial policy. What is urgently needed is some strategic thinking about how these talented and highly trained young designers could, with small teams of well-paid and well-trained production workers, create an honest business culture that could survive in the face of global competition. This might well mean working periodically in partnership with the big fashion retailers who occupy such a powerful position in British fashion. But survival should not entail absorption by the big companies, a step that inevitably leads to the demise (or fatal compromise) of independent creative design.

**Education and training** should also play a role in this new survival strategy. British fashion education rightly has an international reputation for energetically encouraging young talent. It has expertise and knowledge in its academic staff, many of whom are prestigious figures on the international scene. Fashion academics also lobby hard on various official bodies. However, there are some points at which fashion education could play a more effective role in improving the performance of the design industry. At present, fashion design education is too committed to defending the fine art status of fashion to be interested in the messy business of

# no sweat

manufacture and production. As a "feminine" field in the high-culture world of the art schools, and traditionally worried about being seen as merely teaching "dressmaking," educators in fashion have looked upwards to the fine arts for legitimacy and approval. The persona of the fashion designer is consequently modeled on that of the painter, sculptor, or auteur (noncommercial) filmmaker. The aura of creative genius provides a cultural framework for talking about, exhibiting, or "showing" the work.

While this attitude makes some sense both as a utopian strategy for personal reward in work and for psychological survival in a deindustrialized economy, it means that art students spurn and disavow the whole business of actually making clothes. Often it is a mark of professional pride not to know how to put in a zip. Fashion students never visit a factory throughout the course of their training. Perhaps it is convenient for them not to know about how orders are put into production and who makes them up, since this would raise unpleasant questions about pay and working conditions. As one fashion academic said to me, "It would take all the romance out of it." But ignorance of production can only be detrimental to this creative economy if the whole point of fashion design is to realize the original (or prototype) on a scale that reaches beyond the runway. Fashion educators would thus be doing their students a favor by overcoming the bias toward fine art and introducing core courses on fashion as a labor process. Apart from anything else, this would also make designers less vulnerable to exploitation by unscrupulous suppliers who ruthlessly overcharge on production costs while brutally underpaying their subcontracted labor force.

**British fashion retailing.** There is no space here to enter into a full discussion of retailing save to explain that, despite the scale of this sector—estimated at £234 million in 1994, out of £7 billion for all clothing sales[6]—trade union representation has barely survived the Thatcher years. The Union of Shop Distributors and Allied Workers (USDAW) now reports an uphill struggle to hold on to a dwindling membership even in food retailing. There is no significant membership in fashion and clothing. What this means is that the early 1980s boom in retail culture (including new design-oriented chains like Next, the Gap, Jigsaw, Whistles, Hobbs, and in men's wear, Woodhouse and Paul Smith), complementing the ideologically driven consumer confidence championed by the Thatcher government, was entirely based on the employment of a nonunion work force. This is the reality that labor campaigners and policy makers now have to

*Sonnentag and Mulligan.*

accept. One strategy is to work with more progressive retailers like Paul Smith to ensure better careers in fashion retail for the thousands of young people now employed in this sector, and at the same time to expose the atrocious working conditions that prevail in many other outlets in the hope that political attention and bad publicity might force employers to take action.

For example, in my conversations with a number of young women who had worked in these outlets, it became clear that in many downmarket fashion shops in North and East London, owners paid their managers and assistants cash to avoid tax and insurance and on the "understanding" that staff could also claim unemployment benefits. Thus we see petty capital colluding to defraud the welfare state. By paying minimum wages of £3.50 an hour to single mothers as well as unqualified school-leavers, such employers oblige them to "fiddle" the social security. This raises a further political hot potato which no Labour or Tory politician can bear to confront, which is the pervasiveness of the hidden economy, itself the result of Britain's emergence as a low-pay and part-time workers economy. It seems quite absurd for New Labour to invest political energy in the aim of creating a "stakeholder society" based on the assumption that firms and companies will continue to employ hundreds of thousands of full-time workers. The reality could not be further from this vision. As even the biggest companies like British Telecom and the banks announce redundancies on a monthly basis, economic forecasts suggest that in the next ten years, by far the majority of British companies will be comprised of flexible units employing less than twelve people! Flexible here also means free-lance. In some respects, this puts the design industry at the forefront of the U.K. economy. As an ideal type in the growing sector of cultural industries, there is more and more reason to take it seriously.

Of course, the scant prospect of a resurgence of trade unionism among shop workers does not mean that there are no possibilities for labor reform. I suspect this is more likely to happen if the work force who adorn the floor at Donna Karan can be brought into better contact with some newly constituted fashion industry forum or lobby group that would better represent the interests of shopfloor workers than other forms of labor organization. After all, they tend to see themselves as fashion people first and shop workers second. But what kind of job exactly is it to work for Paul Smith or for Whistles? Paul Smith is proud of his record of training up shop assistants to managerial positions in his now vast and highly successful company. But with a complete absence of research on this subject, it is impossible to say how the average shop assistant working in the local branch of Next or, for that matter, behind the counter at Calvin Klein, navigates a career in this field. What is clear is that part-time contracts are increasingly the norm and this in itself has consequences for sickness and maternity pay, pensions, and even holidays. Who knows what will happen when this currently youthful labor force needs maternity leave or days off to look after sick children. It may well be that workers in this sector will have recourse to the law to defend their rights rather than to the now largely defunct (and patriarchal) British trade union organizations.

**The fashion magazines.** Fashion magazines are astoundingly timid when it comes to any form of social criticism. As Roland Barthes pointed out many years ago, everything in their pages has to be therapeutic and reassuring so that nothing unpleasant intrudes on the wearing of fashionable clothes.[7] Nowadays, British fashion editors and their journalists play this card by professing "loyalty" to the U.K. fashion industry. They would not write about low pay and sweatshop conditions at home or abroad because their duty is to support the industry, an already fragile edifice as we have seen. But this could easily change with a few more adventurous editors or a little pressure from young journalists to run intelligent writing on the fashion industry, which would actually do justice to their increasingly well-educated and discerning female readership. In fact, such a strategy could push the magazines into a position of greater power and prominence. If they took the lead in cleaning up the fashion industry, they might be seen by policy makers and politicians as responsible players in this important field.

There is an additional incentive here. The women's magazine sector remains a low-status field of journalism. It is considered the trivial end of the commercial mass media and it is rare for a journalist (or indeed an editor) on a women's magazine to make the quantum leap into the national (even tabloid) press. Nor do the women who work on these magazines get many opportunities to move laterally into television except perhaps as a fashion commentator in a daytime magazine slot. The result is that there are limited jobs, and the great majority of these are free-lance. The turnover of writers is very high, since many become disillusioned and give up. These are sufficient reasons for the magazine industry to reconsider its role, function, and format. The current taste in fashion-oriented magazines like *Marie-Claire*, *Looks*, and *Company* for downmarket tabloid-style sleaze and sensationalism stands in contrast to their timidity when it comes to considering the option of speaking more intelligently to well-informed readers. The fear, of course, is that critical reportage on the fashion industry will lose advertising revenue (and top editorial jobs depend on keeping advertisers happy). But in an age when corporations are desperate to put an ethical gloss on their activities, these magazines should see the commercial incentive involved in supporting campaigns that would extend human rights to all garment workers. This dimension could also be understood as adding diversity to the rather formulaic menu of feminine commercial culture found in magazines rather than, as editors and journalists currently fear, putting themselves out of a job.

**The practices of consumption**. The logic of conventional left and feminist thinking on issues of consumption is as follows. Having recognized how consumerism is the crucial means by which capitalism pulls us all into its unrelenting grip, we have to learn how to detach ourselves from its allure, break the spell of seduction, and become cautious, ethical, even parsimonious consumers. By the mid-1980s, this lofty, moralistic stance was coming under fire from feminists and those on what might be described as the cultural left. Suddenly, it was necessary to better understand our own and other people's participation in consumption and then to recognize the importance people attach to acts of consumption as markers or expressions of their own identity.

Now, in the mid-1990s, this endorsement of consumption (notably fashion consumption) by many feminists has gone too far. Celia Lury, Mica Nava, and others have suggested that consumption affords women a certain degree of power and authority to make choices.[8] But it is important to differentiate the power of boycott, for example, from the power or authority of the female consumer to treat the girl behind the counter as though she were a servant. The weakness of the new feminist consumer studies is that they tend to avoid questions about class relations in consumption. The general tendency is to narrowly focus on the activities of those who can afford to consume while neglecting to address the limits of consumption of those largely excluded from this realm. Lury and Nava each fail to recognize that for the vast majority of women, consumption, including fashion consumption, is an intensely frustrating economic activity.

The justification for this focus on what I would argue are affluent consumers is twofold. First, to counter the puritanism of the (now old) new left and feminist approaches, and second, to appear to be up-to-date in recognizing that with the decline in heavy industry, changes in class structure have produced a more aspiring, consumer-oriented working-class and lower-middle-class strata. Indeed, Lury seems to be suggesting that because production is now more or less out of sight, tucked away in the free trade zones, it is easier for consumers to participate unconstrained by a bad conscience or by the memory or direct experience of being a producer, since there is now a "relative independence of practices of consumption from those of production."[9]

It has to be acknowledged that most people, especially fashion-conscious youth, enjoy shopping for clothes and find it hard to reconcile their own pleasure in finding a bargain at Whistles or Agnes B with the political reality of the low wages and long hours involved in making these clothes. There is considerable psychological pressure to block out such thoughts; indeed, the pleasure of shopping depends on it. If this mindset is to change, then it cannot be left up to consumers alone. Garment companies would not be running scared of bad publicity if they did not take seriously the threat of consumer boycotts mobilized by exposés of superexploitation. But the rag trade has been associated with poverty wages for over a century, and this fact alone does not persuade people to make their clothing purchases with labor conditions in mind.

One of the problems of trying to develop a politics of consumption in relation to fashion is that so many people are involved at so many different locations that it is difficult to coordinate or think through such an analysis in an organized or manageable way. The only solution is to break down or disaggregate the practices of consumption to a more localized level, to contextualize particular forms of consumption in particular communities, cities, regions, or even neighborhoods. This then allows us at least to explore the social relations connecting producers with consumers. We can see signs of a closer dialogue between fashion producers and consumers where they each inhabit a shared cultural milieu, as they do for example in the club culture of Britain in the 1990s.

Currently, the latter is one of the few sectors of the small-scale design industry that is doing well. It comprises British designer/producers who share an involvement in the dance scene with their fellow dancers and with the musicians, DJs, producers, and promoters who in turn often put up the capital from club profits to set the designers up in business (usually with a store). The clothes are thus an integral part of the club circuit and can be bought from these new outlets or else from unit-type outlets across the country, including Hyper-Hyper, Covent Garden, and Camden Market in London, and the Lace Market in Nottingham. Club designer labels like Sign of the Times, Sub Couture, and Wit and Wisdom all produce relatively cheap clothes for those young people for whom dancing has become a primary leisure activity. Sharing the same cultural values as the consumers gives the designer/producers (most of whom, with a couple of friends, design, sew, and sell themselves) a different kind of relationship with their market. Their services are more personal, and they function not unlike the corner store in the traditional working-class neighborhood, or indeed like the local dressmakers mentioned earlier. They survive by their ability to shape and anticipate what people want to be wearing inside and outside the clubs. Inevitably the big retail outlets pick up on these "innovators" and put copies of their styles into mass circulation, but that does not negate the cultural and economic significance of the original, nor can it replicate the active role of the original consumers who contribute directly to the vitality of the subculture. Where would punk have been if the customers hadn't come flooding into Westwood and Maclaren's Sex (then Seditionaries) shop on the Kings Road? This retail transaction was a crucial stage in the production of punk culture, just as the boutiques of Carnaby Street had been a crucible for pop in the 1960s.

What I have outlined above is an approach that insists on seeing fashion production and consumption in the economic context of leisure spaces. Club culture, in particular, has now become an important source of livelihood in what is arguably Britain's most profitable cultural sector. There is no doubt that some of the attraction of the club scene lies in its capacity to provide an economic as well as symbolic model for a more engaged sense of community than that offered by mainstream capitalist consu-merism. But the dispersed, small-scale, survi-valist economics of this model must be set alongside the dynamics of the global labor market and the toil it has exacted on the domestic work force. The situation of the garment industry in the U.K. raises the much larger question of the extension and penetration of low-wage economies in First World countries. In this respect, there is a smaller gap between the highly qualified designers and the low-skill producers than is commonly imagined. Neither group is well paid, and they survive on a casualized, free-lance, or semi-self-employed basis. Most are female, live

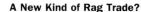

*Model with Sonnentag and Mulligan.*

in cities, find themselves disad-vantaged in regard to health and welfare benefits, mortgage applications, maternity benefits, and even holiday pay. Although they are not well represented by the trade union, nor by any lobby or pressure group or trade organization, there is no good reason why designers and producers should not be allies in pursuit of common self-interest.

All it would take is a shared sense of frustration and the desire to utilize existing talents, skills, and expertise. It would be easy to establish some kind of fashion-forum pressure group with teeth (since such affinity groups remain one of the few real sources of political energy in Britain today). Government could then play its role. The Labour party would score points by supporting (even initiating) such a move, especially since most voters these days have a daughter, son, or relative who has some involvement in the vast culture industries. This would entail a commitment by Labour to find ways of helping fashion workers translate their skills and commitment as well as creative talent into a sustainable fashion design industry which can match international renown with living wages.

*UNITE Demonstration at Macy's and Lord and Taylor, New York City,. December 1996.*

FOR CUSTOMER USE

0  12502 05166  4

Andrew Ross

after the year of the sweatshop
**postscript**

**291**

At the busiest part of the 1996 Christmas shopping season, Santa Claus was arrested in Midtown Manhattan in the full glare of TV cameras.

The charges were not what you would expect: shoplifting or sexual abuse of children. His crime was civil disobedience in front of Lord & Taylor, where he tried to deliver a lump of coal to the store managers, and where he was joined by over a thousand labor unionists and workers protesting the sweatshop conditions that had produced many of the clothes being sold in the upscale department store. The massive demonstration, which had begun at Macy's and was organized by UNITE, marked the release of an investigative exposé detailing sweatshop contractors manufacturing private-label merchandise for stores owned by the May and Federated department store chains. The exposé targeted sweatshops in the heart of New York's Garment District as well as in far-flung locations in Indonesia and Nicaragua. Nationwide antisweatshop protests in all the major cities of North America followed, making this Christmas season an especially anxious one for the apparel industry. Days later, Girls Club members dressed as Show White's Seven Dwarves besieged the Disney store in Sacramento and kicked off a "Disney Week" of protest. Organized by the National Labor Committee (NLC), Disney Week involved over sixty organizations, participating in over sixteen states, in addition to Haiti, the U.K., Japan, and Canada. School children were especially active in the campaign, sending over 6,000 letters to Disney, as were clergy who denounced the company in churches and synagogues all across the country.

The story about Santa was rushed into a five o'clock news slot, and the activities of the anti-Disney children also made good copy. There had been a noticeable lull in media interest after the Kathie Lee story died down, but the Year of the Sweatshop ended with the apparel trade once again bathed in the accusatory glare of the cameras and news headlines.

By this point, the media template was well established and the public were by now conditioned to respond with well-rehearsed outrage. Some veteran activists were quick to sense an air of normalization. But these events were different from the NLC and UNITE exposés that had triggered the media frenzy of the summer. While spearheaded by the NLC, the Disney Week events were the outcome of a grass-roots campaign that had come to embrace hundreds of organizations, local, regional, and national. Disney, after all, had refused to respond to NLC's Haiti campaign earlier in the year, opting to sit out the bad publicity. As a result, the press lost interest, but returned in force when the campaign gained momentum at the end of the year. In addition, Disney took a big blow when the company's claims for its codes of conduct were graphically rebutted by an NBC "Dateline" report, which discovered children making toys for children behind barbed wire in Indonesia and China for Disney, Mattel, and Eden Toys. In Xiangjiang Province in China, where over a million migrant females eat, sleep, and work in factory compounds for 13 cents an hour, producing one out of every two toys sold in America, "Dateline" found workers without protective clothing, laboring in extremely hazardous conditions. Since all these toy products enter the U.S. tariff-free, it was estimated that the markup to Disney was 1000 percent.

Something new was also happening within the company structure itself, thanks to a burst of shareholder activism. Large shareholders in Disney include the Presbyterian Church, the United Methodist Church, and Progressive Asset Management (a socially responsible investment fund). They challenged Disney to allow shareholders to vote on a resolution reviewing the company's sourcing guidelines and its offshore monitoring process. Disney argued before the Securities and Exchange Commission that workplace issues—working conditions, wages, benefits, respect for human rights—fell under "ordinary business operations" and were thus solely the domain of corporate management. But public and media pressure over their subcontracting operations in Haiti, China, and Burma (where they pulled out) forced the company to back down. A proposal for shareholder review was placed in the annual proxy. A "Resolution Requesting Contract Supplier Standards" called upon Disney management to "report on its contract supplier standards, and review the compliance mechanism for vendors, subcontractors and buying agents in the countries where it sources." The resolution also called for the company to guarantee not only "a living wage," to be decided in conjunction with local nongovernment organizations, but also protection of the workers' right to organize. A related resolution, "Financial and Social Accountability in Executive Compensation for Walt Disney Company," was even more unusual. It called for "comparison of compensation packages for company officers with the lowest and average wages for Disney contract workers in the U.S. and three low wage countries, including Haiti." At the shareholders' annual meeting, in late February 1997, the first resolution received the support of 39 million shares (8.5 percent), and the second received the support of 47.9 million shares (10.4 percent). In response, the company declared that it intends to reform its contract supplier system: it will issue a public code of conduct, translated into local languages and posted in factories; it will authorize external audits and inspections at contract facilities; and it will clearly define the right of workers to organize. The surprising success of these resolutions in eliciting a company response represents another line of action, more internal to the operations of corporations, but increasingly viable as the movement for socially responsible investment grows.

In April 1997, a presidential task force—the Apparel Industry Partnership—reached agreement on workplace codes of conduct. This group, which had first convened at the White House in August 1996, included UNITE, the National Consumers League, the Retail, Wholesale, Department Store Union, the Interfaith Center on Corporate Responsibility, and Lawyers Committee for Human Rights, and also had industry representatives from Liz Claiborne, Nike, Reebok, Phillips–Van Heusen, Patagonia, and L.L. Bean. Agreements on health and safety, forced labor, child labor (banning employment under fifteen years, except in certain countries), and antiharassment and nondiscriminatory practices had been reached early on. Accords were eventually reached on limited protections of the right to freedom of association and collective bargaining. Less satisfactory was the task force's acceptance of a sixty-hour work week as the industry norm—forty-eight plus twelve hours overtime. Its recommendation of a sixty-hour maximum, which could, however, be exceeded "in extraordinary business circumstances" (i.e., any rush order), and its commitment to a cap on "mandatory" overtime were both loose and imprecise gestures in an industry where employers and managers already find it all too easy to declare that workers are putting in "voluntary" overtime, or are working under "extraordinary" circumstances. In addition, the agreements required only that workers be paid "at a rate at least equal to their regular hourly compensation" for overtime.

Predictably, the biggest split among the task force participants had been over wages and the issue of independent monitoring. The labor and human rights groups had pushed for a "basic-needs" standard for a "living wage," rather than the legal minimum wage, which in most offshore countries is purposely set well below subsistence level in the hope of attracting foreign investment. The task force accords did little to discourage the maintenance of these minimum wage levels, incapable of sustaining a healthy, dignified life for most workers. In rejecting the pressure for a livable wage, the industry representatives also pushed for a system of "external monitoring" (as opposed to "independent monitoring") that would allow them to use large auditing companies like Ernst & Young, SGS, and Peat Marwick to assess and adjudicate local and international standards that might apply to any area of compliance with the codes. Transnational corporate auditors would thus be playing the role hitherto pioneered by local NGOs familiar with the social and cultural conditions of people's working lives. While the task force's accords advised the external monitors to consult with those institutions that are likely to have the trust of workers and knowledge of local conditions, they did not oblige companies to establish independent monitoring relationships with the labor, human rights, and religious groups in the region. Nor, since the agreements are voluntary, do they carry the threat of penalties for companies that violate the provisions of the code. The large loopholes in the agreements lent themselves to criticism that the Partnership had failed to propose meaningful standards or codes that can be effectively implemented. Elaine Bernard, director of Harvard's Trade Union Studies Program, suggested that the agreements merely gave the "good housekeeping seal of approval to a 'kinder, gentler sweatshop.'" Jay Mazur, UNITE president, declared that the Partnership was a significant first step toward corporations' acknowledgment of their responsibilities in a global economy, but acknowledged that there was still "a long way to go" in the fight to implement the accords.

As part of the accords, the Apparel Industry Partnership agreed to convene an association in order to recruit new members and to develop a mechanism of approval—such as a "No Sweat" label—for informing customers about which companies are abiding by the codes and the monitoring commitments. It remains to be seen who will sign on to this voluntary accord, and who, in practice, will observe the codes—whether the accords will have teeth, or whether they will merely serve as a public relations device to obscure rather than eliminate workplace abuses. The feasibility of the accords may prove to be the first real test of a Clinton administration returned to power partly as a result of the labor movement's campaign war chest. These developments—in government, in civil society, in the media, and within corporate practice itself—were all significant steps forward. Much more typical, however, was the behavior of Guess, Inc., the first company to be put on indefinite probation from the Department of Labor's Fashion Trendsetters List for illegally firing workers and for using homeworkers. The California company, which makes $450 million a year from the sale of $75 jeans, responded by announcing, in mid-January, that it was moving 70 percent of its production to Mexico. A highly successful campaign against its production base in the U.S. lost much of its relevance when the facilities moved across the border that straddles the world's largest income disparity between neighboring regions. Hourly wage estimates for 1996 (including benefits) range from $9.56 in the U.S. to $1.08 in Mexico, even though, in the case of garment companies like Guess, they move simply from paying $2 an hour illegally to Mexican workers in Los Angeles, to paying $1 an hour legally to workers in Mexico. (The global spread ranges from 26 cents in Pakistan, 28 cents in China, 30 cents in Kenya, and 34 cents in Indonesia, to $18.43 in Germany, $16.29 in Japan, and $14.32 in Italy.)

For Guess, and others who beat the same retreat, there will always be cheaper labor, but they are still dependent on their ability to sell in the middle- and high-income markets. Their labels and names cannot afford to be tainted by bad publicity, and the markets for their clothing cannot be relocated. This is why the high-risk game of public relations is so important, for companies and activists alike, and there is no question that the Year of the Sweatshop further dramatized the stakes involved.

The global game of finding the cheapest labor has become much more cruel. It is much more difficult to persuade companies to stay and do the right thing after conditions at their offshore facilities have been exposed. In the case of Disney's Burmese factories, virtually run by the military dictatorship, there were obvious reasons not to be there in the first place. As Aung San Suu Kyi, Nobel Peace Prize recipient and human rights advocate in Burma, put it: "We oppose investment in Burma today because our real malady is not economic but political. Until we have a system that guarantees rule of law and basic democratic institutions, no amount of investment will benefit our people. We do not think now is the time for any foreign company to invest in Burma." But in countries where foreign companies have been present for some time, there is a responsibility to clean up the mess, and ensure that when illegal conditions are exposed, workers are not further penalized through loss of their jobs to another region or country.

In the year when the revived U.S. labor movement was "officially" back in the saddle, garment labor turned out to be the main story. The Year of the Sweatshop registered many successes on behalf of labor, but it also introduced a new conceptual problem—the growing

# no sweat

tendency to see sweatshops, however defined, as an especially abhorrent species of labor, and therefore in a moral class of their own. One unfortunate consequence of this special status is that people are then more inclined to accept or tolerate the existence of labor conditions that cover the legal standards, but only barely. Sweatshops are seen to be morally and politically apart from the lawful low-wage sector, which is condoned as a result. The fact is that virtually every low-wage job, even those that meet minimum wage requirements and safety criteria, fails to provide an adequate standard of living for its wage earner, let alone his or her family. In most respects, it is the systematic depression of wages, rather than conscious attempts to evade labor laws, that is the structural problem. Installing proper fire exits may turn a sweatshop into a legal workplace, but it remains a low-wage atrocity.

All the more reason to define and perceive the "sweatshop" as a general description of all exploitive labor conditions, rather than as a subpar outfit, as defined by existing laws in whatever country the owner chooses to operate. This kind of general definition will allow labor to build on the recent successes. Given its powerful associations with inhumane and immoral treatment, and given its current visibility, the garment sweatshop may be poised, for the second time in modern history, to serve as the crusading vector of the labor movement as a whole.

# no sweat fashion

**1996 Fashion Trendsetters List—U.S. Department of Labor**

The retailers and manufacturers listed below have all pledged to help eradicate sweatshops in America and to try to ensure that their shelves are stocked with only "NO SWEAT" garments.

This list is based on the voluntary efforts of the listed companies. They have agreed to: demonstrate a commitment to labor laws; cooperate with law enforcement agencies when violations of the law are found; and monitor working conditions, for example, by contracting with suppliers who monitor contractors or by conducting supplier site visits. (Companies not on this list may also follow these practices.)

**Army Air Force Exchange**
Services
Post Exchanges
Base Exchanges

**Baby Superstore**

**C.I. Castro**
C.I. Castro
Wayne Copeland
Cookie Crunchers

**Carson Pirie Scott**
Carson Pirie Scott
Boston Stores
Bergner's

**Cee Sportswear**
Cee Sport

**Chorus Line**
All That Jazz
Molly Malloy
Jazz Kids
More Jazz
Jazz Sport

**Gerber Childrenswear**
Gerber
Curity

**Ferell, Inc.**
Ali Myles
Stoneridge
Melissa
Stephanie Thomas
Sandra S.
Lindsey Scott
Victoria Morgan

**Jessica McClintock**
Jessica McClintock
Gunne Sax
Scott McClintock

**Jones Apparel Group**
Jones NY
Jones NY Sport
Jones & Company
Jones Studio
Jones NY Suits
Jones NY Dress
Rena Rowen for Saville
Evan Picone
Lauren Ralph Lauren

**Kellwood**
Robert Scott/David Brooks Outlet
Robert Terry
David Brooks
Robert Scott
DeCorp

**L.L. Bean**

**Lambchop**
Kathie Lee Gifford Product Line

**Lands End**

**Levi Strauss and Company**
Levi's Only Stores
Docker's Only Stores
Levi's
Dockers
Brittania
Slates

**Liz Claiborne**
Liz Claiborne Stores
Dana Buchman Stores
Elisabeth Stores
Claiborne Stores for Men
Liz Claiborne Collection
LizSport
LizWear
LizNight
Liz Claiborne Dresses
Dana Buchman
dana b. and karen
Elisabeth
Liz & Co.
Claiborne for Men
Emma James
Russ
First Issue
Villager

**Malco Modes**

**NFL Properties**

**Nicole Miller**
Nicole Miller Stores
Nicole Miller

**Nordstrom**

**Patagonia**
Patagonia Stores
Patagonia

**Podell Industries Inc.**
Laundry by Shelly Siegel
Shelly Siegel
Laundry Stores

**Quiksilver**
Quiksilver
Que
Pirates Surf
Raison
Leiani
Radio Fiji
Roxy
QSD

**Reebok International Ltd.**
Reebok Stores
Reebok
The Rockport Company
Greg Norman

**Superior Surgical Manufacturing**
Fashion Deal Uniforms
Worklon
Appel Uniforms
Martins Uniforms
Universal Cottons
Superior Surgical International

**Talbot's**
Talbot's Stores
Talbot's

**The Gap**
The Gap
GapKids
BabyGap
Banana Republic
Old Navy Clothing Company

**The Limited**
Express
Lerner
Lane Bryant
Limited Stores
Henri Bendel
Structure
Abercrombie & Fitch
The Limited Too
Gaylans Trading Company
Victoria's Secret Stores and Catalogue
Bath and Body Works
Cacique
Penhaligon's

**Third Generation**

**VF Corporation**
VF Factory Outlet
Wrangler
Lee
Riders
Rustler
Marithe & Francois Girbaud
Cutler's
Jantzen
Jansport
Bassett-Walker
Vanity Fair
Vassarette

Lou
Healthtex
Red Kap
Lee Sport
Big Ben
Bolero
Intima Cherry
Carina
Variance
Gemma
Siltex
Nutmeg
Maverick

**Warnaco**
Olga/Warner Stores
Warners
Olga
Calvin Klein Lingerie
Valentino Intimo
Scaasi
Van Raalte
White Stag
Fruit of the Loom
Speedo
Chaps by Ralph Lauren
Calvin Klein
Hathaway
Catalina

## Introduction

1. Jacob Riis, *How the Other Half Lives* (New York: Charles Scribner's Sons, 1890); Henry Mayhew, *London's Labor and the London Poor* (London, 1851). Leon Stein anthologizes the best accounts at the time in *Out of the Sweatshop* (New York: Quadrangle, 1971).

2. Gus Tyler, *Look for the Union Label: A History of the International Ladies' Garment Workers' Union* (Armonk, N.Y., and London: M.E. Sharpe, 1995), pp. 18–30.

3. This juxtaposition dramatizes the split between craft and industrial unionism that would ultimately pit the AFL against the CIO. See Steve Fraser, *Labor Will Rule: Sidney Hillman and the Rise of American Labor* (New York: Free Press, 1991). Fraser shows how labor recruitment and organization in the industry, which employed immigrant Jews, Italians, Poles, Slovaks, Bohemians, and Lithuanians, often followed regional patterns of kinship, religion, and locale established in the Russian Pale (the majority of owners and manufacturers were established German Jews), and the political divisions between socialist, anarchist, syndicalist, and Bundist workers followed suit.

4. Peter Kwong, *Chinatown: Labor and Politics, 1930–1950* (New York: Monthly Review Press, 1979); Edna Bonacich et al., eds., *Global Production: The Apparel Industry in the Pacific Rim* (Philadelphia: Temple University Press, 1994); and Paul Ong et al., eds., *The New Asian Immigration in Los Angeles and Global Restructuring* (Philadelphia: Temple University Press, 1994).

5. See Roger Waldinger, *Through the Eye of the Needle: Immigrants and Enterprise in New York's Garment Trades* (New York: New York University Press, 1986).

6. For trade history, see José de la Torre, *Clothing Industry Adjustment in Developed Countries* (London: Macmillan, 1985); Fariborz Ghadar, William Davidson, and Charles Feigenoff, *U.S. Industrial Competitiveness: The Case of the Textile and Apparel Industries* (New York: D.C. Heath, 1987); Kitty Dickerson, *Textiles and Apparel in the Global Economy* (Englewood Cliffs, N.J.: Prentice-Hall, 1995).

7. Annie Phizacklea, *Unpacking the Fashion Industry: Gender, Racism, and Class in Production* (London: Routledge, 1990), p. 9.

8. Cynthia Enloe, *The Morning After: Sexual Politics at the End of the Cold War* (Berkeley: University of California Press, 1993), pp. 102–143.

9. Kathy McAfee, *Storm Signals: Structural Adjustment and Development Alternatives in the Caribbean* (Boston: South End Press, 1992).

10. Press release, May 20, 1996, National Retail Federation.

11. A counter-poll commissioned by the International Mass Retail Association showed that most consumers (46 percent) blame the government's lack of regulation for exploitive labor practices, 29 percent blame the manufacturers, while only 19 percent blame the retailers.

12. See Larry Rohter's article in the *New York Times* on July 18, 1996, for a classic example.

13. The International Labor Organization estimates the global employment of child labor at 73 million, or 13 percent of all children from ten to fourteen years old.

### The Global Resistance to Sweatshops

1. The Nike story is detailed in Richard J. Barnet and John Cavanagh, *Global Dreams: Imperial Corporations and the New World Order* (New York: Simon & Schuster, 1994).

2. For a detailed analysis, see Diane Orentlicher and Timothy Gelatt, "Public Law, Private Actors: The Impact of Human Rights on Business Investors in China," *Northwestern Journal of International Law and Business* 14, no. 1 (Fall 1993).

3. Mitchell Zuckoff, "Taking a Profit and Inflicting a Cost," *Boston Globe*, July 10, 1994.

4. *New York Times Magazine*, April 2, 1995, p. 18.

5. A Clean Clothes newsletter is included in the *News from IRENE* (International Restructuring Education Network Europe), available from IRENE at Stationsstraat 39, 5038 Tilburg, The Netherlands.

6. Bethan Brookes and Peter Madden, "The Globe-Trotting Sports Shoe," *Christian Aid*, December 4, 1995, p. 22.

7. The Safety Charter has been endorsed by the Catholic Institute for International Relations, Trade Union Congress, and World Development Movement, in association with Asia Monitor Resource Center, Association of the Rights of Industrial Accident Victims, Hong Kong Christian Industrial Committee, Hong Kong Confederation of Trade Unions, and the International Confederation of Free Trade Unions.

8. Bob Ortega, "Conduct Codes Garner Goodwill for Retailers, But Violations Go On," *Wall Street Journal*, July 3, 1995.

9. Orentlicher and Gelatt, "Public Law, Private Actors."

10. For an inventory of consumer boycotts ongoing in the United States at any given moment, see the magazine *Co-op America Quarterly's* "Boycott Action News." The list of fifty-seven is from the Fall 1994 issue.

### From War Zone to Free Trade Zone

*My thanks to Barbara Briggs, David Dyson, Charles Kernaghan, Ralph Rivera, and Jack Sheinkman for many hours of discussion. They are all friends, and I hope I have done justice to the personal experiences they shared with me. Thanks also to NLC associate David Cook, who helped me gather documentation on the Gap and Kathie Lee campaigns and other background materials. I am most grateful to Andrew Ross for giving me the opportunity to contribute something from my own life to this book. I have learned a great deal in the process.*

*When I visited El Salvador with the National Labor Committee in 1988, I met Febe Elizabeth Velazquez, a dynamic young garment worker and a leader of FENASTRAS, one of several antigovernment labor federations. In 1989, less than a year after I met her, Febe was killed in a bomb attack on FENASTRAS headquarters. This essay is dedicated to her memory.*

1. See excerpts from the 1926 report of a New York State Governor's Special Advisory Committee, reprinted in *Out of the Sweatshop*, ed. Leon Stein (New York: Quadrangle, 1977), pp. 280–281. This report described the proliferation of contracting and subcontracting in the garment industry and recommended regulating the jobber-contractor relationship, giving the jobber (manufacturer) responsibility for the equitable distribution of work and maintenance of proper working conditions.

2. Major retailers dominating the industry include Liz Claiborne, the Gap, Kellwood, and Wal-Mart, all of whom are consigning production to offshore contractors. See Arthur Friedman, "Fashion's Blame Game: Is Retail Price Squeeze Reviving Sweatshop?" *Women's Wear Daily*, June 11, 1996.

3. Though, at 56 cents an hour, garment workers in El Salvador earn more than those in Honduras, the standard of living in El Salvador is higher than in Honduras. According to figures supplied by the Human Rights Department of El Salvador's Jesuit University, an hourly wage of 56 cents covers only 18 percent of a family's essential needs.

4. An NLC bulletin of May 18, 1995, reports that company guards kicked and beat union activists who were calling for a work stoppage. All 850 workers were locked out, and fifty activists were fired in the incident.

5. The convention ratified a merger between the International Ladies' Garment Workers' Union and the Amalgamated Clothing and Textile Workers' Union into UNITE, a single apparel workers' union.

6. A copy of the agreement was issued by the NLC on December 16, 1995.

7. Claiming they did not have enough orders, Mandarin did not immediately rehire the workers. The Gap has participated in efforts to encourage orders from Liz Claiborne and Eddie Bauer in order to facilitate reinstatement.

8. Viewer statistics are from the research department of WABC–Channel 7.

9. See comments of Ron Konecky, Charles Champlin, and Robert Hall in "The Troublemaker," by Joyce Barrett and Joanna Ramey, *Women's Wear Daily*, May 13, 1996.

10. The joint communiqué was issued by Kathie Lee Gifford, Lafayette Avenue Presbyterian Church, UNITE, and the National Labor Committee on June 6, 1996, following a meeting of the parties at the Manhattan residence of John Cardinal O'Connor.

11. See Barry Bearak, "Stitching Together a Crusade," *Los Angeles Times* (Washington edition), July 25, 1996.

12. The author was an early member of the Committee.

13. Daniel Cantor and Juliet Schor, *Tunnel Vision: Labor, the World Economy, and Central America* (Boston: South End Press, 1987), pp. 41–47.

14. Ibid., pp. 1–3.

15. Ungo and Zamora were members of the Revolutionary Democratic Front (FDR), the political arm of resistance during the civil war. They later founded the Democratic Convergence, a socialist

alliance party that opposed the Christian Democratic party of President José Napoleon Duarte in elections in 1988. The Christian Democrats and Duarte were defeated in that election by the reactionary right-wing ARENA party of Alfredo Cristiani.

16. On the occasion of their twenty-fifty anniversary in 1993, Dyson returned to El Salvador with his wife, Sally, and was reunited with several of his old comrades. Among them was Hector Recinos, former president of El Salvador's hydroelectric workers' union. Recinos had spent three years in Mariona Prison before NLC obtained asylum for him in Holland, where he lived for four years. Recinos's wife and daughter had been killed by the death squads.

17. NLC reports following *Paying to Lose Our Jobs*: *Free Trade's Hidden Secrets: Why We Are Losing Our Shirts* (1993); *Haiti after the Coup* (1993); and *The U.S. in Haiti: How to Get Rich on 11 Cents an Hour* (1995). A fourth document, *An Open Letter to Walt Disney*, was released in 1996.

18. See Bearak, "Stitching Together a Crusade"; Barrett and Ramey, "The Troublemaker."

### Paying to Lose Our Jobs

**A note on sources:** Research for this report is based on documents and published materials readily available to the public. Interviews were conducted with sources in governmental agencies. The information contained herein is believed to be accurate but does not purport to be complete.

1. *Bobbin* (August 1991).

2. Letter from R. Ray Randlett, assistant administrator for legislative affairs, USAID, to the Subcommittee on Western Hemisphere Affairs, U.S. House of Representatives, September 1991.

3. USAID/El Salvador Project Paper, "Industrial Stabilization and Recovery," March 1991, amendment #2, annex F.2, pp. 5–6 (hereafter, "Industrial Stabilization and Recovery").

4. USAID/El Salvador Project Paper, "Free Zone Development," August 1988, p. 50 (hereafter, "Free Zone Development").

5. FUSADES, "Why El Salvador," June 1989, p. 7. FUSADES' promotional literature is conceived, written, and printed by consulting firms under contract with USAID. For example, in the mid-1980s the Washington, D.C.–based International Science and Technology Institute (ISTI) was contracted by USAID to "prepare special information packets on aspects of doing business in El Salvador for distribution to exhibitors." See USAID contract #519-0260-C-00-5002-00, December 20, 1984.

6. U.S. Department of Commerce, "Investment Climate Report: El Salvador," April 30, 1990, p. 9. The Latin America/Caribbean Business Development Center (LA/C BDC) is described by USAID officials as "an information clearing house and one-stop for U.S. business interested in the region." The Center's director, Walter Bastian, sees LA/C BDC's role as responding to the Bush administration's initiatives on trade—such as CBI, NAFTA, EAI—by trying to "convert these into business opportunities for U.S. and foreign firms."

7. USAID, "Trade and Investment Strategy, El Salvador," July 1991, p. 2.

8. "Free Zone Development," p. 2.

9. "Industrial Stabilization and Recovery," amendment #2, p. 14. See also "Free Zone Development," annex 6, p. 5, and annex H, p. 6. Food for Peace Aid (Title I, PL480) provides U.S. food shipments to recipient governments at extremely concessionary rates, and often payment is never made. The government sells the food at market rate and keeps the local currency that is generated. The money is typically used for balance of payments support. However in this case, USAID directed the government of El Salvador to use PL480–generated funds to build factory space at the government-run San Bartolo free trade zone.

10. USAID grant agreement with the Foundation of Entrepreneurs for Educational Development, Project #519-0315, August 1987, p. 1, and "Free Zone Development," p. 11.

11. USAID's worker training program in El Salvador is funded under two USAID projects: Training for Productivity and Competitiveness (#519-0315), which has received $20 million in obligations, and Training for Productivity and Competitiveness II (#519-0390), for which $7 million has been obligated. See USAID/El Salvador, "Action Plan, FY 1991–1992," March 1990, annex A, p. 8, and "Action Plan, FY 1992–1993," February 1991, annex A, p. 12.

12. Interview with John Sullivan, deputy director of USAID/El Salvador's Trade and Investment Office, San Salvador, July 1, 1992.

13. U.S. Department of Commerce, "Investment Climate Report: El Salvador," April 30, 1990, p. 5, and "Industrial Stabilization and Recovery," p. 27.

14. USAID/El Salvador Project Paper, "Industrial Stabilization and Recovery," August 1984, p. 18.

15. FUSADES, "Country Profile: El Salvador," information handout, 1991.

16. "Free Zone Development," annex 6, p. 4.

17. USAID Policy Paper, "Private Enterprise Development," March 1985, p. 1.

18. Address by Vice President Bush to the Sixth Annual Miami Conference on the Caribbean, December 1982. The conference was sponsored by Caribbean/Central American Action, which has since changed its name to Caribbean/Latin American Action.

19. Address by Vice President Bush to the Ninth Annual Miami Conference on the Caribbean, November 1985.

20. USAID, "Trade and Investment Strategy, El Salvador," July 1991, pp. 3–4.

21. USAID Policy Paper, "Private Enterprise Development," March 1985, p. 10.

22. All figures are from the U.S. Department of Labor, Bureau of Labor Statistics.

23. American Apparel Manufacturers Association, *1992 Focus/An Economic Profile of the Industry* (Washington, D.C.: AAMA, 1992).

24. When 936 began, it was meant as an incentive for U.S. companies to develop manufacturing operations and create badly needed jobs in Puerto Rico. But today, 936 has become a massive tax loophole for the largest U.S. Fortune 500 companies. 936 loans are available at interest rates 1.5 to

2 percent below the London Interbank Borrowing Rate (which is the international standard for determining global interest rates), the lowest available anywhere in the world. According to Stephen H. Long, Citibank's top executive in the Caribbean region, 936 loans amount to a 20 to 25 percent saving in today's market. This allows a company investing in Central America or the Caribbean to build in lower debt-service payments over the life of the project. For example, on the $80 million 936 loan DuPont is about to receive, the corporation will save approximately $1.6 million in lower interest rate costs.

### Labor, History, and Sweatshops in the New Global Economy

*The author wishes to acknowledge the invaluable collaboration of UNITE colleagues Michele Briones, Muzaffar Chishti, Susan Cowell, Mike Donovan, Brent Garren, Art Gundersheim, Peter Goldberger, Desma Holcomb, Keir Jorgensen, Jo-Ann Mort, and Ellie Spielberg in the preparation of this article.*

1. John Commons, in *Out of the Sweatshop: The Struggle for Industrial Democracy*, ed. Leon Stein (New York: Quadrangle, 1977), pp. 44–45.

2. *The Daily Forward*, November 21, 1900.

3. Gus Tyler, *Look for the Union Label: A History of the International Ladies' Garment Workers' Union* (New York: M.E. Sharpe, 1995), p. 73.

4. *Foreign Affairs* (Fall 1992): 135–154.

5. Isabelle Grunberg, *Rival States, Rival Firms: How Do People Fit In? The Global Unemployment Challenge*, United States Development Programme, Office of Development Studies (Discussion Paper Series, 1996).

6. Jay Mazur, testimony before the Commission on the Future of Worker-Management Relations, Washington, D.C., July 25, 1994.

### New York: Defending the Union Contract

1. The names of some individuals and workplaces have been changed to prevent embarrassment, but all the people and workplaces described are real.

2. It is more profitable for a union contractor to work for union manufacturers, since the union then bills the manufacturer directly for benefit payments. When a union contractor takes orders from nonunion sources, they must assume benefit costs themselves.

3. Not the actual name.

4. "Real" unemployment in 1993, including discouraged and involuntary part-time workers, was estimated at 16–19 percent, and for dropouts at 35 percent. Since then, official unemployment has fallen from 10.5 to 8.5 percent. See *The New Workforce: Investing in New York City's Competitiveness*, a report prepared by the New York City Workforce Development Commission, 1993.

5. U.S. Bureau of the Census, 1992 Census of Manufacturers.

6. Only 1,500 establishments employ more than twenty people. Very small firms include both designer showrooms and small contractors.

7. Florence Palpacuer, "Development of Core-Periphery Forms of Organization: Some Lessons from the New York Garment Industry," unpublished manuscript, Eisenhower Center for the Conservation of Human Resources, Columbia University.

8. Women's wear employment outnumbers men's by more than five to one in the New York City industry, which is driven more by fashion than by the technology-intensive demands of relatively standard men's apparel. Even in the men's sector, there are more jobs in the fashion-driven neckwear industry than in more standardized suits and coats.

9. See "The Outside System of Production in the Women's Garment Industry in the New York Market," an unpublished study for the ILGWU prepared by Emil Schlesinger, 1951.

10. Sample-makers and cutters are among the best paid and most secure production workers. Skilled cutters commonly earn $20,000 or more annually; some sample-makers earn in excess of $50,000 per year.

11. The extent of contracting may vary considerably. Jobbers may maintain an inside shop, do their own cutting and sample production, and own their trucks or distribution center. Others go to the opposite extreme, contracting out even the production of the first pattern and sample garments.

12. Palpacuer, "Development of Core-Periphery Forms of Organization."

13. See "Keeping New York in Fashion," a New York market and technology study by Kurt Salmon Associates, Inc., for the Garment Industry Development Corporation, 1992, p. 27.

14. Teams, Total Quality Management, Total Preventive Maintenance, advanced ergonomic practices, onsite English classes, and expensive training for management and production workers are all part of the package at Sequins International, the world's largest supplier of sequins and sequined trim, employing 200 workers in Long Island City, Queens. But though positive and significant, the inclusive and modern business approach is hardly a trendsetter in New York industry.

15. Ming Lam, producing skirts, slacks, and shorts for Ralph Lauren Womenswear, among other customers, owns other high-volume, high-standard New York contractors.

**The Structure and Growth of the Los Angeles Garment Industry**

1. Edna Bonacich, "Alienation among Asian and Latino Immigrants in the Los Angeles Garment Industry," in *Alienation, Society, and the Industrial*, ed. Felix Geyer and Walter Heinz (New Brunswick, N.J.: Transaction, 1992).

**Fashion as a Culture Industry**

1. Frances Williams, "Poorer Nations Plan Attack on Textile Barriers," *Financial Times*, July 25, 1996,

p. 5; Sheel Kohli, "Territory Teams Up with WTO Delegates to Criticise Policy on Textiles," *South China Morning Post,* July 27, 1996.

2. Kym Anderson, ed., *New Silk Roads: East Asia and World Textile Markets* (Cambridge: Cambridge University Press, 1992).

3. Karl Marx, "The British Rule in India," in *Surveys from Exile: Political Writings* (London: Penguin Books, 1973), vol. 2, pp. 304–306.

4. Elizabeth Wilson, *Adorned in Dreams* (London: Virago, 1985), p. 87.

5. Colin MacInnes, *Absolute Beginners* (London: Allison & Busby, 1980), p. 12; see also Colin MacInnes, *England, Half English* (London: Hogarth Press, 1986).

6. Roger Tredre, "A Name That Should Never Have Died," *The Observer,* April 7, 1996, p. 8.

7. The literature on Fordism is now an extensive one. The classic source is Michel Aglietta, *A Theory of Capitalist Regulation* (London: New Left Books, 1979). See also Alain Lipietz, *Mirages and Miracles* (London: Verso, 1987), and especially D. Leborgne and Alain Lipietz, "New Technologies, New Modes of Regulation: Some Spatial Implications," *Environment and Planning D: Society and Space* 6 (1988): 263–280. For recent review articles, see Martin Kenney and Richard Florida, *Beyond Mass Production: The Japanese System and Its Transfer to the U.S.* (New York: Oxford University Press, 1992); N. Albertsen, "Postmodernism, Postfordism, and Critical Social Theory," *Environment and Planning D: Society and Space* 6 (1988): 339–365; Riahon Mahon, "From Fordism to…? New Technology, Labor Markets, and Unions," *Economic and Industrial Democracy* 8 (1987): 5–60; Kevin Robins, "Reimagined Communities? European Image Spaces, Beyond Fordism," *Cultural Studies* 3, no. 2 (1989): 145–165.

8. P. J. Lloyd, "Structural Adjustments in the Textile and Clothing Industries," in *Industrial Policies for Pacific Economic Growth,* ed. Hiromichi Mutoh et al. (Sydney: Allen & Unwin, 1986).

9. Gloria Bianchino et al., eds., *Italian Fashion* (Milan: Edizioni Electa, 1987), vol. 1, p. 8.

10. Ibid., vol. 2, pp. 36–39.

11. José de la Torre, *Clothing Industry Adjustment in Developed Countries* (London: Macmillan, 1985). I have used this work extensively in the following sections as well.

12. Ibid., p. 128.

13. Robert Reich, *The Next American Frontier* (Harmondsworth: Penguin, 1984).

14. I. M. Destler, *Textile Wrangle: Conflict in Japanese-U.S. Relations* (Ithaca, N.Y.: Cornell University Press, 1979).

15. Torre, *Clothing Industry Adjustment,* pp. 190–194.

16. Lloyd, "Structural Adjustments," p. 193.

17. Ylonda Gault, "Recent Job Cuts Leaving Apparel Industry Threadbare in NY," *Crain's New York Business,* December 18, 1995, p. 3.

18. Philip Lentz, "Fashion Bid Styles Trade Zone of Its Own—District Would Cut Import Duties, Give Edge," *Crain's New York Business,* September 23, 1996, p. 36.

19. Susannah Frankel, "Behold the Man—and His Clothes," *The Guardian*, April 3, 1996, p. 8.

20. Gault, "Recent Job Cuts."

21. Torre, *Clothing Industry Adjustment*; Lindsay Hay, *Management and Design in the Women's Fashion Industry* (London: Design Council, 1976).

22. Nik Cohn, "Today There Are No Gentlemen," in *Ball the Wall* (London: Picador, 1989); George Melly, *Revolt into Style* (Harmondsworth: Penguin, 1972); Dick Hebdige, *Subculture: The Meaning of Style* (London: Methuen, 1979); Nigel Whiteley, *Pop Design: Modernism to Mod* (London: Design Council, 1987); Nicholas Coleridge, *The Fashion Conspiracy* (London: Heinemann, 1988), pp. 117–157.

23. See Simon Frith and Howard Horne, *Art into Pop* (London: Methuen, 1987).

24. Catherine McDermott, *Street Style* (London: Design Council, 1987), pp. 22–56; Lesley White, "The Fall and Rise of Bodymap," *The Face* (May 1985): 61; S. Hoare, "Ritfat Ozbek: The Young Turk of British Fashion," *The Face* (June 1986): 74; C. Franklin, "The Changing Face of the British Fashion Industry," *i-D* 52 (October 1987); J. Scott, "Paris Passion: An Interview with Maria Cornejo," *i-D* 71 (July 1989).

25. Coleridge, *The Fashion Conspiracy*, pp. 112–116.

26. Motoko Rich, "Britain's Textile Manufacturers Cotton on to Cheaper Labour," *Financial Times*, April 16, 1996, p. 23.

27. Ginny Dougary, "Mother of Invention," *The Times*, May 11, 1996.

28. Robin Murray, "Life After Henry (Ford)," *Marxism Today* (October 1988).

29. McDermott, *Street Style;* Hebdige, *Subculture*, pp. 155–180.

30. See Peter Hall, "The Difficult Economics of French Socialism," in *The Mitterrand Experiment*, ed. George Ross et al. (Cambridge: Polity Press, 1987), pp. 59–60.

31. Coleridge, *The Fashion Conspiracy,* pp. 169–194.

32. S. Mower, "Jean-Paul Gaultier: French Dressing," *Arena*, July 4, 1987.

33. "Will This Be Dior's New Look?" *The Independent*, August 14, 1996, p. 3.

34. Folker Frobel, Jürgen Heinrichs, and Otto Kreye, *The New International Division of Labour* (Cambridge: Cambridge University Press, 1980).

35. For a study of the Japanese machine tool industry, see David Friedman, *The Misunderstood Miracle* (Ithaca, N.Y.: Cornell University Press, 1988). However, Friedman does not see the special nature of the capital goods sector in relation to other sectors of the economy, for which it provides a very particular kind of intermediate good.

36. Young-Il Park and Kym Anderson, "The Experience of Japan," in *New Silk Roads*, pp. 28ff.

37. Ronald Dore, *Flexible Rigidities: Industrial Policy and Structural Adjustment in the Japanese Economy, 1970–80* (Palo Alto, Calif.: Stanford University Press, 1986), p. 171.

38. Noburo Makino, *Decline and Prosperity: Corporate Innovation in Japan* (Tokyo: Kodansha International, 1987), p. 19.

39. On postmodernism in Japan, see Yoshio Sugimoto, "Taking the Sociological Pulse of Japan," paper presented at the Sixth Conference of the Japanese Studies Association, Sydney University, July 6, 1989; Gavan McCormack and Yoshio Sugimoto, *Modernization and Beyond: The Japanese Trajectory* (Cambridge: Cambridge University Press, 1988); *South Atlantic Quarterly* 87, no. 3 (1988); Victor Burgin, "Seiburealism," *New Formations* 7 (1989); McKenzie Wark, "From Fordism to Sonyism: Perverse Readings of the New World Order," *New Formations* 15 (1991): 43–54.

40. Kenney and Florida, *Beyond Mass Production*; Ronald Dore, *Taking Japan Seriously* (Palo Alto, Calif.: Stanford University Press, 1986); Friedman, *The Misunderstood Miracle*.

41. Penny Sparke, *Modern Japanese Design* (New York: E.P. Dutton, 1987); Frederick Shodt, *Inside the Robot Kingdom* (Tokyo: Kodansha International, 1988); Leonard Koren, *New Fashion Japan* (Tokyo: Kodansha International, 1986).

42. Koren, *New Fashion Japan*.

43. Roberto Campari, "Film and Fashion," in *Italian Fashion*, vol. 1, pp. 198ff.

44. T. Jones, "Mr. Fiorucci: 20 Years of Global Pollination," *i-D* 51 (September 1987).

45. Charlotte Cooper, "Italian Designers Pay Damages in Bribery Trial," Reuters News Service, June 18, 1996.

46. "Textile Regions Spin to New Highs," *Daily News Record*, October 16, 1995, p. 8.

**Tommy Hilfiger in the Age of Mass Customization**

1. "Top 40 Focus," *Bobbin* (June 1996).

2. "No Need to Trade in Conscience for Affordable Clothing," *San Francisco Chronicle*, July 21, 1996.

3. All the quotes in this and the following paragraph are from the various executives interviewed, and all information has been "mined" from the account of the interviews in "Views from the Top," *Daily News Record*, May 29, 1996.

4. "June Spend on Cards Hits 6.9bn," *Electronic Telegraph*, July 29, 1996.

5. PR Newswire, August 7, 1996.

6. Darcy Frey, *The Last Shot* (Boston: Houghton Mifflin, 1994).

7. Quoted from CNN Headline News Channel, July 17, 1996.

8. Streetsound's board can be accessed on <<http://streetsound.clever.net/style/fashhiphop.html>>. It is worth keeping in mind here that the Internet itself, however much its advocates (myself included) want to think of it as a means toward a certain cultural freedom and even resistance, is also at the same time part of the expansion of the means of consumption that I've been referring to.

1. Angela McRobbie, *Feminism and Youth Culture: From Jackie to Just Seventeen* (London: Macmillan, 1991), and *Postmodernism and Popular Culture* (London: Routledge, 1994).

2. Rozsika Parker, *The Subversive Stitch: Embroidery and the Making of the Feminine* (London: Women's Press, 1984).

3. Sheila Rowbotham and Swasti Mitter, eds., *Dignity and Daily Bread: New Forms of Economic Organising among Poor Women in the Third World and the First* (London: Routledge, 1994); Jane Tate, "Homework in West Yorkshire," in ibid.; Annie Phizacklea, *Unpacking the Fashion Industry: Gender, Racism, and Class in Production* (London: Routledge, 1990).

4. Stuart Hall, "The Meaning of New Times," in *New Times: The Changing Face of Politics in the 1990s*, ed. Stuart Hall and Martin Jacques (London: Lawrence & Wishart, 1989), p. 131.

5. Angela McRobbie, *Fashion and the Image Industries* (London: Routledge, 1997).

6. Government and Trade Association Statistics, KSA.

7. Roland Barthes, *The Fashion System* (New York: Hill and Wang, 1967).

8. Celia Lury, *Consumer Culture* (Oxford: Polity Press, 1996); Mica Nava, *Changing Cultures: Feminism, Youth, and Consumerism* (London: Sage, 1992).

9. Lury, *Consumer Culture*, p. 4.

# contributors

**John Cavanagh** is co-director of the Institute for Policy Studies, a fellow at the Transnational Institute, and co-author (with Richard J. Barnet) of *Global Dreams: Imperial Corporations and the New World Order*.

**Ginny Coughlin** works on the Stop Sweatshops campaign of UNITE.

**Robin Givhan** covers the fashion industry for the *Washington Post*. She has also written about the beauty business, men's style, women's wear, and popular culture for the *Detroit Free Press*, the *San Francisco Chronicle*, the *Washington Post Magazine*, and the *International Herald Tribune*.

**Alan Howard** is a longtime labor activist and journalist. Since 1992, he has worked as assistant to the president of UNITE.

**Charles Kernaghan** is executive director of the National Labor Committee, an independent, nonprofit human rights and workers' rights organization focused on workers assembling garments and other products for the U.S. market in Third World countries, including those of Central America and the Caribbean. He is also a photographer whose photos appear throughout this volume.

**Kitty Krupat** was an editor and journalist at *Esquire* magazine and Simon & Schuster for thirteen years before joining District 65 of the UAW as an organizer of publishing and other white-collar workers. She has also served as education director of the International Ladies' Garment Workers' Union and is presently a doctoral student in the American Studies Program at New York University.

**Angela McRobbie** is reader in sociology at Loughborough University, and author of a number of books, including the forthcoming *Rag Trade or Art World? British Fashion Design in the 1980s and '90s*. She is also editor of the forthcoming *Back To Reality? Social Experience and Cultural Studies*.

**Jo-Ann Mort** is a writer and director of communications at UNITE. She is a member of the editorial board of *Dissent* magazine, where her article in this collection first appeared.

**Steve Nutter** is the international vice-president and regional director of the Western States Region of UNITE. An experienced labor attorney, founding member of Sweatshop Watch, and a board member of several U.S.–Central American labor organizations, he also serves as vice-president of the California Federation for Labor.

**Michael Piore** is professor of economics at MIT, and the author of several books, including *Birds of Passage: Migrant Labor and Industrial Societies*, *The Second Industrial Divide*, and *Beyond Individualism*.

**Eyal Press** is a New York–based journalist who writes frequently for the *Nation*, the *Progressive*, and other publications.